TEACHING TEACHERS

Questions about the Purpose(s) of Colleges & Universities

Norm Denzin, Joe L. Kincheloe, Shirley R. Steinberg
General Editors

Vol. 3

PETER LANG
New York • Washington, D.C./Baltimore • Bern
Frankfurt am Main • Berlin • Brussels • Vienna • Oxford

TEACHING TEACHERS

Building a Quality School of Urban Education

EDITED BY

Joe L. Kincheloe, Alberto Bursztyn,
Shirley R. Steinberg

PETER LANG
New York • Washington, D.C./Baltimore • Bern
Frankfurt am Main • Berlin • Brussels • Vienna • Oxford

Library of Congress Cataloging-in-Publication Data

Teaching teachers: building a quality school of urban education /
edited by Joe L. Kincheloe, Alberto Bursztyn, Shirley R. Steinberg.
p. cm. — (Higher ed; v. 3)
Includes bibliographical references and index.
1. Critical pedagogy—United States. 2. Teachers, Training of—United States.
3. Teaching—Philosophy. I. Kincheloe, Joe L. II. Bursztyn, Alberto.
III. Steinberg, Shirley R. IV. Series.
LC196.5.U6T428   370.7'1'1—dc22   2003027172
ISBN 0-8204-4929-6
ISSN 1523-9551

Bibliographic information published by **Die Deutsche Bibliothek**.
Die Deutsche Bibliothek lists this publication in the "Deutsche
Nationalbibliografie"; detailed bibliographic data is available
on the Internet at http://dnb.ddb.de/.

Cover art by Alberto Bursztyn
Cover design by Lisa Barfield

The paper in this book meets the guidelines for permanence and durability
of the Committee on Production Guidelines for Book Longevity
of the Council of Library Resources.

© 2004 Peter Lang Publishing, Inc., New York
275 Seventh Avenue, 28th Floor, New York, NY 10001
www.peterlangusa.com

Printed in the United States of America

In Memory of Nina Wasserman

Dedication

to Lois Biesky
from Joe and Shirley

to Carol, Dan, and Josh
from Alberto

Contents

Foreword ix
Shirley R. Steinberg

Preface xi
Nicholas M. Michelli

Chapter One
The Bizarre, Complex, and Misunderstood
World of Teacher Education 1
Joe L. Kincheloe

Chapter Two
Teachers as Philosophers:
The Purpose of Foundation Courses in Education 51
Mordechai Gordon

Chapter Three
A Tree Grows in Brooklyn: Schools of Education as
Brokers of Social Capital in Low-Income Neighborhoods 65
Wayne A. Reed

Chapter Four
Race and Education in New York City: A Dilemma 91
Haroon Kharem

Chapter Five
Who I Am Informs My Teaching 103
Alma Rubal-Lopez

Chapter Six
Community Knowledge–Centered Teacher Education:
A Paradigm for Socially Just Educational Transformation 113
Nora E. Hyland and Shuaib Meacham

Chapter Seven
Special Education, Urban Schools,
and the Uncertain Path to Social Justice 135
Alberto Bursztyn

Chapter Eight
Run Jane Run: Researching Early Childhood
Teacher Practice Frame by Frame 157
Carol Korn-Bursztyn

Chapter Nine
The Graduate Program in School Psychology:
Imparting Responsive Practice. 179
Florence Rubinson

Chapter Ten
The Changing Faces of Literacy 195
Carolina Mancuso

Chapter Eleven
Toward a Counterhegemonic Multicultural Grammar. 209
Lee Elliott Fleischer

Chapter Twelve
Students' Perceptions of Schools of Education 229
Koshi Dhingra

Chapter Thirteen
The Experience of Experience:
Haphazard Stories about Student Teaching. 241
Philip M. Anderson

Afterword
Working on the Future: Concluding Thoughts. 251
Alberto M. Bursztyn

Contributors 263

Index 267

Foreword

Shirley R. Steinberg

Is it arrogant to suggest that we have an idea of how to build a quality school of education? Hopefully our readers will take the title in the spirit that it was created: We are all builders and we are all engaged in quality education. Unfortunately, the immediate past, present, and possible future of teacher education may not be enveloped in the quality we seek.

I used to believe that teaching children was the most difficult profession in the world; however, I am amending that to suggesting that teaching the teachers who teach children holds that distinction. The responsibility of democratically introducing young men and women into the teaching profession is daunting, daunting in its volume but even more so in the fact that it is a responsibility that is constantly obfuscated by governmental interference.

The fact that our nation has been ravaged by an incompetent administration led by a "Blame the Teacher" coalition of the Secretary of Education's office, the Christian Right, textbook publishers, and quick-fix educational solutions adds to the chagrin that many of us feel. The No Child Left Behind Act terrorizes school administrators as it promises to remove needed funding from budgets unless schools are compliant with the quantitative standards-driven agenda. Added to the stress and fear from the new act is the obsession that most colleges of education enter into as they attempt to adopt the National Council for Accreditation of Teacher Education (NCATE) guidelines in order to have "national recognition." While many scholars may argue that, indeed, NCATE recognition is essential, the fact remains that many schools are occupied with dealing with the regulations of the association and not as occupied with the concerns surrounding pedagogy and the best education for children and youth. Ironically, some of the top colleges of education within the United States do not seek national certification; rather they rely on their reputations and scholarship to guarantee the best available teacher education.

Beloved teacher Paulo Freire always insisted that teachers were cultural workers. I would like to take up that label, to be a cultural worker who is engaged in the development of the pedagogy and profession for young cultural workers. The context of cultural work expands the school into a learning site that is added to the other contextual learning sites: the home, the community, and the media. As a teacher of teachers, I hope that I am able to create the contextual, the wholistic, the connected vision of curriculum for a democratic and socially just pedagogy.

While certainly implicit in this book is a critique of colleges of education, we believe that most of us engaged in this work are attempting to facilitate good teaching. What I find tragic is that colleges of education are singled out over and over again as that institution that has caused the problems within teaching while colleges of arts and sciences have been exonerated from the process. Colleges of Education are not the only academics who are responsible for the education of teachers. Arts and sciences have equal responsibility in that area. Unfortunately, teacher educators must take up the slack and remediate much of what could have been taught in the first years of university. We hope that our colleagues outside of colleges of education will listen, rather than ignoring questions of educational purpose and pedagogical practice.

The teachers who have contributed to this volume have all worked together in one way or another. They have connections through the City University of New York system; some have left the system, while most still remain. I left the system for a time, only to return to Brooklyn College this year . . . I guess to join forces in the constantly challenging battle of gaining recognition and respect from both government and other departments—respect that teaching teachers is not for the weak or pedagogically challenged . . . it is for the best of the best. It is the most difficult job on this planet, and we all love it.

Preface

Nicholas M. Michelli

Teacher education is one of the central issues in American public education as we begin the new millennium and for good reason. Increasingly, we have evidence that the quality of the teacher—in terms of content knowledge, pedagogical knowledge, and knowledge of child development—is the most important variable in the success of children in school. It is a variable that is more powerful in predicting success than is socio-economic class or the education of parents. This is not to negate the deep social inequities in our society—inequities apparent to the faculty in each of the twenty colleges of the City University of New York every day. We do need to examine, understand, and redress those inequities, but they will not be erased overnight, and so our focus must be on control over what we know to be the most important variable affecting the education of future generations. Teacher quality is that variable.

Now, there is no question that there are disputes over how to achieve teacher quality and what *teacher quality* actually means. Proposals range all the way from strengthening college-based programs by adopting high state standards and requiring national accreditation, as New York State has done, to letting the market determine who teaches and who doesn't, without regard to qualifications. Across the country, as states interpret one of the most intrusive bits of federal legislation in our history, the No Child Left Behind Act of 2001, educators are scrambling to meet a federal mandate that all teachers be of "high quality" by 2004. The term "high quality" is being defined by state certification requirements, including alternate routes to certification. As this volume is nearing completion, we know that New York City will need 11,000 new teachers within a few months. In New York State, where teacher quality is tied to meeting high state certification standards, the need is to replace currently uncertified teachers by September to meet the terms of a court order.

And so the work represented here by urban faculty members in colleges and departments of education provides some insight into what the thinking is in a college-based teacher education program under tremendous pressure to meet the needs of urban children. What you will find is a vision that is emerging across the campuses of the CUNY schools, for example, with a central theme of teaching for social justice. It cannot be otherwise. For the 1.1 million children in New York City, as well as for those in urban schools across the nation, and I might add in rural schools, public education is the only route to personal fulfillment that society offers—and education for social justice depends on highly qualified teachers. Why do I add rural schools in with urban schools? I believe that there is the potential for a powerful coalition between urban and rural schools because of the poverty, isolation, difficulty in attracting teachers, and mainstream cultural deprivation that are often shared by inner-city and rural schools. But our mission at CUNY is clearly focused on urban schools.

As you read through these reflections on the full range of programs to prepare educators for our schools, it is fair to ask whether we are preparing teachers who will meet the needs of children. You will find limited mention of high-stakes testing, which has permeated conversations about education in the first decade of this century. It isn't that the writers here are unaware of the role of such tests but rather that we know that the public purpose of education is not to have children pass tests. We believe that the public purpose is threefold:

- to provide children with equitable access to knowledge and understanding so that they can assume their place in the economy at the highest possible levels,

- to prepare students to be active, critical participants in our emerging political and social democracy, and

- to provide students with the understanding they need to lead rich and fulfilling personal lives.

Many will read this list of purposes and say, of course, that is why we have public schools. It is what we should be preparing teachers to be doing. But it is clearly out of synch with much of the pressure that schools are under due to the relentless focus on tests. Tests may be a proxy measure of whether or not students are prepared to meet certain goals, but the test is not the substitute for life. It is as Ivan Illich reminds us: We cannot mistake the institution for the goal—mistaking the presence of schools for education, of police for safety, or of hospitals for health care. We need to educate teachers in such a way that they do not mistake preparing students to pass tests for preparing them to lead rich and fulfilling personal and public lives.

As Joe Kincheloe points out, we cannot have teachers who are merely technicians, and we must convince schools that they need much more than technicians. To this end, another aspect of our work at the City University of New York is to develop deep and equitable partnerships with the schools we work with, as well as with the U.S. Department of Education. This is hard work, because the personnel we must work with change regularly, and we often have to begin again to complete collaboration that we already thought was established. Witness the transition of chancellors in New York City every three years or so and the parallel transitions of school leaders in urban schools across the United States.

The enterprise of teacher education is complicated as well because we must negotiate our standing and existence within our own institutions. Phil Anderson writes of the conflict between powerful experiential learning and the standing of experiential learning within institutions of higher education. We expect faculty to work in schools, but we often do not have reward systems that recognize the value of that work. We think of research in a rarefied, pure way and consider it somehow tainted if it is applied and leads to a higher quality of life. Our arts and science colleagues suffer even more from the mismatch of the reward system with such work, and we need them to join with education faculty in a common goal of recognition. We want and expect our presidents and provosts to make teacher education central to the mission of the university, and yet they aspire to keep their institutions safe from politically volatile programs like teacher education.

Teacher education is a difficult, bizarre, complex, and misunderstood world indeed, and the contributors to this volume raise some of the most difficult and critical questions to be faced. Each of them raises a series of such questions around curricular issues. For example:

Mordechai Gordon: Can we prepare teachers to think philosophically about the meaning of education?

Wayne Reed: Can schools of education find new meaning as brokers of social capital in the neighborhoods they serve?

Alberto Bursztyn: Is trust the missing link for meaningful renewal in education leading to social justice?

Carol Korn-Bursztyn: Can teachers learn to view their teaching with the eye of a researcher? Can they learn to identify and use the frames that explain their actions to achieve greater understanding of themselves as teachers?

Carolina Mancuso: Can we sustain a focus of critical literacy in future teachers in the face of the current positivist perspectives on literacy?

Lee Elliott Fleischer: Can teachers conceptualize grammar that reflects the multicultural reality of the city?

Koshi Dhingra: Can the school of education bridge the gap between theory and practice by capitalizing on the complex interrelationships that exist between arts and science and education faculties in universities, between cultural institutions and the public in neighborhoods and cities, and between formal and informal learning?

Phil Anderson: Can we find new models for the interaction of teacher education institutions with schools?

All of these questions are framed in Joe Kincheloe's careful analysis of the forces that direct schools of education away from these important questions. How can we find the time and space in an increasingly positivist world to be reflective about what is important for our children and our society? The question for me ultimately is, how can we NOT find the time and space? Kincheloe and the others whose work make up this volume believe, as I do, that our moral responsibility as educators—a responsibility to children and to society—mandates the kind of reflection and subsequent action we see in the work of these educators.

Chapter One

The Bizarre, Complex, and Misunderstood World of Teacher Education

Joe L. Kincheloe

In a speech I presented recently to a wonderful group of professors of education and teachers in South Carolina, I began by saying, "I don't trust schools." What I was trying to get across involves the understanding that those of us concerned with studying schooling and improving education in this country have to be very wary of the goals that schools embrace and the ways they engage particular individuals and groups. To illustrate my point, I asked how many audience members had studied at any point during their schooling the story of the European colonization of Africa and the effects of the slave trade—a process that killed at the very least tens of millions of Africans. When it was revealed that none of the teachers had encountered this human tragedy in any systematic detail in their schooling, I was not surprised, for I had encountered the same response numerous times before. I pointed out that I simply could not trust an institution that routinely ignored such information, that would not rate it as one of the most important events of the last millennium, and that would not engage students in wrestling with the moral responsibilities that accompany acquaintance with such knowledge.

I use this anecdote to set the tone for this book on teacher education. From the outset, readers need to know that I don't think teacher education in the United States has been especially successful over the last century and a half. At the same time that I assume such inadequacy, I also am dissatisfied with the history of U.S. higher education in general. For many of the same reasons, teacher education and the liberal arts and sciences have often failed to engage their students in a rigorous, complex, critical education that prepares them for professional and civic competence in a democratic society. With these biases admitted up front, it is our effort to induce teacher educators and teacher education students to join in a meta-dialogue about the nature and purposes of teacher education. We want to seduce readers into an examination of what constitutes a good college/school/department of teacher education and how they might contribute to and benefit from it. The authors of this book assert that good teacher education and in turn good teachers are central to our very survival as a democratic society.

The first decade of the twenty-first century is an exciting and frightening time for supporters of a rigorous, practical, socially just, and democratic teacher education. It is a time of dangerous efforts to destroy teacher education and of brilliant attempts to reform it. A sense of urgency permeates discussions of the topic, as studies indicate that presently there is a need for more teachers in a shorter time frame than ever before in U.S. history. About 1,025 teacher education programs graduate around 100,000 new teachers annually. The problem is that over the next few years 2 million teachers will be needed in U.S. elementary and secondary schools. Many analysts argue that the problem will be solved by lowering standards for teacher certification or simply doing away with the certification process and admitting anyone into the teaching ranks who breathes regularly (U.S. Department of Education, 1998). Such capitulation to short-term needs would be tragic.

Addressing the Condescension toward Teacher Education and Pedagogy

I wish I had a dollar for every time someone in higher education or the professions reacted condescendingly upon learning that the individual with whom he or she was conversing was a professor of teacher education or pedagogy. Understanding the history of teacher education, one is provided with plenty of reasons to look at the domain askance—but not any more so than other elements of higher/professional education. Too often, condescension toward teacher education and teacher educators is harbored for all the wrong reasons. Contempt for teacher education and pedagogy emanates not from knowledge of their historical failures but from a generic devaluing of the art and science of teaching, to the level of an unnecessary contrivance. "As long as one knows her subject matter," the clichéd argument goes, "she doesn't need anything else to teach." Anyone who makes such an assertion should be mandated to teach the fourth grade for six weeks. Such a crash immersion may induce a reconsideration of this platitude, as the complexity of doing such a job well becomes apparent.

Indeed, the complexity of the pedagogical process and the intricacies of a rigorous teacher education are central concerns of this book: What is a good college/school/department of education? What is a critical complex teacher education? In its devaluation, pedagogy has been rendered invisible in many higher educational settings. Teacher educators, teachers, and teacher education students must not only understand the complexity of good teaching, but stand ready to make this known to political leaders and the general population. If we are not successful in such a political effort, we will witness the death of the scholarly conception of teacher education to the degree it now exists. While such articulations of the importance of teacher education are not dominant, many scholarly, rigorous, and democratic teacher education programs exist and produce excellent teachers. At the same time, in countless mediocre programs, great teacher educators ply their trade in unfavorable conditions, turning out good teachers despite the circumstances.

Nevertheless, the dominant disdain for teacher education has undermined support for scholarly teacher education in general, induced closings of university teacher education programs, removed teacher educators as players in school reform, catalyzed the movement to alternate forms of teacher certification, and moved governments around the country and the world to legislate how teacher education should operate while they slash funds for colleges/schools/departments of education.

In this legislative context, numerous examples of punitive measures exist, threatening teacher education programs with punishment if they don't meet certain mandated standards. For example, from the New York State Regents Task Force on Teaching:

Teacher education programs will be subject to deregistration if:

- fewer than 80 percent of their graduates who completed their teacher education programs pass one or more teacher certification examinations; and
- deficient programs do not demonstrate significant annual improvement to reach the 80 percent target.

The Regents will review the 80 percent standard periodically with the goal of raising it to 90 percent. (Regents Task Force, 1998, p. 24)

The objects of these threats are not institutions with great prestige and power.

One of the many factors contributing to the public perception of the weakness of teacher education involves the historic lack of understanding of exactly what teacher education is and what it should do. Not only is there public confusion, but teacher educators themselves have never agreed upon their mission. Historians typically identify four distinct orientations toward teacher education:

THE ACADEMIC TRADITION. Teachers learn how to transform the knowledge of disciplines into curriculum material for students.

THE SOCIAL EFFICIENCY TRADITION. Teachers are taught the correct way to teach based on empirical research.

THE DEVELOPMENTALIST TRADITION. Teachers study how students grow and develop in relation to behavior and cognition.

THE SOCIAL RECONSTRUCTIONIST TRADITION. Teachers study their own teaching in relation to the ways they reflect the larger society's tendency to reproduce oppressive race, class, and gender dynamics (Hatton and Smith, 1995).

Of course, merit can be found in all of these positions, and at different historical moments some have held sway over others. In the critical complex conception of teacher education offered here, all of these orientations are considered worthy except for the social efficiency tradition, with which we have particular objections. From our perspective, a rigorous teacher education should

- help teachers learn how to transform the knowledge of disciplines into curriculum material for students while appreciating counterdisciplinary knowledges and their curricular role

- engage teachers in the study of student development, not merely in a white, male, upper-middle-class context but in a variety of cultural, gender, and class domains

- facilitate teachers' study of their own practice in relation to race, class, or gender oppression, making use of new ways to do this that have been developed over the last few decades

- employ research on teaching to help teachers operate, but use research produced within diverse paradigms of knowledge production and often generated by teachers themselves

Throughout this chapter, I will develop ideas about the purposes of a critical complex teacher education for a democratic educational system and a democratic society. Perhaps, as we begin to articulate and employ such a rigorous mode of professional education, teachers and their educators can begin to undermine the historical condescension toward teacher education and pedagogy.

Undermining the Practitioner as Scholar:
The Teacher as Technician

In all of these historical orientations to teacher education, with the exception of the social reconstructionist tradition—the most marginalized and reviled of the four standpoints—the teacher to varying degrees has been viewed as a technician. The most unfortunate feature of this tendency is that over the past twenty years of conservative educational reforms, political and educational leaders have promoted the technician model with a vengeance. In the contemporary top-down standards movement, for example, the teacher is little more than an implementor of curricula devised by faraway experts. In the most egregious cases—which are becoming more and more common in the first decade of the twenty-first century—actual scripts are provided for teachers to follow. Teacher educators, teachers, and teacher education students dedicated to upholding the dignity of their professional calling cannot sit passively by while such degradation takes place.

Such technical orientations imply a hierarchical impulse that is incompatible with an inclusive, democratic worldview. In such a hierarchy a small elite group at the top of the pyramid conducts the scholarly decision-making work while a larger corps of worker bees at the bottom carry out their directives. Such totalitarian organizational models are disturbing, as they perpetuate an elitist mode of scientific management that positions teachers as interchangeable cogs in a machine that turns out students as standardized products. Questions of individuality, the right of critique and dissent in a democratic society, and the complexities of knowledge production and interpretation are conveniently swept under the industrial-strength carpet of the education factory. In a chilling language of "excellence," "quality," and "accountability," all of these reforms are justified as functions of democracy.

Teacher education students can sense this technician orientation in some of the literature and coursework they encounter. My colleagues and my highly motivated and intelligent students ask me in relation to such encounters: "Do they think we're brain dead? I don't know if I can stay in such a Mickey Mouse operation." Notions of teachers as scholars and self-directed professionals are further undermined by elementary and secondary schools that are less than interested in promoting and rewarding the intellect of their teachers (Howley, Pendarvis, and Howley, 1993). My best and brightest teacher education students often return depressed after student teaching experiences or their first year of teaching. "I love my students and the times I get to direct my own teaching," they report, "but I'm so depressed by the curricular controls I face. And I'm so lonely there. I miss intellectual stimulation." Such reports are disconcertingly common in my experience of teaching teachers. I am profoundly affected by them, and as I age I find such stories increasingly emotionally wrenching and difficult to listen to; the frustrations and cynicism that many teachers feel as a result of their exclusion from the culture of scholarship, research, and policymaking are often misread as a lack of concern with these dynamics. An observer of this process must understand that too many teachers are still enculturated by a technically rational teacher education and teaching workplace (begging questions of what we should be doing and why we are subservient to "proper" techniques of doing it). Such enculturation rarely allows for explorations of the social and political roles of schooling and how they might be problematic. When I talk to some groups of teachers about such concepts, it becomes quickly apparent that they have never been exposed to analyses of the way schooling has historically and contemporaneously hurt particular individuals and groups of people.

When teachers are viewed as technicians, there is little expectation that they will operate, as John Goodlad (1994) puts it, "as critically inquiring stewards of schools" (p. 17). The idea that teachers would be central agents in educational policymaking is silly in the technician motif—policy deliberation and teaching exist in two separate worlds (Elmore, 1997; Hatton and Smith, 1995). In the rarefied circles of contemporary technically rational policymakers, the idea that teachers should be educated as professional leaders and decision makers is not simply wrongheaded but is deemed beyond the capabilities of such low-status individuals. Rarely are teacher education students or practicing teachers intellectually challenged.

The time has come for this to change. Because of such elitist attitudes and assumptions, too many teachers are deprived of the opportunity to study the larger social, political, cultural, and economic contexts of schooling and their relation to educational purpose and classroom practice. In the technician context, many have not had the chance to develop a language or conceptual schema for discussing education as a moral and ethical operation. A critical complex teacher education sees these dimensions as central aspects of every portion of teacher education, in-service education, and the teaching act itself. Without these dynamics systematically infused into all elements of professional education and practice, the degradation of teaching will expand in the coming years.

Politics and Teacher Education: Regulating Teachers

Issues of teacher education and the degradation of teaching cannot be separated from the domain of power and politics. Many of the seemingly irrational reactions to democratic policies and teacher self-direction cannot be understood outside of a larger social, cultural, economic, and political context. Since the mid-1970s Americans have witnessed a deliberate, systematic, and successful attempt to reeducate citizens around issues of race, class, gender, sexuality, and social justice (Kincheloe, Steinberg, Rodriguez, and Chennault, 1998; Gresson, 1995; Apple, 1996; McLaren, 2000). Teacher education has been profoundly affected by this reactionary project. Reacting to perceived social, cultural, and educational changes of the 1960s, guardians of dominant power relations sensed a good opportunity to promote their cultural-political agenda of:

- a return to "traditional values"

- the formation of a neoclassical market-driven economic policy

- the reassertion of long-standing racial and gender relations

- the establishment of a school curriculum grounded on the transmission of "the truth," not on inquiry and interpretation

- the authorization of a top-down, fragmented, accountability-friendly, teacher-as-rule-follower system of public education

In this new context, the protectors of tradition promoted a new cultural story that played well to white male audiences uncomfortable with the social alterations taking place around the world and in the United States. Using the power of this "new story," the guardians of tradition engaged these white men and their allies in what has been labeled the recovery of white supremacy and patriarchy perceived to have been lost in the Civil Rights movement and the women's movement. The reeducation process was directly connected to this notion of what had been lost. In this "recovery" context, Aaron Gresson (1995, 2004) argues that this new white story inverts a traditional black narrative. Because of the dominant culture's portrayal of the economic success of blacks and other minority groups—a portrait much less accurate than represented—many whites believe that nonwhites in the last three decades of the twentieth and the first decade of the twenty-first centuries have greater power and opportunity than whites.

This fallacious position contends that new African American, Latino, and Native American privileges have been achieved at the expense of more deserving white Americans—especially upper-middle-class white males. The narrative is promoted in a variety of spheres, including education and teacher education, and in a variety of ways, but always with the same effect: the production of white anger directed at nonwhites and women in particular. We can see this very clearly in the condemnation of teacher education curricula that ask students to question the democratic and justice-related nature of American education around issues of race, class, and gender. This white anger operates, of course, to divide poor and working-class people of all races and genders, to support the interest of privileged power wielders, and to shape the nature of what occurs in schools. It works to limit what can be questioned by teacher educators and to contain critical examination of the purposes and outcomes of education in the United States.

This conservative reeducation project, operating under the well-worn rubrics of "less government" and "freedom," has established highly politicized bureaucracies in state and local governments. Such organizations have worked hard to undermine the ability of teachers to assert their professionalism, to use their professional judgment in dealing with issues of curriculum, motivation, evaluation, and teaching style. Obviously, such top-down mechanisms of control raise serious questions about the nature of schooling and the role of the teacher in a democratic society. A critical complex conceptualization of teacher education and teaching most definitely does not want to force teachers or schools to operate in particular ways. The point is to engage teachers in the study of particular questions about education in a democracy—concerns with justice, the demands of egalitarianism and equality of opportunity, and the nature of the scholarly act. Teachers in democratic schools must have the professional freedom to deal with these questions in their own ways.

If these conversations and questions were out front for everyone to see and ponder, we should not be in such a mess. In the present political climate, the ideological forces behind the conservative reeducators purposely fly below the radar, denying their own existence as they insidiously shape the content of the curriculum and the role of teachers. Often, advocates of imposed hierarchical reforms operate in collusion with corporations such as McDonald's, Exxon, Coca-Cola, RJR Nabisco, Pizza Hut, and Citicorp to contain dissent and questioning, to shape sociopolitical perspectives, to train future citizens as cooperative employees and consumers, and to tap into the uniquely exploitable children's market. If corporate advertisers can reach children, they know that children will buy their products, children will shape their parents' consumption, and children will consume as future adults (Grimmett, 1999).

As I mentioned in the opening paragraph of this chapter, I don't trust schools. In this case I particularly don't trust schools that are comfortable with these political dispositions. In the market-driven discourse described here, individuals are not agents who work to build democratic, inclusive educational, political, and economic institutions—they are potential consumers. Not only is this problematic in general, but when it comes to schooling, teaching, and teacher education, it upsets the very heart and soul of education for free and self-directed people. When the political and economic elite, with its privatized, free-market socioeducational vision, controls the "schooling enterprise," we have entered a new and frightening era. In such a competition-based system, there must be distinct winners and losers. Unfortunately, who wins and who loses is predetermined by forces of race and class. Teachers are forced to make their evaluations using criteria developed far away from the classroom by people who have no understanding of where particular students come from or what they have had to face.

Such educational policy serves to regulate and domesticate teachers and teacher educators. What do colleges/schools/departments of teacher education tell students about these political processes? Often a climate of fear is produced in which in the name of meeting the standards, teacher education students are taught merely to do the right thing, to follow the rules, to be good boys and girls. In this context of domestication, concepts of teacher empowerment and of teachers as self-directed scholars and assertions of teacher professionalism perversely mutate in the eyes of the guardians into manifestations of misbehavior. Teacher educators who raise questions of social justice, democracy, and diversity are placed under suspicion as agents whose motives are questionable and underhanded. As an associate dean in Louisiana once described my efforts to engage our teacher education students in questions of racism, class bias, sexism, and homophobia in relationship to teaching and learning: "Joe appeals to the worst instincts of our students."

Specifying the Regulations: Standardizing the Effort to Stupidify Teachers

Indeed, the very enterprise of contextualizing the processes of teaching and learning, examining the political, cultural, philosophical, and epistemological assumptions behind them, has been called into question by the reeducators now shaping public school and university teacher education policy. Historical and social contextualization, many are now asserting, can promote subversion (Snook, 1999). The use of *subversion* in this context is fascinating, as it seems to be equated with the scholarly ability to analyze and evaluate educational proposals, mandated curricula, and pedagogical methods. These abilities rest at the center of the notion of empowered teacher scholars, who we believe are necessary to the long-term improvement of education. I deduce from these objections to teachers engaging in such scholarship that many of the leaders of the reeducation movement and school policymakers actually do not want teachers to be scholars.

The less informed and analytical teachers are, the less likely they will cause problems for the reeducators. Amazingly, we have reached an educational epoch in which a politics of stupidification is sometimes being employed in relation to the teaching profession. As I experienced when I was first looking for a teaching position at the high school level, my scholarly aspirations and experience in the sociology and history of curriculum development were liabilities and not assets in my job search. After several rejections by principals, a wise and sympathetic social studies supervisor in the school district told me, "You can't talk about these scholarly concerns in your interviews. You're going to have to play dumb." I took her sage advice and during my next interview, where I mumbled crass clichés about "loving the children," I was offered a position.

As the contextualizing dimensions of teacher education become relics of previous eras, philosophical and historical analyses of educational purpose are replaced by a state-mandated hodgepodge of topics. Study of the aims of a democratic education is replaced by reductionistic proficiencies and competencies articulated in the language of behavioral objectives or outcomes. An actual example in teacher education: "The student will be able to (TSWBAT) begin each component of a lesson plan with TSWBAT"—no kidding. Many states carefully limit the number of courses in which teacher education students study the so-called professional aspects of education, where scholarly questions of purpose, context, politics, and culture are analyzed in relation to school organization, curriculum development, and cultural practice.

In the place of these experiences, states mandate specific content, such as how to construct proper lesson plans and correctly administer standardized texts. Concerned with meeting the crazy-quilt requirements, colleges/schools/departments of education without visionary and gutsy leadership begin to lose sight of the scholarly dimension of teacher education. The organizations find themselves becoming more and more technicianized, dehumanized, and standardized and less and less scholarly, learning oriented, and student centered. Observing what is passing for coursework in such a college/school/department of education, professors in liberal arts and sciences find new ammunition for accusations of anti-intellectualism in teacher education. Most of the time such professors are less than sympathetic with teacher education's attempts to deal with the politicized, shortsighted state intrusions into their professional practice. The cycle of degradation is exacerbated.

In the pathological climate created by corporate-embedded state regulation of teacher education, professors are inundated with activities related to strategic planning. In this new context, colleges/schools/departments of teacher education are expected to delete non–revenue generating "sectors" such as foreign language education. Numerous highly paid consultants are brought in to advise administrators on how to profitably focus their attention. Open discussion by faculty about the political dynamics and moral/ethical dimensions of teacher education do not resonate with the spirit of the new regulations. Innovative teacher education and the production of knowledge about the pedagogical cosmos are less important in the regulated world than sustaining the organization and bowing to the private interests involved. In such a domain, becoming a "team player" elicits the greatest rewards, as it contributes to an uncomplicated flow of activities and the standardization of the teacher education product. Even as regulated teacher educators attempt to play the game, they find less support, more closures of university teacher education programs, and their exclusion from formulation of school reform policies (Cochran-Smith, 2000; Vavrus and Archibald, 1998; Getzel, 1997; Grimmett, 1999).

Problems and Possibilities in Teacher Education: Welcome to the Dollhouse

Simply put, teacher education is ensnared in a swamp of complications. Those of us concerned with the future of the teaching profession and its central role in promoting a healthy, democratic society have no choice but to make sense of these complexities. Understanding what is of worth and what is fluff, the problems resulting from regulation, and the problems that are self-generated is a daunting task. With these difficulties in mind, I have often made the statement that the worst pedagogy and the best pedagogy I have observed in higher education have been in colleges/schools/departments of education. When teacher education is good, it is truly a work of pedagogical artistry. The adept education professor brings a variety of knowledges and conceptual frameworks together to engage students in a both intellectual and practical exercise in the act of teaching and the understanding of forces shaping education.

The reductionistic technician orientations referenced above are self-generated problems that reflect positivistic ways of conceptualizing professional practice. While teacher education must take responsibility for such mistakes, it is not alone. All professional education has been plagued by such technicism. In this construct, teachers need be provided only with the technical skills of teaching. Such goals have nothing to do with politics and little to do with culture, and philosophical/historical understandings are irrelevant. Indeed, being a well-educated, informed individual is not a requirement here. Advocates of such traditional technical approaches to teacher education, Gary Fenstermacher (1994) argues, have missed the boat. University-based teacher education has a central role in the improvement of teaching, but it must find its way in the complex morass previously described. The only way out of the wilderness is to construct a vision of educational practice around democratic principles, ethical concerns, and a rigorous notion of teachers as scholars.

To the degree that teacher education is associated with behavioral training and mechanistic procedures, it will fail. Great teaching is not now and has never been grounded in the mastery of routinized functions. Practicing teachers have long understood the muddleheadedness of teacher education directives about the *proper* way to teach issued in university classrooms. It docsn't require great practice in ethnography to discern such teachers' attitudes toward such technical "how to teach" courses. How many times have I recorded practicing teachers saying, "My teacher education methods courses were worthless. They had nothing to do with the world I've faced in schools." Yet, in this technicianized world of professional education, such teachers possessed little experience with analyses of educational purpose, the consequences of education for differing groups of students, the nature of knowledge production and its influence on curriculum, the ways the political economy shapes the form that school takes, or their roles as teacher and democratic agent in relation to these dynamics. The technicists are traveling a lost highway. Improving teacher education and reforming schools requires far more than technical fine-tuning.

We all need to be cognizant of the vicissitudes of professional teacher education. No one needs to understand these complexities more, however, than teacher education students. Not only do teacher education students typically not know anything about these issues, they rarely are even provided an institutional welcome to the college/school/department of education. What is a college of education? Why does it exist? What are its components? How does it fit into the university? What are its goals? Are there differences in opinion about the answers to such questions? Where does the student fit into this teacher education matrix? These are only a few of the orientation queries to which students should be exposed. The technicist ethic assumes that in their role as rule followers and passive receptors of truths about teaching, teacher education students don't need such a conceptual overview. Such an introduction to colleges of education lays the foundation for the more rigorous critical complex form of teacher education advocated here.

Teacher education students begin to understand that pedagogical methods and classroom management techniques are not isolated, rule-driven, universal procedures but parts of larger articulations of educational purposes. The "critical" aspect of critical complex teacher education involves the ability to view everyday teaching practice from a variety of contextual vantage points—including social justice and power. Such an ability engages teacher education students in a process of self-education and the development of the ability to discern the origins and effects of existing educational arrangements (Davidovich, 1996). Here teacher education students learn that what presently exists did not have to be the way it is. The educational status quo was formed by human beings and thus can be re-formed by them. This critical dimension of the teacher education process is the one most often missing.

One can uncover this important absence and its negative effects on many planes of pedagogical practice. One example involves the ways teacher education students and practicing teachers often accept existing arrangements of schools as givens, as if they could have been constructed in no other way. Knowledge is provided to teachers, who subsequently demonstrate their ability to retransmit the unproblematized data back to teacher students on standardized evaluation instruments. How could it be any other way? Another example involves teacher education students' and practicing teachers' attention to individuals and aggregations of individuals and ways of "disciplining" them in classroom settings. Concerns with the formation of students' identities, their ways of seeing the world, and the effects of their membership in ethnic, racial, religious, socioeconomic, or gendered groups is less important.

In no way is this meant to belittle the concern of teacher education students about survival skills such as the ability to adeptly manage their students, to not be "eaten alive" in their classrooms. I am very sensitive to such anxieties. Such concerns arise when teacher education students are denied access to systematic observation and analysis of school and classroom practice. Students are not told that they will not learn how to manage classrooms in university teacher education classrooms. Propositional knowledge that is presented in five-step packages displayed on an overhead projector will not help them. Critical complex teacher education programs get this point across early in the orientation process and get students into research-oriented school placements as early as possible.

In such programs, students don't walk into university teacher education classrooms asking for four surefire steps to effective classroom management. They understand that the concepts engaged in the university classroom involve a different type of knowledge, a more sophisticated epistemology of practice that moves beyond providing steps to particular classroom activities. This makes for a much smoother operation of a teacher education program—a program in which students' expectations are not at odds with the purpose of particular teacher education experiences. Professionally schooled in this manner, teachers develop a far more sophisticated sense of their personal need for lifelong teacher education. In this context, such in-service experiences can be developed by teachers themselves and not imposed on them by hierarchical superiors. In this way, in-service education might become a source of pleasure and practicality, not a mandated pain to be endured. The pathway to such critical improvements can be constructed in the first orientation experiences in a college program.

Dealing with Positivism

A key aspect of understanding the bizarre and complex world of teacher education involves an appreciation of the rationalistic, scientific-managerial, and positivistic forces that have too often shaped colleges/schools/departments of education. In these intersecting traditions, we can observe the ways objectivity, hyperrationality, efficiency, and accountability have molded both the purpose of teacher education and the components of teacher education programs. A central concept in this book involves the understanding that teacher education students who don't grasp the influence of the epistemology of positivism will not gain the larger conceptual overview being promoted in a critical complex orientation. A brief description of positivism is in order.

Positivism is an epistemological position. Epistemology is the branch of philosophy that studies the nature of knowledge. In the context of education—teacher education in particular—epistemology has tacitly shaped not only the organization of schooling but even the way we think about and conceptualize it. Epistemology, especially its positivist variety, even shapes who we are, the way we see the world, and the way we picture ourselves as teachers. The assumptions of positivist epistemology are drawn from the logic and methods of investigation associated with Cartesian-Newtonian physical science. In such a context, the complexity of interpretation holds little status. What is important in the positivistic context involves explanation, prediction, and technical control. Moral and ethical questions about the ways we decide what constitutes a desirable state of affairs are of little consequence. Knowledge, to the positivist, is worthy to the extent that it describes objective data.

Critical complex questions concerning the ways knowledge is constructed are irrelevant when positivists assume that knowledge is objective, value free, and unscathed by hidden assumptions. Critical complex analysts understanding the bogus nature of claims to objectivity study the codes, media, ideologies, cultural inscriptions, discursive rules, and socioeconomic structures that shape "facts" and the political interests that direct the selection and evaluation of all data. Since the hidden values that shape all knowledge are unexamined by positivism, the positivistic cult of objectivity suppresses moral, ethical, and political concerns in research, analysis, and practice. For example, in the culture of positivism, the cultural inscriptions and political effects of IQ tests are not relevant. From a positivist perspective, an IQ test is an objective scientific instrument—end of story. Thus, positivism is silent about its own political nature. It is incapable of gaining insight into how power asymmetries hide in the language of teacher education, teaching, and everyday life. Since it is incapable of reflecting on the political dimension of its own thinking, it ultimately offers uncritical support for the status quo and its inequities (Kincheloe and Weil, 2002; Giroux, 1997; Aronowitz, 1988).

Central to the understanding of positivism and its effects on teaching and teacher education is the notion that differing epistemologies may be required in diverse areas of knowledge production. For example, ways of seeing and thinking about the world appropriated from the physical sciences simply do not fit neatly in the humanities, psychology, and education. Focusing on the goals of prediction and control, the positivism of the physical science discourse emphasizes exactness and precision. In an educational context operating within the orbit of positivist discourse, the concern with exactness and precision overrides the latitude and flexibility needed for teaching in a complex and ever-changing classroom setting. The positivistic effort to devise precise, universally applicable rules for what a teacher is supposed to do in such a setting is futile—the situation is far too mercurial and complex. Indeed, this is why we use *complexity* and *complex* to describe our approach to teacher education and teaching.

Thus, positivist teacher educators attempt to produce exact forms of empirical proof for concepts and methods of acting that are nonempirical in nature. How might a critical complex teacher educator measure a student teacher's ability to discern and respond to individual students' emotional needs in an appropriate manner? This is a complex question because we would have to define what constitutes an emotional need—not an empirical question. We would have to define "in an appropriate manner"—not an empirical question. Once we have agreed on these issues, we would have to devise an instrument to measure the quality of the responses. Could it be possible that to make it measurable we might have to simplify this complex operation to the point that we lose its very meaning? Such reductionism affects every positivistic attempt to measure the teaching act.

Many students of pedagogy recognize the inadequacy of positivism in teacher education. All too often, however, political and educational leaders who devise regulations for colleges/schools/departments of education do not share such insights. As long as such assumptions remain unchallenged at the policymaking level, teacher education will be mired in epistemological quicksand. The efforts of teacher educators, teachers, and students to pursue complex and troubling dimensions of educational practice will be impeded by policies grounded in an unquestioned positivism. Teacher education and professional educational practice involve far more than a body of neutral interactions governed by universal and unchangeable laws. Social, psychological, and educational activities and experiences do not proceed with a lawlike predictability. Contrary to the assertion of positivism, unchanging laws do not govern education. The role of the educational scholar is not to uncover these laws and pass them along to teacher educators who then in turn teach them to their students. There are no universal statements to be made about the correct way to teach. These are moral, ethical, and political issues that cannot be put to rest by empirical investigation. There is more than one good way to teach. How we decide to teach depends on a plethora of value decisions all teachers are required to make either consciously or unconsciously. Again, these are complex issues.

What we are attempting to avoid is the positivistic, technicist tendency in teacher education to take unproblematized universal truths, transform them into fixed pedagogical procedures, and pass them along to students.

After years of research and analysis undermining the sanctity of this reductionistic model, there persists the idea in many corners of university teacher education and in-service teacher education conducted by school districts that if teachers just learned the "correct teaching methods," everything would be okay (Novick, 1996; Munby and Russell, 1996). I see this daily in New York City, where teachers are subjected to parroting the correct teaching methods in Success for All (SFA) and other degrading positivistic teacher *training* programs. Many teachers rebel against such programs and refuse to buy into their view of teaching or the deskilled role of teacher.

Other teachers and teacher educators accept the programs and their assumptions and become nervous, right-answer deliverers or receivers. In my teacher education classes, I always encounter a cadre of teachers who are preoccupied with "getting it right." They view teacher education as the provision of correct methods and are uncomfortable with encounters with complexity and the effort to raise questions about the political, moral, ethical, and epistemological assumptions embedded in particular practices. Their experiences in school, in teacher education, and in-service have made it difficult for them to conceptualize teaching as a lifelong journey into new domains and new teaching and learning experiences (Noone and Cartwright, 1996). In positivistic modes of teacher education, such lifetime learning orientations are squashed under the weight of immediate practicality. Technical teacher education is not a quest for meaning and modes of engaging students in this great search as much as it is a flirtation with crass applicability. Too many teachers continue to be victimized by this positivistic subversion of democratic modes of conceptualizing a complex pedagogy.

Engaging University Arts and Sciences in a Critical Complex Teacher Education

There seems to be lots of empirical data supporting the assertion that too many teachers leave college academically unprepared to teach effectively (Regents Task Force, 1998). As long as this is true, teacher education cannot be improved. While there are many complex social, cultural, philosophical, economic, and pedagogical causes of this reality that will take decades of reform to alter, there are some factors that can be addressed immediately. One of these involves the quality of the university coursework teachers receive. The authors of this book are keenly aware of the problems in colleges/schools/departments of education and direct many of their comments, inquiries, and analyses to improvement in this domain. What is often missed in the public bashing of professional education, however, is that this is only one dimension of university teacher education. Colleges/schools/ departments of liberal arts and sciences also educate teachers. In many programs, teachers spend more of their time in arts and sciences than they do in colleges of education. Arts and sciences must accept their share of the blame for the miseducation of our teachers.

All students—teacher education students in particular—need to come away from university arts and sciences courses with understandings of contemporary societies and their pasts so they can appreciate the social, cultural, and political contexts that shape these societies and that shape individuals as members of groups. Such students are better prepared to understand connections between these contexts and schooling. With such awareness, they are empowered to develop a moral and ethical vision of politics that relates to their professional goals as educators. In addition, knowledge in these domains helps students enter into conversation about social values and civic responsibilities both in general and in relation to the role of schools in a democratic society.

With these abilities and understandings, potential teachers are ready to study the complexities of knowledge production, the forces that shape its character, and how these dynamics influence the nature of things. Here potential teachers begin to conceptualize power in a sophisticated manner and develop the skills to transfer such insight into wider historical, scientific, and political appreciation of the complex forces shaping their profession. University arts and sciences, to say the least, often fail to provide prospective teachers with such experiences (Ferreira and Alexandre, 2000). Too often, undergraduate arts and sciences grant students little more than a smattering of unproblematized and unconnected "basic facts" about an academic domain. As a complex act, teaching demands a rigorous and conceptually sophisticated education for teachers.

Grounded in the same technicism described above, arts and sciences have excluded sophisticated strategies of meaning making and conceptual analysis from their undergraduate programs. As they pass along predigested empirical truths for memorization by students, they have too often ignored processes of analysis, research abilities, and skills of interpretation. Such processes and many of the academic traditions that have produced them have been consciously excluded from the arts and sciences curriculum. Most students graduate from college unfamiliar with phenomenology, epistemological studies, hermeneutics, critical theory, discourse analysis, and even diverse modes of knowledge production (Shaker and Kridel, 1989; Pinar, 1994). This must change in the effort to graduate better academically prepared teachers, as well as businesspeople, doctors, social workers, chemists, journalists, criminologists, and engineers.

To assert our position directly: Too many university arts and sciences programs are still oppressed by the same archaic notion of scientific epistemology that has dominated university teacher education. The education that results from such technicism fails to equip students with the skills needed by the various professions. In this context, the normative, ethical, and moral dimensions of professional practice are ignored. Graduates are on their own when applying the information they have learned to complex social settings. Obviously, people are ingenious and inventive and many learn to deal with such complex operations. But they could be so much better prepared for the process by exposure to and detailed analysis of what happens when academic knowledge collides with the complex exigencies of the lived world.

One of the greatest epistemological and thus pedagogical mistakes of university education in general has involved the isolation of knowledge from experience. In technicist, positivist teacher education. we have separated knowledge about teaching from the everyday experience of teaching. Teacher educators have failed to ask what happens when teachers take this knowledge about teaching into the fast-moving, complex, multidimensional, contextually inscribed, ever-changing world of the classroom (Fischer, 1998; Munby and Russell, 1996). Teacher education students and practicing teachers understand this complex epistemological dynamic well. The language they use to express it is very familiar to teacher educators:

"All this is good on paper, but when you get to the classroom it's useless."

"That may be good in theory."

"You've been living in the ivory tower too long—this isn't going to work with real students."

"I've been around a while and this is just another fad that will be replaced by something else next year."

As students in technicist arts and sciences programs and teacher education programs move into the domain of practice, these insights often engender anger and cynicism. Many of them return to professional education only when required to by various vocational and financial incentives. I understand their exasperation.

Imbued with bodies of isolated facts about the world but devoid of the conceptual connections that are essential to the development of worldviews, visions of educational purposes, and the development of a teacher persona as ethical agent, many teachers flounder. They are unequipped to see the connections between social context and educational setting or the relationship between student performance and the multidimensional forces that shape student consciousness, identity, and relation to the school. They end up comfortable with decontextualized, individualistic notions of student behavior:

"Maria's so lazy."

"Jack has a bad attitude."

"Donnie is just not capable of doing well in school."

"The students in this class just can't learn."

Such perspectives result from a consistent lack of exposure to the ways human beings are shaped by specific historical, social, economic, and cultural forces. Many teachers learn to see only the immediacy of school and student experience. They have not encountered ways of seeing the power of forces not immediately visible in everyday interactions. This ability is central to a critical complex conception of teacher education.

The appreciation of such complex ways of seeing should be cultivated in both arts and sciences and in teacher education, neither of which typically discusses the idea that the development of such analytical abilities should be a function of their undergraduate curricula. Moreover, little thought is given to the responsibilities of colleges of arts and sciences in the education of teachers in their first two years of higher education. Deans of arts and sciences often assert that their curricula hold no special responsibility to teacher education. But when medical and engineering schools speak of premed and pre-engineering students' needs in these first two years, such arts and sciences leaders often respond quickly and decisively to adjust the curriculum. Status differences are exposed in multiple ways in the academy.

In teacher education the result of such dynamics operates to position many prospective teachers in the den of passivity constructed by formal learning, with its memorization exercises. Such students sometimes find it extremely difficult to move to a more active learning venue. When first confronted with notions of learners as researchers, as skeptics in relation to the delivery of unproblematized knowledge, as interpreters rather than receivers of professorial pronouncements, as self-directed explorers of knowledge production, as perceivers of complexity and ambiguity, they experience profound discomfort. Arts and sciences professors should be distressed when teacher education or any students leave their classrooms in this frame of mind. Again, a critical complex teacher education is not only the responsibility of colleges/schools/departments of education.

The Collision of the Craft Culture and the Research Culture of Teacher Education: The Panic over "Systemic Functions"

As if all of these problems in the bizarre, complex, and misunderstood world of teacher education did not make the improvement of teaching hard enough, teacher educators and teachers have had to deal with the existence of two competing cultures in the educational profession. Even casual involvement with teacher education will reveal the existence of both a "craft culture" and a "research culture." The research culture exerts little impact on the craft culture, and many times educational researchers seem quite unconcerned by this reality. Such a disconnection from research ultimately has a negative impact on members of the craft culture. It must be admitted, however, that because of the separation of the two domains, the craft culture has escaped the worst of the positivist delineation of correct procedures to follow. Skilled teachers in the craft culture develop profoundly sophisticated ways of multitasking while managing the everyday chaos of a classroom (Bereiter, 2002). There are varying degrees of success and failure in this context, and changing cultural conditions profoundly affect the nature of the process.

Nevertheless, skilled teachers perform these complex tasks adroitly. Where the negative consequences of the cultural split show up for members of the craft culture is in deficiencies in their expertise in relation to such issues as:

- educational purpose

- cultural context

- knowledge production

- curriculum development

- cognitive understandings

- epistemologies of practice

- evaluation of student abilities

- political inscriptions on reform measures such as context standards

- social justice

- teachers as knowledge producers

Here the craft culture is complacent and comfortable with the political and educational status quo. The cultural chasm in this case works to isolate teachers from compelling ideas and active minds engaged with dynamic issues. The breach removes researchers from the complexity of practice and the needs of teachers in this complicated context. A critical complex vision of teacher education attempts to create a new culture, in which an egalitarian spirit, a concern with practice, a social vision of what could be, and an awareness of the relation of education to the world of cultural politics operate to bring the two groups together.

There is no doubt that such a task will be difficult. The attempt to induce educational researchers to think about the interrelationships among empirical knowledge about education, the normative understandings that provide direction and vision, and classroom experience will not be easy. The effort to enjoin members of the craft culture to view education as an intellectual pursuit and teaching as a learning profession will be stressful. But I am confident that it can be done. Indeed, we can find numerous examples where a synergy or synthesis of the two cultures has already taken place successfully. Teachers will have to be provided time to engage in systematic learning and various forms of inquiry. Collaborative learning and interchange among teachers will have to be valued and rewarded. Teacher educators whose research is concerned not only with the traditional empirical methodology of higher education but with normative knowledges and analyses of practice must not be punished by positivistic conceptions of "proper research" held by university tenure and promotion committees. Indeed, universities must make it as easy as possible for university teacher educators to produce valued knowledge about education and connect it to teaching practice (Elmore, 1997; Grimmett, 1999; Britzman, 1991; Cole and Knowles, 1996).

Teacher education students are, of course, the most victimized players in the two-culture profession. As they find themselves ensnared in the middle of the conflict, they often encounter conflict between what they were told to do in their university courses and the demands of the school district in which they are student teaching. I have seen this conflict manifest itself on numerous occasions. For example, as the cultures came into conflict in one setting, student teachers were removed from their field placements for employing pedagogical approaches learned in university courses that were at odds with school mandates. While I was a professor at Penn State I had to struggle to get a student back into a teacher education program who had actually been removed from candidacy for employing "unacceptable" teaching methods on the first day of his placement.

He had learned these strategies in a language and literacy methods course. No diligent teacher education student should have to experience the stress and anxiety this conscientious student endured.

No wonder teacher education students are often so nervous about student teaching and the mechanics of surviving their classrooms, filled with diverse and restless students. It should not be surprising to anyone that they tell teacher educators over and over about their perceived need for practical classes—courses on classroom management and ways to teach. Caught in the middle of the professional two-culture conflict, they find out that it is these practical types of courses that elicit so much debate among the various interest groups in teacher education. The type of hands-on practical experiences desired by nervous teacher education students are best taught within elementary and secondary schools, not in university classrooms. Indeed, a critical complex teacher education recognizes the dissonance students perceive in their professional education and works to address it. Teacher education students need to learn as early as possible in their program that there are different types of knowledges to be learned about teaching and education. In this context the distinctions made previously in relation to empirical knowledge about teaching, moral or ethical (normative) knowledge about education, and knowledge derived from teaching experience become profoundly important.

These epistemological understandings—contrary to the conventional wisdom—are not meant only for teacher educators. With these distinctions in mind, teacher education students should get into school settings as soon as possible. They should be involved with Gary Fenstermacher's (1994) notion of the "systemic functions of school." It is this systemic knowledge that students worry so much about (Munby and Russell, 1996). The systemic functions are not empirical or normative knowledges although the knowledges do interact and affect one another. These functions involve skills that are necessary to the function of the educational system, such as:

- setting up a classroom

- dealing with administrators

- planning a lesson

- managing a classroom

- communicating with parents

- obtaining materials

- administering tests

- determining and recording grades

- taking attendance

- dealing with emergencies

When university teacher education courses operate simply to transmit these systemic skills, an epistemological mistake is made. The university classroom is not a good venue for teaching such experiential types of knowledge. We know too much about the epistemology of practice to allow these problems to continue. The two cultures need to discuss what each does well and then discern what each can learn from the other.

The Critical Complex Vision: Teachers as Scholars and Policymakers

The vision on which this work is based involves the empowerment of teachers. I want universities to produce rigorously educated teachers with an awareness of the complexities of educational practice and an understanding of and commitment to a socially just, democratic notion of schooling. Only with a solid foundation in various mainstream and alternative canons of knowledge can teachers begin to make wise judgments and informed choices about curriculum development and classroom practice. In this context they can craft a teacher persona that enables them to diagnose individual and collective needs of their students and connect them to their pedagogical strategies and goals. It is naive and dangerous to think that teachers can become the rigorous professionals envisioned here without a conceptual understanding of contemporary and past societies and the sociocultural, political, and economic forces that have shaped them. Such knowledges are essential in the process of both understanding and connecting the cultural landscape of the twenty-first century to questions of educational purpose and practice (Bruner, 1996; McGuire, 1996; Ferreira and Alexandre, 2000; McNeil, 2000).

Few seem to understand the demands of high-quality teaching of a critical democratic variety in the twenty-first century. After listening, for example, to former mayor of New York Rudolph Giuliani and other high-ranking city officials chastise and degrade New York City teachers over the last decade, I understand the anger and cynicism these teachers harbor as they open their classroom doors to start the day. The emotional complexity of their lives haunts me as I engage them in rigorous graduate school analyses of the various knowledges demanded by the critical complex vision. "Why learn this," they sometimes ask me, "when the system won't let us apply it in our deskilled classrooms?" This is a tough question. I struggle for the right words, for inspirational words to let them know the value of the vision. Literally, there is no hope for educational reform if they do not gain detailed insight into:

- the context in which education takes place

- the historical forces that have shaped the purposes of schooling

- the ways dominant power uses schools for antidemocratic ideological self-interest

- how all of this relates to the effort to develop a democratic, transformative pedagogy

- the specific ways all of these knowledges relate to transformative classroom teaching in general and to their particular curricular domains in particular

Only with these and similar insights and skills can teachers build rigorous communities of practice that empower them to develop more compelling ways of teaching and conceptualizing pedagogy. And just as importantly, in these communities of practice they can mobilize the political power to educate the public about the nature of a rigorous, democratic education and the types of resources and citizen action that are necessary to make it a reality. Given the political context of the twenty-first century, with its "reeducated" public and corporatized information environment, the friends of democracy and education have no other choice. Thus, critical complex teaching involves teachers as knowledge producers—knowledge workers who pursue their own intellectual development. At the same time, such teachers work together in their communities of practice to sophisticate both the profession's and the public's appreciation of what it means to be an educated person. They ask how schools can work to ensure that students from all possible backgrounds achieve this goal (Horn, 2000; Smyth, 2001; Bereiter, 2002). In this context such educators engage the public in developing more sophisticated responses to questions such as:

- What does it mean "to know" something?

- What is involved in the process of understanding?

- What are the moral responsibilities of understanding?

- What does it mean to act on one's knowledge and understanding in the world?

- How do we assess when individuals have engaged these processes in a rigorous way?

Teachers as scholars demand respect as they engage diverse groups in these and other questions about education in a democratic society. They alert individuals to the demands of democratic citizenship that require the lifelong pursuit of learning. In such a context, no teacher and no concerned citizen is ever fully educated; he or she is always "in process," waiting for the next learning experience. As they claim and occupy such an important sociopolitical role, critical complex teachers dismantle the Berlin Wall that separates educational policy from practice. Those who make educational policy almost never engage in classroom practice. These policymakers, especially in the recent standards reforms, have in many cases completely disregarded the expertise and concerns of classroom teachers and imposed the most specific modes of instructional practice on them (Schubert, 1998; Elmore, 1997). This type of imposition is unacceptable. Teachers in a democratic society have to play a role in professional practice, the education of the public, and educational policymaking.

Categorizing the Multiple Forms of Pedagogical Knowledge: Developing a Meta-epistemological Perspective

We are asking teachers and teacher education students to gain complex understandings not previously demanded of educational practitioners. The following is a delineation of the types of knowledges required in a critical complex teacher education. This delineation is conceptually wrapped in what might be called a meta-epistemological package that grounds many of the categories of knowledges teachers need to know. What follows is a review and categorical conceptualization of some of the issues already discussed. A meta-epistemological perspective is a central understanding in a critical complex conception of teacher professionalism (Strom, 2000). Simply put, such an insight helps us approach the contested concept of a "knowledge base for education." In our meta-epistemological construction, the educational knowledge base involves the recognition of different types of knowledges of education, including but not limited to empirical, experiential, normative, critical, ontological, and reflective-synthetic domains.

Such an assertion challenges more traditional and technical forms of teacher education that conceptualized teaching as a set of skills—not a body of knowledges. Thus, in the framework promoted here, teaching, before it is anything else, is epistemological—a concept that wreaks havoc in the pedagogical world. As an epistemological dynamic, teaching, as Hugh Munby and Tom Russell (1996) contend, "depends on, is grounded in, and constitutes knowledge." If the teaching profession doesn't grasp and embrace this understanding, as well as the different types of knowledges associated with teaching and the diverse ways they are taught and learned, teacher education will continue to be epistemologically bankrupt and viewed as a philistine vocation. In the meta-epistemological domain, critical complex teacher educators avoid this philistinism by analyzing the epistemological and other types of tacit assumptions embedded in and shaping particular articulations of practice.

Such teacher educators work to discern where such assumptions emerged and the types of knowledges upon which they draw. With this in mind they seek to identify the different types of knowledges either overtly or covertly operating in the profession (Schubert, 1998; Munby and Hutchinson, 1998). Accompanying such identification is the effort to develop critical complex forms of such knowledges—in the process, studying the ways they interact with and inform one another. The teaching profession needs a clear delineation of these dynamics; practitioners need to know how knowledges are produced and applied in the pedagogical cosmos. With these insights, technicist and deskilling tendencies can be thwarted, oppressive ideologies in neutral wrappings can be exposed, and modes of regulation disguised as validated practices can be confronted.

In this meta-epistemological context, teacher educators and teachers connect such knowledges to paradigmatic awareness. The paradigm that dominated teacher education over the last half of the twentieth century involved employing universal disciplinary knowledge to ground particular types of teaching skills and practices. As noted previously, this positivistic or technically rational model has found itself criticized from a variety of angles over the last few decades. A meta-epistemological cognizance of paradigms has allowed teacher educators and teachers to appreciate the results of this rationalistic overemphasis of an unproblematized version of empirical knowledge. Such a narrow version of empiricism excluded interpretive, phenomenological, philosophical, historical, and even ethnographic forms of research data from the negotiating table of professionalism. Such paradigmatic narrowness profoundly harmed and, unfortunately, continues to harm teacher education and the quality of teaching.

Thus, meta-epistemological analysis reveals that the technically rational, positivist paradigm has been challenged because it fails to recognize the complexity of knowledge production as well as the complexity of the teaching act. It is difficult to produce universal knowledge about education when we recognize that much of the expertise of teachers rests in the particular contexts in which pedagogical action takes place. Because of these failures, much of the educational research produced over the last fifty years has exerted little effect on the everyday lives of teachers. In the epistemological recognition of complexity, critical complex teacher educators understand that there is no culminating moment of certainty when we understand teaching and the pedagogical process. We do not finally connect all the pieces of the jigsaw puzzle; there are simply too many ill-defined problems, to say nothing of the never-ending source of questions about teaching. All critical complex teacher educators will have to explain these complications to many teacher education students reared in an educational culture of positivism—these students will not be especially happy with such news (Hoban and Erickson, 1998; Strom, 2000; Noone and Cartwright, 1996; Munby and Hutchinson, 1998).

Our concern with democratic teacher empowerment demands a reconceptualization of teacher knowledge. The practitioner knowledge that teachers develop alerts them to the complexity and chaos of the classroom and the school. Such an understanding signals the innate problems with technicist attempts to produce empirical generalizations about the best way to teach. Even though the limitations of these empirical generalizations are well understood, it is impossible to escape the shadow of their scientific authority. In their perpetual vulnerability to the whims of public opinion, teachers are unable to prove their competence through their practitioner experiential knowledge. Because it has not been "scientifically" validated, this knowledge holds no legitimacy in the court of public opinion. Thus, state legislatures demand scientific validation of teaching practice. As a result, teachers are forced to abandon practitioner knowledge in favor of practices scientifically endorsed by the research base—practices that may directly contradict subtle practitioner understandings (Smyth, 2001; Kincheloe and Weil, 2002; Altrichter and Posch, 1989; Garrison, 1988). Meta-epistemological understandings of pedagogical knowledge are necessary in this and many other professional educational contexts.

Our meta-epistemological knowledge alerts us to the process that produces the narrow technical teaching skills demanded by state accreditation organizations and legislative bodies. Some colleges/schools/departments of education are required to merely deliver particular required courses, irrespective of the guiding philosophy of their programs. Such a positivist process of knowledge production about teaching banishes alternative modes of information because the positivist process is grounded in a premise of "certainty." Thus, the complexities and contradictions that mark pedagogy are summarily dismissed as lesser, unvalidated knowledges. In light of a meta-epistemological appreciation of diverse pedagogical knowledges, the reductionistic model of applied positivistic knowledge is no longer defensible in professional medical, legal, business, social work, or teacher education. Epistemological awareness in all of these domains has moved professional educators to be wary of the impositional relationship between positivist knowledge and practice.

In this rationalized situation—usually spoken of in terms of theory and practice—positivist knowledge is applied to practice. The hidden curriculum of this technicist process promotes a passive view of teachers. Indeed, practitioners become rule followers who are rendered more "supervisable" with their standardized lesson plan formats and their adaptation to technical valuation/accountability plans. Talk in such a positivistic context about democratic education when teachers occupy the role of disempowered technicians rings hollow. In the complex lived world of teaching, this situation has typically resulted in practitioners rebelling against such outside regulation and rejecting "theory" outright. This countermove by practitioners often results in an exclusive reliance on the authority of experience (Vavrus and Archibald, 1998; Lomax and Parker, 1996; Ferreira and Alexandre, 2000).

Because of these knowledge-related problems in teacher education, many have looked askance at colleges of education and the educational field in general. In addition to viewing teacher education as an immature academic discipline, observers in higher education have maintained that there is no knowledge base to the field. These concerns are central to our meta-epistemological analysis. In light of the different knowledges of education that we are documenting here, it may be important for critical complex teacher educators to argue that the education knowledge base is a contingent notion (Lester, 2001; Ferreira and Alexandre, 2000; Strom, 2000). What constitutes "essential education knowledge" always depends on one's view of pedagogical purpose—a normative form of knowledge.

Indeed, the ways we connect normative knowledge to empirical knowledge profoundly affect what might be defined as a knowledge base. Thus, what we label a knowledge base for education may have more to do with the concepts involved in a meta-epistemological analysis of the different categories of knowledge involved with pedagogy than with the delineation of a body of empirical facts. This recognition is central to the critical complex view of teacher education. With this understanding, teacher educators, teachers, and students are empowered to gain a far clearer picture of the complex demands of teacher education, develop the ability to understand the use value of particular types of information, and discern ways that great teachers connect the various categories of pedagogical knowledge.

Empirical Knowledge about Education

Empirical knowledge comes from research based on data derived from sense data/observations of various aspects of education. Throughout this chapter I expressed reservations about the positivist version of empirical knowledge and its uses—but not about the concept of empirical knowledge itself. A critical complex teacher education demands more sophisticated forms of sense observational knowledges of education. A thicker, more complex, more textured, self-conscious form of empirical knowledge takes into account the situatedness of the researcher and the researched—where they are standing or are placed in the social, cultural, historical, philosophical, economic, political, and psychological web of reality. Such insight respects the complexity of the interpretive dimension of empirical knowledge production.

A critical complex empiricism understands that there may be many interpretations of the observations made and the data collected, that different researchers, depending on their relative situatedness, may see very different things in a study of the same classroom. Power dynamics such as ideological orientation, discursive embeddedness, disciplinary experience, ad infinitum, may shape the research lenses of various researchers in diverse and even contradictory ways. Once we understand these dynamics, we can never be naive researchers again. Empirical knowledge about education enters into an even more complex realm when educators ask what it tells them about practice. Since such knowledge has such a complex interaction with and multidimensional relationship to practice, there will always be diverse articulations of its practical implications. Too many teacher educators have not understood these dynamics. Serious consequences occur when this happens.

A critical complex empiricism understands that knowledge about humans and their social practices is fragmented, diverse, and always constructed by human beings coming from different contexts. Such a form of knowledge does not lend itself to propositional statements—i.e., final truths. Indeed, a critical complex empirical knowledge does not seek validation by reference to universal truths. Rather it remains somewhat elusive, resistant to the trap of stable and consistent meaning. The way it is understood will always involve the interaction between our general conceptions of it and its relationship with ever-changing contexts. Thus, our conception of empirical knowledge is more dialectical than propositional. Simply put, there is not one single answer to any research question, and no one question is superior to all others. Particular empirical descriptions will always conflict with others, tensions between accounts will persist, and alternative perspectives will continue to struggle for acceptance.

The technical rationality of positivism failed to heed the warning that this stuff is complicated. In the technical-rationalist articulation of the empirical project, there was nothing too complex about educational knowledge production and its role in teacher education: Researchers defined educational problems and solved them by rigorous fidelity to the scientific method. These solutions were passed along to practitioners who put them into practice. A critical complex empiricism avoids this technical rationality and the certainty that accompanies it. It never prescribes precise content and validated instructional techniques for teachers' use. In the critical complex perspective, there is no certain knowledge about what subject matter to teach, the proper way to develop a curriculum, the correct understanding of students, or the right way to teach (Pozzuto, Angell, and Pierpont, 2000; Report of Undergraduate Teacher Education Program, 1997; CPRE, 1995). The relationship between such knowledge and practice in its complexity is open to discussion and interpretation.

In this discussion, a critical complex empiricism refuses to undermine other types of educational knowledges and exclude them from the process. For example, the experiential knowledge teachers derive from teaching is deemed very important in this context. Traditional positivist perspectives created a chasm between empirical knowledge and experience, as they excluded teachers from the knowledge-production dimension of the profession. The concept of great teachers as virtuosos who produce brilliant pieces of pedagogical performance/knowledge was alien to the positivist conception of empirical knowledge about education. In a positivist context, teachers were expected to follow empirical imperatives, not to produce masterpieces (Segall, 2002; Britzman, 1991; Horn, 2000). If teachers don't belong at the conference table of knowledge production in education, then the table deserves to be dismantled.

Critical complex empirical knowledge about education avoids the positivist tendency to represent itself as a distinct, autonomous object—a thing-in-itself. Here critical complex knowledge always acknowledges the contexts of its production and interpretation. Valuing the relationships that connect various knowledges, researchers in the complex domain ask how education experience is constructed and educational meaning is made (Denzin and Lincoln, 2000; Day, 1996). In such explorations, they walk through a gate into a more pragmatic dimension of empirical research. Understanding the contexts of knowledge production and the nature of its relation to practice, critical complex educational researchers study the half-life of their data in terms of the implementation of the knowledge. How could it be used to improve education? How is educational improvement defined? Does it promote professional awareness? How does professionalism relate to practice? Within such analyses, reflections, and inquiries, a new dawn breaks for the role of empirical knowledge in education.

Normative Knowledge about Education

Normative knowledge concerns "what should be" in relation to moral and ethical issues about education. What constitutes moral and ethical behavior on the part of teacher educators and teachers? How do we develop a vision of practice that will empower educators to embrace these behaviors without fear of reprisals? Such questions began the theoretical work necessary to the development of a democratic, egalitarian sense of educational purpose. Such normative knowledge is central to the effort to establish just and rigorous colleges/schools/departments of education and schools of various varieties. Such knowledge is not produced arbitrarily but in relation to particular social visions, power relations, and cultural/historical contexts. With these concerns in mind we ask questions about the nature of education, the role of schools in a democratic society, and the philosophical issues raised in this process.

The "critical" in our critical complex teacher education is directly related to normative knowledge. Critical theorists such as Max Horkheimer,

Theodor Adorno, and Herbert Marcuse directly addressed this normative dimension when they wrote about the concept of "eminent critique." Moral and ethical action, they argued, cannot take place until one can envision a more desirable state of affairs, alternatives to injustice. In this context, they argued, any domain of study is ethically required to examine not only "what is" but also "what could be"—the notion of eminence. In critical pedagogy—the educational articulation of critical theory buoyed by the work of feminist theorists and the Brazilian educator Paulo Freire—advocates have confronted on normative grounds the positivistic, decontextualized, and depoliticized education often found in mainstream teacher education and in educational settings from elementary school to higher education. These institutional contexts, critical analysts maintain, have often failed to develop an ethical vision for the pedagogical process in a democratic society.

From the critical complex perspective developed in this chapter, educational rigor and social justice cannot be ethically separated. Questions of oppression and empowerment are always implicated in visions of scholarship. For example, when positivistic schools are set up to serve the needs of individuals abstracted from their social, cultural, political, and economic context(s), the privileged will be rewarded and the marginalized punished. Thus, the critical perspective develops a language of critique to expose the way that contemporary democratic societies maintain disparate social relations and in turn how these relations shape pedagogy. The complex part of the critical complex equation insists that these dynamics are even more complicated than originally understood and that advocates of critical pedagogy must be consistently vigilant about their own oppressive tendencies. The complex normative context must always be reflective about modes of oppression growing up around its advocates' own relationships to issues of race, class, gender, sexuality, religion, geographic place, etc.

As critical professionals develop these modes of normative knowledge, they begin to understand how ethical concerns are often hidden in everyday life and professional practice. They observe such masking processes at work in many cultural sites, in many colleges of education, and in secondary and elementary schools. In this cloaking process, educators are induced to accept the organizational structure and daily operations of schools as if they could be no other way. This hidden normative curriculum moves critical complex teacher educators to be concerned about positivist forms of educational knowledge production and the role such forms play in this great denial of the moral and ethical dimensions of pedagogy. Moved by this concern, criticalists argue that all of the other educational knowledges must be produced in close connection to normative knowledges.

Empirical knowledge produced outside of such normative concerns takes on the pseudo-neutrality of positivism, which promotes an unexamined normative agenda even as it claims it does not. Moreover, as we clarify the distinctions between normative knowledge and empirical knowledge, we begin to realize that positivistic requests for empirical proof of what are normative questions are epistemologically naive and misguided. One cannot "prove" a normative statement about educational purpose or professional ethics (Fischer, 1998; Goodlad, 1994; Giroux, 1997; Hinchey, 2001). No study empirically proves the inadequacy of an educational purpose—this is a different form of knowledge. Teacher educators concerned with social justice and democracy have been confronted with such epistemological inconsistencies for decades. In my own work around issues of social justice in teacher education, I have often been asked by colleagues to provide empirical evidence of the validity of such concerns. From the perspective of such educators, there was only one form of professional knowledge about education—empirical. If pedagogical insights could not be empirically proved or disproved, then they were relegated to the epistemological junk heap.

All educational programs and curricula are built on a foundation of normative knowledge—even if such knowledge is hidden or not fully understood. This is so often an inchoate awareness in teacher education and schooling. Thus, a key dimension of the work of teacher education is to bring these norms, these ethical and moral assumptions, these visions, to the light of day so they can be analyzed and discussed. Because many in teacher education have not conceptualized and talked about normative knowledge, those operating within a positivist culture of neutrality often view this analytical process with great discomfort. Discussing concepts such as a political vision undergirding teaching is often construed as a "politicization of education." More attention to normative types of knowledge can sometimes clear up these misunderstandings.

When one claims neutrality and promotes a view of education that doesn't attend to effects of human suffering, exploitation, and oppression in relation to the teaching act, a serious contradiction arises. By failing to address such issues, one has taken a distinct moral position. Such orientations in the analysis of normative knowledge are revealed and problematized. Indeed, critical complex educators consider it an ethical duty to disclose their normative perspectives, to admit their value structures, and to help students understand how such allegiances affect their teaching. Critical complex teacher education openly embraces democratic values; healthy visions of race, class, gender, and sexual equality; and the necessity of exposing the effects of power in shaping individual identity and educational purpose. This is not an act of politicization of education; education has always been politicized. Critical complex teacher educators are attempting to understand and act ethically in light of such politicization.

Critical Knowledge about Education

Critical knowledge is closely associated with normative knowledge, as it focuses on the political and power-related aspects of teacher education and teaching. In the context of critical knowledge, the charges of politicization hurled against the normative domain grow louder and often more strident. Critical complex teacher educators maintain that it is impossible to conceptualize curriculum outside of a sociopolitical context. No matter what form they take, all curricula bear the imprint of power. When teacher education students are induced to study the curriculum outside of an awareness of such horizons, they are being deceived by a claim of neutrality concerning the production of knowledge. The culture of positivism defines the curriculum as a body of agreed-upon knowledges being systematically passed along to students as an ever-evolving, but neutral, instructional process.

Critical complex teacher educators know too much to be seduced by the sirens of political neutrality. As a deliberate process, the curriculum is always a formal transmission of particular aspects of a culture's knowledge. Do we teach women's and African American history in eleventh-grade social studies? Do we read Toni Morrison and Alice Walker in twelfth-grade literature? In colleges of education, do we teach the history of Horace Mann's crusade for public education from a political-economic perspective? These are all sociopolitical questions—this means they involve power and its influence. In this context, critical complex teacher educators understand the need to build a teacher education that infuses this critical knowledge into all phases of professional education. As this takes place, teacher education students gain a far more rigorous and nuanced understanding of why education exists in its present form.

Teacher educators don't have to look very far to uncover critical knowledges in education, the exercise of power in shaping the way things are. Colleges of education are themselves implicated in power relations shaped by interest-driven legislative intervention in academic life. Responding to the needs of business and corporate leaders, legislators often impose policies presupposing a view of the educational profession that acts in the power interests of managerial elites. Appreciating such dynamics, critical complex teacher educators ground their curriculum in the notion that the socioeducational world has been constructed by the dominant power and thus can be reconstructed by human action and savvy political organization. Thus, critical complex teacher educators inject a literacy of power into their professional education curriculum. Such an orientation studies critical knowledges such as hegemony, ideology, discursive power, regulatory power, disciplinary power, and so forth.

With these critical knowledges, critical complex teacher educators gain greater familiarity with diverse cultural expressions and the ways teacher education and schooling brush against them. As researchers and knowledge workers, they develop the analytical ability to expose the insidious ways that dominant cultural inscriptions on educational contexts marginalize culturally diverse and lower-socioeconomic groups. Always mindful of race, class, and gender differences, critical complex practitioners survey their classes for patterns developing along these lines. Their critical respect for diversity allows such teachers to conceptualize multiple perspectives on issues such as intelligence, student ability, evaluation, community needs, and educational justice. Such perspectives allow for the acceptance of a diversity of expressions that exposes the fingerprints of power—in the process, bringing more parents and students to the negotiating table of educational purpose.

Appreciating that all knowledges about education, and all disciplinary knowledges, are produced in discourses of power, critical complex teacher education understands that there is no neutral ground. Imbued with such critical knowledges, it sees through positivistic technical rationality and its claim that objective researchers produce educational knowledge and theory that is then applied to neutral sites of practice. In the technical-rational context, the assumption of ideological innocence on the part of researchers and educational policymakers leads to unproblematized hierarchical assumptions between the educated and the uneducated. Wearing the badge of neutrality, such hierarchies can quickly mutate into schooling as a neo–White Man's Burden, where educational missionaries attempt to deliver the civilizing gospel of European high culture to the poor and/or nonwhite masses.

The culture of these masses is a disease to be cured, and the Western canon is the magic bullet. A central tenet of a critical complex pedagogy and of teacher education thus emerges. Such an educational orientation attempts to reclaim the cultural capital and critical knowledges of the oppressed. Using this understanding to facilitate the struggle of marginalized individuals to reappropriate their histories, linguistics, and cultures, critical complex teachers and teacher educators learn from these knowledges. In this process, teachers and learners join together, transforming this cultural capital into a new form of knowledge—a powerful and ever-dangerous subjugated knowledge (Semali and Kincheloe, 1999; O'Sullivan, 1999; King and Mitchell, 1995; Kincheloe and Steinberg, 1997; Gresson, 1995). With these ideas in mind, we come to see that critical knowledges are always interacting with the other educational knowledges, forcing teacher educators and teachers to think about experiential knowledge and practice—a profoundly complex matrix—from new angles. After engagement with critical knowledges, teacher educators and teachers can never look at the other educational knowledges in the same way.

Ontological Knowledge in Education

There is nothing new in asserting that the ways in which teachers teach, the pedagogical purposes they pursue, are directly connected to the way that teachers see themselves. At the same time, the ways that teachers come to see themselves as learners shape their teacher persona—in particular the ways in which they conceptualize what they need to learn, where they need to learn it, and how the process should take place (CPRE, 1995). Such a persona cannot be separated from the various forms of knowledge delineated here and the larger notion of "professional awareness." Too infrequently are teachers in university, student teaching, or in-service professional education encouraged to confront why they think as they do about themselves as teachers—especially in relation to the social, cultural, political, economic, and historical world around them. Teacher education provides little insight into the forces that shape identity and consciousness. Becoming educated, becoming a critical complex practitioner, necessitates personal transformation.

With such dynamics in mind, critical complex teachers are asked to confront their relationship to some long-term historical trends rarely discussed in the contemporary public conversation. Critical complex teacher educators maintain that these trends hold profound implications for the development of both professional awareness and a teacher persona. In my own case, the understanding of my personal historicization in light of five centuries of European colonialism—and of the new forms of economic,

cultural, and educational colonialism picking up steam in the contemporary era—is essential knowledge. Indeed, everyone in the contemporary
United States is shaped by this knowledge in some way, whether or not
they are conscious of it. We cannot contemplate our professional awareness without reference to these last 500 or so years and their effects. I was
born in 1950, in the middle of the postcolonial rebellion against this half-
millennial colonial violence against Africa, Asia, and Latin America, and
throughout the native lands of indigenous peoples.

While anticolonial activity continues into the twenty-first century,
postcolonial discontent reached its apex in the United States in the 1960s
and early 1970s, finding expression in the Civil Rights, women's, antiwar,
gay rights, and other liberation movements. By the mid-1970s (with its
roots in the early mid-1960s), a conservative reaction was taking shape,
with the goal of "recovering" what was perceived to have been lost in
these movements. Thus, the politics, cultural wars, and educational
debates, policies, and practices of the last three decades cannot be understood outside of these efforts to "recover" white supremacy, patriarchy,
class privilege, heterosexual "normality," Christian dominance, and the
European intellectual canon. I must decide where I stand in relation to
such profound yet muffled historical processes. I cannot conceptualize my
teacher persona outside of them. They are the defining macroconcerns of
our time, as every topic is refracted through their lenses. Any view of education, any curriculum development, any professional education conceived outside of their framework ends up becoming a form of ideological mystification.

Once we turn our analysis to the examination of ontological knowledges vis-à-vis such historical processes, we put the teacher "self" in question. Inherited dogmas and absolute beliefs are interrogated as self-
images, and teachers begin to see themselves in relation to the world
around them. They perceive the school as a piece of a larger mosaic. With
such a conceptual matrix, teachers start to see an inseparable relationship
between thinking and acting, as the boundary between feeling and logic
begins to fade from the map of teacher thinking—a map redrawn by the
cartography of teacher education and its ontological knowledges. In such
an ontological context, teachers derive the motivation to produce their
own knowledge. If teachers hold power to produce their own knowledges,
then they are empowered to reconstruct their own consciousnesses. The
top-down tyranny of expert-produced interpretations of tradition and its
oppressive power can be subverted and our futures can be reinvented
along the lines of a critical complex system of meaning making.

If positivism prevails and successfully excludes ontological, normative, and critical knowledges from professional education, teaching will too often remain a technical act. These issues of self-production will be removed from the consciousness of prospective teachers, as they memorize the generic theories and the fragments of the "knowledge base." Relegated to a static state of being, teachers in the technicist paradigm are conceived as a unit of production on an assembly line—historically abstracted outside of a wider social context. Standards reforms that decontextualize students in this manner are molded by the dynamics of history and social structure (Kincheloe and Weil, 2002). Identity is never complete and is always subject to modification in relation to prevailing ideologies, discourses, and knowledges. Critical complex teacher education encourages desocialization via ideological disembedding. Critical complex professional education coursework and practicum experiences focus on the ways in which the values of power-driven, information-saturated hyperreality of the twenty-first century shape the consciousness of both students and teachers (Britzman, 1991; Macedo, 1994; Carson, 1997; Apple, 1999; Gordon, 2001; Malewski, 2001a, 2001b). The rigorous study of cultural and historical context alerts prospective teachers to the ways that dominant myths, behavior, and language shape their view of the teacher role without conscious filtering.

Experiential Knowledge about Education

Obviously, there are experiential knowledges of education. Educators need knowledges about practice; teacher educators need to take these knowledges seriously and place them neither above nor below other forms of knowledges about education. Knowledges about practice are inherently problematic, however, because the nature of what constitutes practice is profoundly complex. There are many different forms of educational practice, such as:

- classroom teaching

- teacher leadership involving areas of curriculum and instruction

- educational administration

- educational policymaking

- teacher education

- knowledge production in education

- political activism

The point here is that there are many types of educational practice—these are just a few. Yet too often the only type of practice signified by teaching and teacher education involves classroom teaching. We have to be very careful about this type of reductionism as we work to develop and put into practice a critical complex teacher education. Thus, the form of teacher education advocated here recognizes that not only are there numerous forms of practice, but that all of them are complex. Donald Schön (1983) has used the term "indeterminate zones of practice" to signify the uncertainty, complexity, uniqueness, and contested nature of any practice. The positivistic epistemology of the contemporary university often is incapable of coping with the complexity of practice, as it applies scientific theories to practical situations. Instead, Schön promotes a practice grounded in reflection-in-action. Here practitioners engage in conscious thinking and analysis while "in practice." They have no choice, they have to do this, Schon argues, because each situation a practitioner encounters is unique. This demands a rigor that falls outside of the boundaries of positivistic technical rationality and its reductionistic rule following. I actually endured this lesson in an undergraduate teacher education class in 1971:

> Look to the overhead projector, class. Here are the five steps to writing on the chalkboard:
>
> 1. Always keep chalk longer than two inches readily available in the chalk tray.
> 2. Before writing, adjust windowshades to minimize glare on board.
> 3. Hold chalk at a 45-degree angle relative to the board.
> 4. Write letters at least five inches tall.
> 5. Dust hands before leaving the board so as not to wipe them inadvertently on clothing.

I am still trying to recover.

Thus, our meta-epistemological understanding reasserts itself here in the context of experiential knowledge. From such a perspective, the knowledge derived from practice about education is shaped by an epistemology significantly different from the one shaping propositional empirical knowledge. The experiential position undermines the technically rational notion that teacher education researchers should continue to produce positivist empirical knowledge about educational practice until they can tell teachers how to do it correctly (Hatton and Smith, 1995; Munby and Russell, 1996). Experiential knowledge in the critical complex paradigm is rooted in action and informed by a subtle interaction with the empirical, normative, critical, ontological, and reflective-synthetic knowledges. There is no way to specify these interactions and routinize practice accordingly. Professional practice is always marked by surprises. Such interruption forces the practitioner to restructure her understanding of the situation. Critical complex practitioners learn to improvise and develop new ways of dealing with the new circumstances and new modes of action.

A new teaching situation, for example, may be created by a particular student's behavior or by a reprimand of the teacher by the principal. How do I address the needs that are moving the student to be so violent? How do I work with the principal productively when she holds views of educational purpose so different from my own? Schön contends that such reflection-in-action brings the medium of words to the action orientation of practice. And this is the context in which experiential knowledge begins to come into its own as one of many knowledges related to education. Valuing this knowledge—not as its only important form—brings practitioners to the negotiating table as respected participants in the professional conversation. With practitioners at the table, no longer will education be subjected to mandated "expert-produced systems" with rules and scripts for teachers to follow (Goodson, 1999; Schön, 1983; Capra, 1996).

A critical complex teacher education is dedicated to making sure that experiential knowledge is not deemed second-class information about education. As previously argued, given its importance and student teachers' eagerness to obtain it, beginning teacher education with experiential knowledge of school experience may be desirable. Such an approach by teacher educators would challenge the debasement of experiential knowledge while helping students deconstruct the positivist view that we can only do after being told what to do. This epistemological assumption must be challenged before a critical complex teacher education can get students to analyze the diverse forms of knowledge involved in becoming a professional educator. In this context, critical complex teacher educators listen carefully to the experiential knowledge of teachers and other types of educational practitioners. We must be sensitive to not only the value of such knowledge, but the ways it is obtained, altered, and sophisticated in lived contexts. Understanding these features of experiential knowledge, we are better prepared to teach it and integrate it with the other forms of educational knowledge (Quinn, 2001; Munby and Russell, 1996; Munby and Hutchinson, 1998).

Such an effort involves close and difficult work to help student teachers, and all teachers for that matter, construct their own views of teaching and their own experiential knowledge about practice. This work must take place both in and out of the classroom. The authority of experience is important; but critical complex experiential knowledge is best developed when experience is submitted to reflection and analysis. Without such an adjunct to the process, the authority of experience can become a tyrant. We know that positivist empirical knowledge can become oppressive. Questioning its authority does not mean a tail-tucked retreat to the tyranny of experiential knowledge. I've watched such experiential despotism arise when it is not widely understood that the meaning of experience is never self-evident. It must always be interpreted for insight into what it tells us and, just as importantly, what it does not tell us.

Reflective-Synthetic Knowledge about Education

Acknowledging our debt to Donald Schön's notion of the reflective practitioner, a critical complex teacher education includes a reflective-synthetic form of educational knowledge. Since our purpose is to not indoctrinate practitioners to operate in a particular manner but to think about practice in more sophisticated ways, a central dimension of teacher education involves reflecting on and examining all of these knowledges in relation to one another. A reflective-synthetic knowledge of education involves developing a way of thinking about the professional role in light of a body of knowledges, principles, purposes, and experiences. In this process, we educators work to devise ways of using these various knowledges to perform our jobs in more informed, practical, ethical, democratic, politically just, self-aware, and purposeful ways. At the same time, they work to expose the assumptions about knowledge that are embedded in various conceptions of practice and in the officially approved educational information they encounter.

In the reflective-synthetic context, the practitioners' purpose is not to commit various knowledges to memory or to learn the right answers. Instead, teachers and other practitioners work studiously to avoid generic forms of educational knowledge purported to be applicable in all situations. Neither does their reflection on and synthesis of all the knowledges we have described reduce the uncertainty of the profession. The recognition of such uncertainty and complexity elicits humility, an understanding that all teachers and teacher educators agonize over the confusing nature of everyday practice. To do otherwise would involve a reductionistic retreat to the dishonesty of positivism's veil of certainty. In the reflective-synthetic domain, practitioners learn they cannot separate their knowledges from the context in which they are generated. Thus, they study their own usage of such knowledges and the schemas they develop in this process.

In the reflective-synthetic domain, teacher educators engage teacher education students and teachers in an examination of not only the contexts in which teaching has taken place but the various forces and cultural knowledges shaping everyone involved with the teaching act. How do cultural knowledges of educational purpose connected with racialized and class-inscribed definitions of what it means to be an "educated person" shape the pedagogical act? How do folk knowledges about the nature of children and the ways they must be treated insert themselves into pedagogy? How do craft knowledges of the proper role of the teacher shape practice? How does the larger depoliticization of American culture shape teachers', parents', and the public's view of the political role of schools in a democratic society? How does the public's view of the "ideal teacher" influence who chooses education as a career path? How do all of these dynamics intersect to shape education in the United States writ large as well as in the individual lives of teachers and students?

All teacher educators, educational leaders, and friends of democratic education must make sure that all teachers have the time and opportunity to cultivate such reflective-synthetic knowledges. Such knowledges help them come to terms with their early anxiety over survival skills so that they can move to a more sophisticated understanding of the diverse factors that shape teaching and the broad contexts that must be accounted for as pedagogy proceeds. When positivism reduces teacher education to training in methods of transferring knowledge in light of the demands of standards, a teacher possessing reflective-synthetic skills knows that such teacher education has already embraced many political assumptions about knowledge. Synthesizing a variety of the educational knowledges we have studied, such a teacher begins to piece together the complex ways these political assumptions have shaped the purposes of schools, the image of the "good teacher," the validated knowledge about "best practices" he is provided, and the ways he is evaluated. In this synthetic context, this teacher knows that the way in which particular knowledges are transmitted reflects a variety of value positions and hidden assumptions.

Critical complex teachers thus use their insights to connect their students to these understandings. Such teachers get to know their students and help their students know them by producing a form of authentic dialogue. They analyze and reflect with students on classroom conversations (how do we talk to one another?), the nature of classroom learning (what do we call knowledge?), curriculum decisions (what do we need to know?), and assessment (is what we are doing working?). In these conversations with students, they ask how the macrolevel decisions about larger educational, political, and moral issues shape these everyday classroom dynamics. When thinking advances and the dialogues grow in sophistication, students come to reflect on the sociopolitical, moral, and epistemological dimensions of their school experiences. When this happens, a new level of learning has been reached.

Again, the concept of teachers as researchers becomes extremely important in critical complex practice. If teachers and eventually students are to be able to engage in these types of exercises, they must become researchers of educational contexts. Bringing the various educational knowledges together with research skills, all parties are empowered to reveal the deep structures that shape school activities. In this process, they develop a reflexive awareness that allows them to discern the ways that teacher and student perception is shaped by the socioeducational context, with its accompanying linguistic codes, cultural signs, and tacit views of the world. This reflexive awareness, this stepping back from the world as we are accustomed to seeing it, requires that the prospective teachers construct their perceptions of the world anew. For teachers this reconstruction of perception is not conducted in a random way but in a manner that undermines the forms of teacher thinking that the culture makes appear natural.

Reflexively aware teacher researchers ask where their own ways of seeing have come from—in the process, clarifying their own meaning systems as they reconstruct the role of the practitioner. The ultimate justification for such reflective research activity is practitioner and student empowerment. In this context, teachers gain the skills to overcome the positivist tendency to discredit their integrity as professionals who are capable, reflexively aware, and self-directed (McLaren, 2000; Wesson and Weaver, 2001; Carson and Sumara, 1997; Diamond and Mullin, 1999; Hatton and Smith, 1995).

Conclusion: Motivating Teachers to Advance Their Knowledge

With a constant awareness of these various knowledges of education, a critical complex teacher education helps teachers reject the antischolarly role so often foisted upon them. Teacher educators inform their students that they can't learn everything the profession demands via bachelor's or master's degrees, so they must become lifelong learners. This is a key charge of a critical complex teacher education: to persuade students that in order to become great teachers they must continue studying all the educational knowledges throughout their careers. A good place to begin this process might be in the study of social, historical, and philosophical foundations of education or curriculum theory courses. Drawing upon a variety of disciplinary and transdisciplinary knowledges, such courses study the various contexts in which education takes place. While separate courses in these domains are essential, the questions they raise must be infused into every aspect of teacher education.

Sadly, such courses dealing with foundations and curriculum theory are often neglected in many colleges/schools/departments of education. Even in such institutional settings where they are important aspects of the teacher education curriculum, forces are at work to undermine their efforts to broaden the knowledges to which professional education students are exposed. Because of the larger social, cultural, and political tendencies to construct a deskilled view of teachers, as well as the immediately practical concerns of teacher education students, such courses are viewed as irrelevant. Much too often, such narrowly focused student perspectives are encouraged by other faculty in teacher education settings who focus on only functionalist dimensions of learning to teach. The less related to the immediate needs of the classroom such curricula are deemed to be, the less respect they receive in technicist programs. If critical complex teacher education is to motivate teachers to pursue lifelong learning of the various knowledges of education, such pedestrian perspectives must be challenged (Goodlad, 1994; Snook, 1999; Schubert, 1998).

A central concern for foundation and curriculum theory courses—to say nothing of the liberal arts and sciences dimensions of teacher education—involves engaging teachers in the appreciation of the ways the larger society shapes the perception of teacher education and teaching. Much of my own work has involved studying the ways that forces of power in the larger society shape not only educational institutions but the individual lives of teachers, students, parents, and citizens (Steinberg and Kincheloe, 1997; Kincheloe and Steinberg, 1997; Kincheloe, Steinberg, Rodriguez, and Chennault, 1998; Cannella and Kincheloe, 2002). The philosophical orientations that individuals bring to the conversation about education are not arrived at serendipitously but are constructs based on the perspectives they have had access to in the larger culture. In this informed context, teacher education students and teachers would understand that the positivist tendency to frame teaching as an act of working with individual students in individual classes is a desecration of the complexity of the act. There is so much more to it. Critical complex teacher educators have their work cut out for them. Their effort to engage teachers and many other groups in this understanding will be tough, as it swims against the tide of many contemporary social currents.

References

Altrichter, H., and Posch, P. (1989). "Does the 'Grounded Theory' Approach Offer a Guiding Paradigm for Teacher Research?" *Cambridge Journal of Education*, 19:1, pp. 21–31.

Apple, M. (1996). "Dominance and Dependency: Situating *The Bell Curve* within the Conservative Restoration." In J. Kincheloe, S. Steinberg, and A. Gresson, eds., *Measured Lies: The Bell Curve Examined*. New York: St. Martin's.

Apple, M. (1999). *Power, Meaning, and Identity: Essays in Critical Educational Studies*. New York: Peter Lang Publishing.

Aronowitz, S. (1988). *Science as Power: Discourse and Ideology in Modern Society*. Minneapolis: University of Minnesota Press.

Bereiter, C. (2002). *Education and the Mind in the Knowledge Age*. Mahwah, NJ: Lawrence Erlbaum.

Britzman, D. (1991). *Practice Makes Practice: A Critical Study of Learning to Teach*. Albany: State University of New York Press.

Bruner, J. (1996). *The Culture of Education*. Cambridge, MA: Harvard University Press.

Cannella, G., and Kincheloe, J. (2002). *Kidworld: Childhood Studies, Global Perspectives, and Education*. New York: Peter Lang Publishing.

Capra, F. (1996). *The Web of Life: A New Scientific Understanding of Living Systems*. New York: Anchor Books.

Carson, T. (1997). "Reflection and Its Resistances: Teacher Education as Living Practice." In T. Carson and D. Sumara, eds., *Action Research as a Living Practice*. New York: Peter Lang Publishing.

Carson, T., and Sumara, D., eds. (1997). *Action Research as a Living Practice*. New York: Peter Lang Publishing.

Cochran-Smith, M. (2000). *The Outcomes Question in Teacher Education*. Paper presented at the annual meeting of the American Educational Research Association, New Orleans, LA.

Cole, A., and Knowles, J. (August, 1996). *The Politics of Epistemology and Self-Study of Teacher Education Practices*. Paper presented at the International Conference on Self-Study in Teacher Education: Empowering Our Future. East Sussex, England.

CPRE (Consortium for Policy Research in Education) (1995). "Dimensions of Capacity." http://www.ed.gov/pubs/ CPRE/rb18/rb18b.html

Davidovich, M. (1996). "Rethinking Reflection: Critical and Creative." *LSU Bulletin*, 10, pp. 3–16. http://sol.aston.ac.uk/lsu/lsub10md.html

Day, R. (1996). "LIS, Method, and Postmodern Science." *Journal of Education for Library and Information Science*, 37:4.

Denzin, N., and Lincoln, Y. (2000). "Introduction: The Discipline and Practice of Qualitative Research." In N. Denzin and Y. Lincoln, eds., *Handbook of Qualitative Research*, 2nd ed. Thousand Oaks, CA: Sage.

Diamond, P., and Mullin, C., eds. (1999). *The Postmodern Educator: Arts-Based Inquiries and Teacher Development*. New York: Peter Lang Publishing.

Elmore, R. (1997). "Education Policy and Practice in the Aftermath of TIMSS." http://www.enc.org/TIMSS/addtools/pubs/symp/cd163/cd163.html

Fenstermacher, G. (1994). "The Knower and the Known: The Nature of Knowledge in Research on Teaching." In L. Darling-Hammond, ed., *Review of Research in Education*, vol. 20. Washington, D.C.: American Educational Research Association.

Ferreira, M., and Alexandre, F. (July, 2000). *Education for Citizenship: The Challenge of Teacher Education in Postmodernity*. Paper presented at the conference on Education for Social Democracies: Changing Forms and Sites. University of London. http://www.ioe.ac.uk/ccs/conference2000/papers/epsd/ferreiraandalexandre.html

Fischer, F. (1998). "Beyond Empiricism: Policy Inquiry in Postpositivist Perspective." *Policy Studies Journal*, 26:1, pp. 129–146.

Garrison, J. (1988). "Democracy, Scientific Knowledge, and Teacher Empowerment." *Teachers College Record*, 89:4, pp. 487–504.

Getzel, G. (1997). "Humanizing the University: An Analysis and Recommendations." http://humanism.org/opinions/articles.html

Giroux, H. (1997). *Pedagogy and the Politics of Hope: Theory, Culture, and Schooling*. Boulder, CO: Westview.

Goodlad, J. (1994). *Educational Renewal: Better Teachers, Better Schools*. San Francisco: Jossey Bass.

Goodson, I. (1999). "The Educational Researcher as Public Intellectual." *British Educational Research Journal*, 25:3, pp. 277–297.

Gordon, M. (2001). "Philosophical Analysis and Standards—Philosophical and Analytical Standards." In J. Kincheloe and D. Weil, eds., *Standards and Schooling in the United States: An Encyclopedia*. 3 vols. Santa Barbara, CA: ABC-CLIO.

Gresson, A. (1995). *The Recovery of Race in America*. Minneapolis: University of Minnesota Press.

Gresson, A. (2004). *America's Atonement: Racial Pain, Recovery Rhetoric, and the Pedagogy of Healing*. New York: Peter Lang Publishing.

Grimmett, P. (1999). "Teacher Educators as Mettlesome Mermaids." *International Electronic Journal for Leadership in Learning*. 3:12. http://www.ucalgary.ca/~iejll

Hatton, N., and Smith, D. (1995). *Reflection in Education: Towards Definition and Implementation*. University of Sydney, Australia. http://www2.edfac.usyd.edu.au/LocalResource/study1/hattonart.html

Hinchey, P. (2001). "Purposes of Education—Educational Standards: For Whose Purposes? For Whose Children?" In J. Kincheloe and D. Weil, eds., *Standards and Schooling in the United States: An Encyclopedia*. 3 vols. Santa Barbara, CA: ABC-CLIO.

Hoban, G., and Erickson, G. (1998). *Frameworks for Sustaining Professional Learning*. Paper presented before the Australasian Science Education Research Association, Darwin, Australia.

Horn, R. (2000). *Teacher Talk: A Post-formal Inquiry into Education Change*. New York: Peter Lang Publishing.

Howley, A., Pendarvis, E., and Howley, C. (1993). "Anti-intellectualism in U.S. Schools." *Education Policy Analysis Archives*, 1:6. Electronic journal at: http://epaa.asu.edu/epaa/v1n6.html

Kincheloe, J., and Steinberg, S. (1997). *Changing Multiculturalism*. London: Open University Press.

Kincheloe, J., Steinberg, S., Rodriguez, N., and Chennault, R. (1998). *White Reign: Deploying Whiteness in America*. New York: St. Martin's Press.

Kincheloe, J., and Weil, D., eds. (2002). *Standards and Schooling in the United States: An Encyclopedia*. 3 vols. Santa Barbara, CA: ABC-CLIO.

King, J., and Mitchell, C. (1995). *Black Mothers to Sons*. New York: Peter Lang Publishing.

Lester, S. (2001). "Working with Knowledge—Learning for the Twenty-First Century: Raising the Level." In J. Kincheloe and D. Weil, eds., *Standards and Schooling in the United States: An Encyclopedia*. 3 vols. Santa Barbara, CA: ABC-CLIO.

Lomax, P., and Parker, Z. (1996). *Representing a Dialectical Form of Knowledge within a New Epistemology for Teaching and Teacher Education*. Paper presented before the American Educational Research Association, New York.

Macedo, D. (1994). *Literacies of Power: What Americans Are Not Allowed to Know*. Boulder, CO: Westview.

Malewski, E. (2001a). "Administration—Administrative Leadership and Public Consciousness: Discourse Matters in the Struggle for New Standards." In J. Kincheloe and D. Weil, eds., *Standards and Schooling in the United States: An Encyclopedia*. 3 vols. Santa Barbara, CA: ABC-CLIO.

Malewski, E. (2001b). "Queer Sexuality—The Trouble with Knowing: Standards of Complexity and Sexual Orientations." In J. Kincheloe and D. Weil, eds., *Standards and Schooling in the United States: An Encyclopedia*. 3 vols. Santa Barbara, CA: ABC-CLIO.

McGuire, M. (1996). "Teacher Education: Some Current Challenges," *Social Education*, 60:2, pp. 89–94.

McLaren, P. (2000). *Che Guevara, Paulo Freire, and the Pedagogy of Revolution*. Lanham, MD: Rowan and Littlefield.

McNeil, L. (2000). *Contradictions of School Reform: Educational Costs of Standardized Testing*. New York: Routledge.

Munby, H., and Hutchinson, N. (1998). "Using Experience to Prepare Teachers for Inclusive Classrooms: Teacher Education and the Epistemology of Practice." *Teacher Education and Special Education*, 21:2, pp. 75–82.

Munby, H., and Russell, T. (1996). *Theory Follows Practice in Learning to Teach and in Research on Teaching*. Paper presented before the American Educational Research Association, New York.

Noone, L., and Cartwright, P. (1996). *Doing a Critical Literacy Pedagogy: Trans/forming Teachers in a Teacher Education Course*. Paper presented at the 1996 conference of the Australian Teacher Education Association, Inc. http://www.atea.schools.net.au/ATEA/96conf/noone.html

Novick, R. (1996). "Actual Schools, Possible Practices: New Directions in Professional Development," *Education Policy Analysis Archives*, 4:14.

O'Sullivan, E. (1999). *Transformative Learning: Educational Vision for the Twenty-first Century*. New York: Zed Books.

Pinar, W. (1994). *Autobiography, Politics, and Sexuality: Essays in Curriculum Theory, 1972–1992*. New York: Peter Lang Publishing.

Pozzuto, R., Angell, G., and Pierpont, J. (2000). "Power and Knowledge in Social Work." http://www.arcaf.net/social_work_proceedings/ftp_files5/pozzuto3.pdf

Quinn, M. (2001). *Going Out, Not Knowing Whither: Education, the Upward Journey, and the Faith of Reason.* New York: Peter Lang.

Regents Task Force on Teaching (1998). *Teaching to Higher Standards: New York's Commitment.* The University of the State of New York, State Department of Education.

Report of the Undergraduate Teacher Education Program Design Team (University of Missouri–Columbia) (1997). http://www.cos.missouri.edu/syllabi/report.html

Schön, D. (1983). *The Reflective Practitioner: How Professionals Think in Action.* New York: Basic Books.

Schubert, W. (1998). "Toward Constructivist Teacher Education for Elementary Schools in the Twenty-first Century: A Framework for Decision-Making." my.netian.com/~yhhknue/coned19.html

Segall, A. (2002). *Disturbing Practice: Reading Teacher Education as Text.* New York: Peter Lang.

Semali, L., and Kincheloe, J. (1999). *What Is Indigenous Knowledge? Voices from the Academy.* New York: Garland.

Shaker, P., and Kridel, C. (1989). "The Return to Experience: A Reconceptualist Call." *Journal of Teacher Education,* 40:1, pp. 2–8.

Smyth, J. (2001). *Critical Politics of Teachers' Work.* New York: Peter Lang Publishing.

Snook, I. (1999). "Teacher Education: Preparation for a Learned Profession." http://www.aare.edu.au/99pap/sno99148.htm

Steinberg, S., and Kincheloe, J. (1997). *Kinderculture: Corporate Constructions of Childhood.* Boulder, CO: Westview.

Strom, S. (2000). "Knowledge Base for Teaching." *Educational Resources Information Center,* Digest no. 88–8. http://www.ericsp.org/pages/digests/knowledge_base.html

U.S. Department of Education (1998). "Improving Teacher Preparation." http://www.ed.gov/pubs/prompractice/title.html

Vavrus, M., and Archibald, O. (1998). *Teacher Education Practices Supporting Social Justice: Approaching an Individual Self-Study Inquiry into Institutional Self-Study Process.* Paper presented before the Second International Conference on Self-Study of Teacher Education Practice, Herstmonceux Castle, UK.

Wesson, L., and Weaver, J. (2001). "Administration—Educational Standards: Using the Lens of Postmodern Thinking to Examine the Role of the School Administrator." In J. Kincheloe and D. Weil, eds., *Standards and Schooling in the United States: An Encyclopedia.* 3 vols. Santa Barbara, CA: ABC-CLIO.

Chapter Two

Teachers as Philosophers: The Purpose of Foundation Courses in Education[1]

Mordechai Gordon

I am observing a fifth-grade reading class in which a student teacher is teaching a lesson on poetry. The teacher begins the lesson by reading to the class a poem about the moon while the students sit at their desks with their heads down and their eyes closed listening to the poem. When she finishes reading the poem, the teacher asks the students to share with the class the kinds of thoughts or feelings the poem has evoked in them. Several students raise their hands and voice a number of different responses, like "sadness," "fear," and "a sense of mystery," which are not questioned by the teacher. Next, the teacher plays an audiocassette of a man reading this poem and then asks the students the same question about what the poem has evoked in them. A number of students contribute thoughts and feelings similar to the ones raised a few moments ago. Again, the teacher makes no attempt to question or "problematize" the students' reactions. Finally, the teacher asks one of the students to read this poem, followed by the same routine of asking the students to share their thoughts and feelings with the class, and a similar uncritical response by the teacher . . .

As I watched this half-hour lesson, a question kept entering my mind: What is the underlying purpose of this lesson? Later, when I met with the student teacher to discuss her lesson, I asked her this question, posing it in several different ways. For instance, I asked: "What, in your opinion, was the main goal of this lesson?" or "Why do you think it is so important to teach fifth graders a lesson on poetry?" She replied that this lesson is part of their curriculum and that is why she chose to teach it. When I challenged her to think about the possible underlying goals for a lesson on poetry, she looked at me dumbfounded and acknowledged that no one had previously asked her such questions.

This true anecdote is rather common, unfortunately, and points to a serious problem in the programs that prepare teachers: the lack of emphasis on *foundational questions in education*. By this, I mean questions such as: What is the main purpose of education? What does it mean to be an educated person?

What is teaching and learning? Do teachers have a right to educate character? Whose interests are served by schooling? and so forth. These are philosophical questions that ask students to reflect on some of the fundamental assumptions underlying teaching and learning at the very time that they are beginning to formulate and experiment with their own "philosophies of education." Foundational questions also raise important ethical concerns that challenge teachers to evaluate specific practices that are used in the classroom as well as broader educational, social, and political issues. Such questions call our attention to the first issue that needs to be emphasized in foundation courses: that students should be required to think in terms of general philosophical goals and problems and not just in terms of concrete instructional objectives. Whether they are designing lesson plans or writing research papers, it is crucial that students of education think philosophically and engage foundational questions.

Thinking Philosophically

Thinking philosophically is not the same as problem solving; it is neither linear nor aimed primarily at finding a practical solution to a pressing problem. According to Martin Heidegger:

> Thinking does not bring knowledge as do the sciences. Thinking does not produce usable practical wisdom. Thinking does not solve the riddles of the universe. Thinking does not endow us directly with the power to act. (Heidegger, in Arendy, 1978, p.1)

Now even if we acknowledge that Heidegger is exaggerating here, I believe that he has hit on a fundamental truth about thinking. The truth is that philosophical thinking is not aimed first and foremost at finding practical results, knowledge, or solutions but rather at clarifying a complex issue or problem that is being discussed. Recall the many Socratic dialogues that go around in circles and end without reaching a clear and definitive answer to the question under debate. Yet, while in these dialogues we never arrive at a precise definition of virtue, friendship, or piety, we do get a better understanding of many of the ideas and misconceptions associated with these concepts. Thinking, in this view, is not evaluated by the product but rather by the process. It is a continuous process of doubting, questioning, critically examining, and revising our beliefs.

Yet why is it so important that students of education be required to think philosophically? Several reasons immediately come to mind. To begin with, there is the idea that education in general and teaching in particular have been reduced in many public debates and schools to a technical endeavor of finding the most efficient means to achieve a set of prescribed ends. For example, in recent discussions on standards and educational reform, the fundamental questions about the nature and purpose of education have been largely ignored. As Jeffrey Kane notes, "The question now is one of means and means alone: how to provide educational experiences that effectively enable children to achieve the desired goals" (Kane, 1998, p. 2). Moreover, Kane argues, the underlying epistemological, moral, ontological, and economic foundations of the new standards are taken for granted rather than debated. Since all efforts are aimed at discovering the most efficient methods of attaining these standards, there is almost no discussion taking place about crucial issues such as "what learning means to the learner in terms of the way he/she develops an understanding of self, other, and the world" (Kane, 1998, p. 2). My experience as well as that of many other teacher educators indicate that if we do not challenge our students to engage such questions, they easily fall into the trap of equating teaching with being a good technician. They may be skilled at writing formal lesson plans and controlling their classes, but know very little about what a worthy education means and how to cultivate it.

Another reason that teachers need to think philosophically is that if we follow Martin Buber, who contends that "education worthy of the name is essentially education of character" (Buber, 1955, p. 104), then all teachers must view themselves not simply, or even primarily, as instructors in a certain body of knowledge or of a particular skill, but rather, as aiming at the person as a whole, including the moral, spiritual, physical, and affective dimensions of his/her being, together with the cognitive aspect that most schools focus on. This means that student teachers need to be prepared to address moral dilemmas that arise in the classroom, whether or not these moral questions are part of the curriculum. For example, a social studies high school teacher who is facilitating a discussion on ancient African civilizations in a global history class should, at the very least, raise the following philosophical questions: What does it mean to be civilized? How well are the leaders and people of our own society living up to this standard? This teacher should also take into account the emotional impact that a discussion examining "the integrity of ancient African civilizations" will have on minority students in general and on African American students in particular. If teachers do not pay attention to the moral, psychological, and political dimensions of the learning process, they have little chance of affecting the whole individual, as Buber inspires us to do. Indeed, they may even do damage to their students by presenting an elitist notion of the concept of civilization and a very nar-row, exclusively Western view of history.

Relating Theory and Practice

The second issue that needs to be emphasized about foundation courses is the relation of theory and practice. When I was a graduate student at Teachers' College, the practice of education and teaching was rarely, if ever, discussed in my classes. Perhaps it was assumed that Ivy League graduate students were generally not interested in questions of practice and, if they were, they could make the connections between theory and practice themselves, after class. I strongly reject this assumption. Following educators like John Dewey, I believe that theory and practice, philosophy and doing, are interrelated and that it is the teacher's respon-sibility to make these connections explicit. Throughout my college teach-ing experiences in both Israel and at Brooklyn College in New York, I have discovered again and again that students of education frequently find it very difficult to make these connections on their own. Thus, in my courses,I not only give many examples that illustrate the relationships between theory and practice. I also require students to practice making such connections in virtually all the assignments they do. In this way, the students are constantly required to reflect on the connections of theory and practice, with the hope that they come to realize that our philosophies shape the way in which we conduct our classrooms and that our educa-tional experiences often help us revise and refine our theories of teaching and learning.

To be sure, many of my students openly ask me to make these con-nections explicit, and they constantly raise questions that indicate that they are trying to make sense of this issue. How else is it possible for stu-dents of education to fully comprehend the things they are doing daily in the classroom? Dewey argues quite convincingly that if modern science has demonstrated anything,

> it is that there is no such thing as genuine knowledge and fruitful understanding except as the offspring of doing. The analysis and arrangement of facts which is indispensable to the growth of knowledge and power of explanation and right classification cannot be obtained purely mentally—just inside the head. Men have to do something to the things when they wish to find out something; they have to alter conditions. (Dewey, 1966, p. 275)

Thus, as Dewey asserts, it is only by experimenting with various teaching techniques and practices that students of education are able to gain genuine knowledge about teaching and learning, knowledge that is tangible and comprehensible to them.

On the other hand, it is only through the power of theory that teachers can make sense of what they and the schools are doing in the often harsh realities of the urban public schools. bell hooks (1994) makes this point very well:

> Living in childhood without a sense of home, I found a place of sanctuary in "theorizing," in making sense out of what was happening. I found a place where I could imagine possible futures, a place where life could be lived differently. This "lived" experience of critical thinking, of reflection and analysis, became a place where I worked at explaining the hurt and making it go away. Fundamentally, I learned from this experience that theory could be a healing place. (p. 61)

Drawing on hooks's insights, we can see that only by theorizing are teachers able to interpret and make sense of the difficulties they encounter in their classes and schools. Theories provide teachers with a frame of reference and a language with which to name and critically analyze many of the problems they face daily. However, as hooks points out, theory is also a place of hope and healing. That is, theories provide teachers with a rich source of understanding of not only what is, but how things could be differently. Teachers and educators who are struggling to make a difference need to become theorists who can imagine and create alternatives to many of the oppressive ideologies, practices, and conditions in America's public schools.

Teaching as a Challenge, Not a Recipe

Third, foundation courses should stress what I call the distinction between a recipe and a challenge. Many of our students come to us looking for recipes, for a bag of tricks that they can take with them and apply in their classrooms. They assume that if they can just acquire these techniques and skills, they will be good teachers or at least survive in the New York City public management. I seriously doubt that knowing these techniques will make them good teachers or even allow them to survive in an urban public school. Of course, such an attitude is understandable given the technocratic, positivistic view of education and schooling that is predominant in our society. Ann Watts Pailliotet and Thomas Callister (1999) point out that

> [b]y making the educational process technical, we pattern the curriculum after a stair-step model of linear fact-by-fact learning, trivialize teaching as a series of

generic "how to's" or formulaic "hints and tips," and too often reduce the act of learning to simple models of behavioral stimulus-response mechanisms. (p. 166)

The problem is that the teacher's role is reduced to that of identifying and managing technical problems. Paillotet and Callister argue correctly that this view not only fails to prepare new teachers for the realities they will face in contemporary schools and society, but it also undermines the attempt to foster teachers who are reflective, compassionate, and ethically minded practitioners. Moreover, the technocratic view of education is in stark contradiction to the way in which most experienced teachers conceptualize their own role and work. Experienced teachers typically describe teaching as a very complex and difficult challenge that cannot be reduced to a bag of tricks or a number of proven techniques. Indeed, much of what makes someone a good teacher, like enthusiasm in the classroom and compassion for students, has very little to do with technique and may not even be teachable. The point is that it is crucial for we teacher educators to encourage our students to think less in terms of teaching recipes and much more in terms of educational challenges. That is, we need to deconstruct our students' false assumption that good teaching involves merely the mastery of certain pedagogical skills. They need to realize that it is more like a craft or an art, which involves constantly challenging oneself with new goals and ideas. As Joe Kincheloe and Shirley Steinberg assert, "Nothing is simple about teaching people to think critically; no set of easy steps can be delineated in some workshop conducted by an expert in educational psychology charging twelve thousand dollars per day" (Kincheloe and Steinberg, 1999, p. 239).

In arguing that teaching cannot be reduced to a recipe or a set of skills, my intention is neither to denigrate technique nor to imply that good teachers do not rely on various techniques in their work. My critique is aimed rather at the technocratic mindset mentioned above, which continues to dominate the educational realm and is obsessed with questions of means, procedures, and mechanical skills. In this context it is interesting to note that the English word technique is derived from the Greek term *techne*, which means art or craft. For the ancient Greeks, it was clear that the mastery of any art or craft, including the art of teaching, involves acquiring certain techniques and skills. Yet, both Plato and Aristotle were aware that these techniques are merely means and methods used by the artist in the service of the fundamental goals of the respective art. They held that artists, unlike people with only practical experience, possess the theoretical knowledge of their craft and are able to think deeply about issues such as relations of cause and effect.[2] Most of the discussions about standards and the educational reform initiatives they have produced indicate that this ancient hierarchy has been greatly distorted. Technique is no longer regarded as merely a necessary condition for achieving the aims of education; it has now been elevated to the status of one of the most important educational goals.[3]

To get a better understanding of the distinction between the "recipe" and "challenge" approaches to teaching, it is fruitful to look at some of their underlying assumptions. By the recipe approach to teaching, I mean a way of conceptualizing teaching based on a mechanistic worldview and a behaviorist educational psychology. This is a reductionist approach to education in that it asserts that a highly complex and nuanced activity like teaching can be understood if we break it down to its constituent parts and then piece them together according to causal laws. Paulo Freire calls this model the "banking concept" of education and claims that it reduces the teacher's role to that of a depositor of information. In this view, the students become containers who are merely expected to receive, file, store, and recall the teacher's deposits. The problem with this approach to education is that it disregards precisely those qualities, like creativity, inquiry, and transformation, that make us truly human. Freire (1994) contends that ultimately

> it is the people themselves who are filed away through the lack of creativity, transformation, and knowledge in this (at best) misguided system. For apart from inquiry, apart from the praxis, individuals cannot be truly human. Knowledge emerges only through invention and re-invention, through the restless, impatient, continuing, hopeful inquiry human beings pursue in the world, with the world, and with each other. (p. 53)

In contrast, the teaching-as-challenge approach I am advocating here is based on an existentialist worldview as well as on some of the insights of critical pedagogy. Existentialists like Buber maintain that not only is every person a unique being in this world, but "every living situation has, like a new born child, a new face, that has never been before and will never come again" (Buber, 1955, p. 114). However, critical theorists like Freire have demonstrated that human beings do not operate outside of history and a social milieu and that our identities are greatly influenced by the existing power structures in the society. Taking these two insights together, we can see that teaching is a challenge in a twofold sense. It is a great challenge for teachers to respond to each student and every situation in the classroom in a unique way. And it is no less of a challenge for teachers to help students expose the ways in which "our identities are fundamentally shaped by our entanglements in the webs that power weaves"

(Kincheloe, 1999, p. 14). The successful realization of these challenges requires that teachers exhibit qualities like creativity, spontaneity, imagination, presence, courage, and self-awareness. The advantage of this conception of teaching is that it enables us to avoid the dangerous tendency of reducing the teacher's role to that of disseminating information and preparing students to take standardized tests. Indeed, it dignifies teachers' role and profession at a time when teachers are coming under increasing attacks by politicians, administrators, and the general public.

Philosophical Rigor

This brings me to the fourth, and final, issue that foundation courses ought to include: challenging student teachers to go beyond the banal exercises and rote learning and demanding that they display *philosophical rigor*. Philosophical rigor implies that prospective teachers need to demonstrate the ability to think critically, to question, doubt, and be able to provide convincing justifications for their stances and answers so that they in turn will require nothing less from their students. Teacher educators should not be content with clichés and stock phrases when eliciting student responses. This is because such use of clichés and hackneyed phrases usually means that a person is avoiding thinking critically and personally about a situation. When my college students use such language, I often find that they have not really reflected on the meaning of a given cliché before using it. For example, when I ask my students about the meaning of equality, as one of the principles of democracy, a common response is that "all humans are created equal." When I challenge them to explain in what sense human beings are created equal or should be equal, many of them find it difficult to respond. My experience indicates that most students have not adequately reflected on the difference between universal equality (as an ideal that is difficult to define) and legal, social, or political equality (which is a standard that democratic societies strive for).

Moreover, I find that clichés and phrases are frequently used by students in order to artificially simplify a problem that is complex. Such language prevents students from viewing a problem from several perspectives and hence from gaining a deeper understanding of the issue. To continue the previous example, most college students who are asked about the significance of equality in a democratic society are able to point to principles such as equal rights and equality of opportunity. However, many of these same students have not critically analyzed the various meanings of these principles. They have never really thought about whether equality of opportunity means that everyone should get the exact same opportunities, regardless of differences of race, gender, nationality, and so forth. Or does it imply, on the other hand, that the government needs to intervene to give certain privileges to various sectors of society that historically have been discriminated against? In short, my experience with college students indicates that while most of them are able to identify democratic principles such as equality, diversity, and freedom, they lack a deep understanding of what these principles denote and how they are related. I am not suggesting that this lack of understanding is a problem, but merely that students use clichés and stock phrases to evade addressing questions critically. Professors need to be mindful that when students use ready-made common quotes, they usually do not have an adequate understanding of the issue.

Dewey, who was vehemently opposed to the mind-numbing practices of traditional education, calls on educators to

> cultivate the habit of suspended judgement, of skepticism, of desire for evidence, of appeal to observation rather than sentiment, discussion rather than bias, inquiry rather than conventional idealizations. When this happens schools will be the dangerous outposts of a humane civilization. But they will also be supremely interesting places. For it will then have come about that education and politics are one and the same thing because politics will have to be in fact what it now pretends to be, the intelligent management of social affairs. (Dewey, 1922, p. 334)

Dewey here points to another aspect of philosophical rigor, which has to do with the interrelation of education and politics. Education, as thinkers such as Paulo Freire insist, is never a neutral, impartial, or objective enterprise. Rather, we should always view the education system as part of a larger social, political, economic, and moral context. Henry Giroux and Peter McLaren (1986) are well aware of this point when they state that

> schools do not merely teach academic subjects, but also, in part, produce student subjectivities or particular sets of experiences that are in themselves part of an ideological process. Conceptualizing schooling as the construction and transmission of subjectivities permits us to understand more clearly that the curriculum is more than just an introduction of students to particular subject disciplines and teaching methodologies; it also serves as an introduction to a particular way of life. (p. 228)

If we accept the view that politics and education, ideology and the curriculum, are closely connected, then it follows that philosophical rigor has to do with exposing the epistemological, political, moral, social, and economic assumptions and interests that support a certain view of education. This means that students of education should be required to reflect on questions such as: Whose interests are served by a particular view of teaching, learning, and intelligence? What kind of ethical issues are raised by the practice of tracking students? Who benefits economically and socially from the fact that many urban schools are crumbling or resemble prisons? Such questions are only seldom raised in teacher education classes and in wider educational policy debates. Yet I submit that engaging such questions is at the core of displaying philosophical rigor and becoming a good teacher. Kincheloe and Steinberg (1999) are correct when they write that

> such an undertaking is not merely an attempt to, in the words of conservative critics, "make students feel good at the expense of becoming educated." On the contrary, it is a content-based, discursively savvy, complex analytical educational process that requires a deep understanding of a wide variety of knowledge systems, the skills to critique them, and the cognitive facility to develop new insights to replace inadequate academic constructs. (p. 242)

In my foundation classes, I call this undertaking the "practice of making the implicit explicit." The point that I try to get across to the students is that it is absolutely crucial for them to make explicit the underlying assumptions of various historical pedagogical theories as well as their own views of education. Students who are never encouraged to examine their basic assumptions all too often come to accept the theories and views they subscribe to as natural, inevitable, and unchangeable. Such students will most likely find ways to adjust to the existing state of schooling in America and become supporters of the status quo. They will only rarely gain those insights and critical abilities that will enable them to become transforming agents and educational reformers.

Above all, in the previous quote, Dewey is talking about the development of a philosophical mindset. And my main point in this essay is not simply that the four issues discussed are essential to include in foundation courses. It is rather, more generally, that schools of education should be committed to fostering this philosophical mindset. Developing a philosophical mindset has to do with acquiring the expertise that will enable teachers to not simply react to the demands of their jobs, but to become scholars of the different and complex factors they are daily faced with, such as students, bodies of knowledge, and pedagogy. We have already seen that the teacher's expertise cannot be reduced to a list of generic how to's. Yet it does include various philosophical skills (among others), such as interpreting texts, analyzing issues from multiple perspectives, applying deductive and inductive reasoning, connecting theory to practice, providing a convincing argument for one's position, and defining a problem in a complex rather than a simplistic way. These skills are the basic standards that we require scholars to demonstrate when they submit an article or a book for publication. And my contention is that given the complex nature of pedagogy and the numerous responsibilites placed on teachers, they should be held to the same standards as scholars.

I would like to conclude this essay with a narrative written by one of my students that, in my view, illustrates beautifully this philosophical mindset and how the foundation courses in education are related to the life of schoolteachers:

I used to say that I loved to teach and I truly did think that. When I was a child I used to place empty chairs and pretend to teach invisible students. At the age of thirteen, I taught my younger sister (who was three) to read, write, and do math. She skipped kindergarten because she was too advanced. I also enjoyed tutoring children at the church. It made me happy and gave me a great feeling of satisfaction when others did better on a test. Then it made me think: I could do this thing, teach. It is my forte, my talent, my joie de vivre. I enjoyed it.

However, teaching high school has been quite an experience. Faced with approximately 150 teenagers per day is enough to make anyone tear their hair out (mine is turning gray). It seems to me that I could never get enough done. Their snide remarks take 15% of the lesson time. They test you every day, in some way or other. They walk in without books, paper, pens (I never knew I had to be everyone's mother). They try to concoct all kinds of ways to get out of class. "My stomach is hurting, I've got to go to the nurse." They stand before you knock-kneed, twisting in every direction: "Ms. Wilson, I've got to go to the bathroom."

I should be focusing on content at that level, not the human factor. The assumption is that by now they have already been taught to be humans and, therefore, now all we have to teach is the subject. Nevertheless, the challenge for me every day is what can I do to improve the human factor so that I can get through the content in a given period of time.

The human factor in teaching is something I had never really considered when I thought I had teaching talent or ability. Now I find myself questioning whether I am a good teacher! What is a good teacher anyway? The ability to just explain the subject? Or is it the ability to get it across to your students and make it somehow relevant to their lives? Or is it turning your students into good people who are willing to learn the subject and achieve? Sure it was OK to teach my little sister and countless others whom I had known all of my life. But teaching others with different backgrounds, levels of aptitude, education, personality, etc. . . . In other words, trying to teach 150 teenage individuals is mind-boggling.

Is it enough to teach the child who lives in a drug-infested area Math 1 or 2? His daily human experience is witnessing others taking drugs and well-dressed dealers with flashy-looking cars. In terms of math, the dealer pulls out wads of bills before him and buys whatever he wants. One way or the other, this will affect his character. Maybe he or she sees school as a waste of time. After all, what does he or she do? Sit everyday in a math class learning geometry, wondering how these calculations are supposed to get him or her flashy cars and a wad of bills. How do I tie it all in with the math, his daily experience? Shouldn't I touch the person before I teach him or her? Wouldn't this make him or her want to listen more intently, and therefore learn?

It becomes a fight of wills, and I don't believe I am going to win. Somehow I have to win these students over. I have to show them what is in my heart. I want them to pass brilliantly. I want them to take their potentially bright futures and make it a reality. But I cannot do this without their participation. I have to show them that teaching is a partnership, not an absolute rule thing.

This is the challenge I face every day. They are just kids. However, every time they walk into the classroom, they and I hold a small yet big part of their futures in our hands. That's not kid stuff. I now know that my ability to deal with people may be just as important as explaining or communicating subject matter.

I strongly believe that schools of education must be committed to cultivating teachers who, like Ms. Wilson, are able to ask philosophical questions, doubt, and critically reflect on education in general and on what they are doing daily in their classes in particular. We need teachers, like Ms. Wilson, who do not have all the "answers" but are struggling to find their own voices/identities in schools in which conformity to established norms, methods, and subject matter is the rule. Schools of education must foster teachers who are aware of the social, political, and cultural embeddedness of the education system and how it affects them as well as students from different backgrounds. Finally, we need teachers who, like Ms. Wilson, approach their vocation as a challenge and are determined to make a difference in the lives of their students.

Notes

1. An earlier version of this essay appeared in the Spring 2000 issue of *Encounter: Education for Meaning and Social Justice*. In choosing to focus on the purpose of the foundation courses, I am deliberately steering away from the issue of the content of these courses. This is, in part, because the question of content is highly controversial

but primarily because my goal here is to delineate four issues that all foundation courses should address regardless of their specific content.

2. Following the example of the Greeks, the word *art* is used here in the broad sense to refer not only to the fine arts but also to the productive arts, like carpentry and architecture, as well as to the service arts such as medicine and teaching. For Aristotle's conception of art, see Richard McKeon's General Introduction, in *Introduction to Aristotle*, ed. by Richard McKeon, (New York: The Modern Library, 1947), pp. xv–xvi.

3. In the current "educational standards reform initiative" of the State of New York, schools of education are required to prepare teachers to "teach their prospective students *how to* write and perform various other literacy skills." While fostering literacy is undoubtedly an important education goal, the State's guidelines emphasize the technical aspect of teaching and learning literacy with little regard to questions like the meaning of literacy, its underlying purpose, or its cultural embeddedness.

References

Buber, M. (1955). "The Education of Character." In *Between Man and Man*. Trans. Ronald Gregor Smith. Boston: Beacon Press.

Dewey, J. (1922). "Education as Politics." In Jo Ann Boydston, ed., *John Dewey: Middle Works*, vol. 13 (p. 334). Carbondale: Southern Illinois University Press, 1986.

Dewey, J. (1966). *Democracy and Education*. New York: The Free Press.

Freire, P. (1994). *Pedagogy of the Oppressed*. Trans. Myra Bergman Ramos. New York: Continuum.

Giroux, H., and McLaren, P. (1986). "Teacher Education and the Politics of Engagement: The Case for Democratic Schooling." in *Harvard Educational Review*, 56:3, p. 228.

Arendt, H. (1978). *The Life Of The Mind* New York: Harcourt Brace Jovanovich.

hooks, b. (1994). *Teaching to Transgress: Education as the Practice of Freedom*. New York: Routledge.

Kane, J. (1998). "The New Language of Reform." *Encounter: Education for Meaning and Social Justice*, 11:1, p. 2.

Kincheloe, J. (1999). "The Foundations of a Democratic Educational Psychology." In Joe Kincheloe, Shirley Steinberg, and Leila Villaverde, eds., *Rethinking Intelligence: Confronting Psychological Assumptions about Teaching and Learning* (p. 14). New York: Routledge.

Kincheloe, J., and Steinberg, S. (1999). "Politics, Intelligence, and the Classroom: Postformal Teaching." In J. Kincheloe, S. Steinberg, and L. Villaverde, eds., *Rethinking Intelligence: Confronting Psychological Assumptions about Teaching and Learning*. New York: Routledge.

McKeon, R. ed. (1947). *Introduction to Aristotle*. New York: The Modern Library.

Pailliottet, A. W., and Callister, T. A. Jr. (1999). "Preparing Postformal Practitioners: Pitfalls and Promises." In J. Kincheloe, S. Steinberg, and L. Villaverde, eds., *Rethinking Intelligence: Confronting Psychological Assumptions about Teaching and Learning*(p. 166). New York: Routledge, 1999.

Chapter Three

A Tree Grows in Brooklyn: Schools of Education as Brokers of Social Capital in Low-Income Neighborhoods

Wayne A. Reed

Schools of education in urban contexts are not typically defined by the role they play in revitalizing low-income neighborhoods. Busy preparing educators for classroom practice, these schools rarely consider the prospect that what they do influences community development, even though the public school is arguably the single most important institution in any poor area and has significant potential to contribute to a neighborhood's quality of life. Because of its central position, the school can generate both human and social capital in an impoverished area and thus influence a neighborhood's economic, social, and cultural well-being. By failing to acknowledge this role for schools, administrators and teachers often miss opportunities to capitalize on the indigenous social connections created by schools and inadvertently obstruct the efforts of other grassroots organizations involved in community development. The problem is that in far too many cases, schools and communities are at odds with each other. This tension has historical, sociological, cultural, and economic roots and has turned many urban schools into places where children are allowed in, but local residents are shut out. Schools of education, as centers for teacher and principal preparation, must examine their role in perpetuating this tension, while locating ways to give urban educators a vision for community revitalization.

The purpose of this essay is to examine the contribution that schools of education can make to the social capital of low-income neighborhoods by brokering a new relationship between urban schools and the communities they serve. My basic premise is that urban schools of education are in a position to negotiate the divide between schools and communities by challenging educators to revise the way schools function in low-income areas. In what follows, I draw on my experiences, both as an adult educator and as a professor, to examine the gulf that exists between schools and communities and suggest ways for schools of education to bridge the divide. I recommend that university education programs help schools become generators of social capital by forming learning communities that incorporate a cluster of schools in a neighborhood with the university. In reporting on my own efforts to form such a learning community, I share some of the challenges faced when community development concepts are introduced into a school of education.

The Divide

Rushing toward a Brooklyn elementary school where I supervise student teachers, I spotted Jacqueline exiting her apartment house and coming my way. Already late for a student teaching observation, my insides froze. I hadn't seen Jackie since her son was shot two weeks earlier; he'd been murdered on this block. When the news first broke, I had attempted to comfort Jackie in a phone call. But now, as she approached, my heart rate increased and I sought words of consolation. We hugged. "I'm so sorry about Shawn," became the only phrase I could muster.

Standing in the sunshine, we were blinded by the brightness reflected from the white wall of the school across the street. Jackie told me of recent events, the court proceedings, how she knew the young men who murdered her "baby," how she was waiting for the trial. Pointing toward a large tree at curbside farther down the street, she said, "That's where it happened. They stood him against that tree and shot him in the back of the head. I haven't been able to walk near there since." We talked a few more minutes and hugged again. I quickly moved on, conscious that a student teacher anxiously awaited my arrival.

Inside, the daily routine of the school appeared as normal. The principal walked the halls checking bulletin boards. Teachers were busy at their tasks. One or two children appeared to be roaming the stairwells, possibly taking a circuitous route to the restroom. Finding the classroom, I moved quickly to the back and sat down, and the lesson began. I tried to stay focused on the observation, but my mind kept drifting back to my encounter outside. How is it possible that former students of a school can kill each other within sight of the classrooms where they once sat, and the school's daily routine marches on as though nothing had happened?

Observations finished, I left the school later in the day. I stopped at the tree. A small, ribbon-wrapped bouquet leaned against the trunk. Through the lower branches, I could see the three-storied, beige-bricked school rising tall across the potholed street. From where I stood, the hundred feet between the tree and the school was more like a hundred miles.

Schools: The View from the Street

Working in one of Brooklyn's poorest neighborhoods the last eight years has helped me to see the chasm that exists between schools and communities. The experience has given me some understanding of the viewpoints that appear on both sides of the divide. Educating adults for nonprofit organizations brought me into numerous relationships with local residents and a chance to see how they view public schools. Recently my position as a professor of elementary education at a public university brought me inside schools where I learned about the challenges faced by teachers, principals, and administrators as they strove to educate children in a low-income, urban, and highly politicized context. Working inside schools, I see more clearly how school personnel view their surrounding neighborhood. Of these two viewpoints—the way communities see schools and the way schools look at their neighborhood—the former is not often explored in schools of education, even though understanding the viewpoint of parents, community leaders, and local residents is critical in transcending the chasm between schools and neighborhoods.

My experience teaches me that adults in low-income neighborhoods are passionate about the success of their children. Parents in poor areas are almost fanatical in their commitment to one recurring idea: "We want to make things better for our kids." Creating a future for the children of the neighborhood seems never to be far from the minds of anyone. When local residents come together to work on community development projects, nine times out of ten they select a project to impact youth. At town hall meetings with civic and political leaders, no topic stirs a crowd more than issues related to young people. Even issues that may not appear directly related to them often have children and youth as a subtext. For example, debates about law enforcement and drug laws are usually based on concern for the safety, security, and quality of life of the children in the community.

Given this passion, it might seem surprising that residents of low-income neighborhoods are equally passionate in denouncing their local schools. When asked, residents are likely to say that the education of their children is of ultimate importance and, in the same breath, comment on their disregard for the school their children attend. As Hyland notes elsewhere in this volume, many in low-income neighborhoods view the school as a fortress, a walled place where local residents send their children but where the parents and other residents are not welcome. Their feelings of alienation foster strong resentment. Parents feel shut out, sense the fact that they are not really wanted in the school, and remain frustrated that they have so little knowledge of what goes on inside and so little say in what happens there. Michelle Cahill describes the situation in many urban schools as follows, "What goes on in these buildings is often a mystery to the people in the homes and businesses down the block. . . . This lack of connection between many urban schools and their communities is bad for both" (Cahill, 1996).

Relationships between low-income parents and schoolteachers are often tense, with parents blaming teachers for their children's lack of academic progress. My observation is that much of this tension is fueled by a loss of power, the lack of control that parents have over the daily activities of their children. The tension is maintained by the patronizing of parents by teachers and principals. The faculty of urban public schools tend to wear their expertise on their sleeve. It's as though these educators are trying to ensure that parents are always aware that those running the school are the educators, the ones who best understand how to teach the parents' children. My experience is that next to the police precinct, the school is the most disliked and distrusted public institution in a low-income neighborhood.

The perception that the school is isolated from the community extends beyond parents. I regularly hear community leaders point out that virtually all of their efforts to strengthen the neighborhood occur without participation or support from the local school. Community events and meetings are rarely, if ever, attended by school personnel. In the weeks following Shawn's murder, for example, community activists organized an antiviolence march through the neighborhood. The march was a call to action, with residents rallying against the shootings that killed local youth. Flyers were distributed throughout the area and posters hung in numerous shops and bodegas. Over a hundred people participated in the march. The marchers passed Shawn's alma mater. No schoolteacher or administrator joined in the march or participated in the campaign.

In my years of work in three different low-income neighborhoods, I have never seen public school teachers or administrators at a community-sponsored event, even though such events are numerous and school leaders have ample opportunity to attend. In the neighborhood where I have the longest history, town hall meetings with political representatives from city, state, and national government are often well attended by the local residents. Easily a quarter of the questions raised at these meetings center on education, the need for improved facilities, questions about standardized testing, hiring and firing of superintendents, an outcry over lack of textbooks. In spite of the demonstration of support by community residents at these gatherings, I have yet to see one principal, teacher, or district administrator there to support the cause. One often hears principals and teachers complaining about the lack of parent participation in school events, e.g., PTA meetings, open school night. What about participation by principals and teachers in community-led meetings? What about teacher involvement in neighborhood events?

Although not all inner-city schools operate with this fortress mentality, the research indicates that the sentiments I hear from these Brooklyn parents is fairly typical of the attitudes in other urban, low-income neighborhoods across the country. This schism between urban schools and parents is well documented and is clearly described by Wendy Glasgow Winters in her study of African American mothers. Winters (1993) writes: "Socioeconomic factors and traditional patterns of interaction frequently mitigate positive exchange between school personnel and their constituents in poor, urban communities. As a result, both, in defense, retreat."

Winters' discussion of this topic is helpful because it refuses to place the burden of responsibility on one party or the other. For a new relationship to form between schools and their surrounding neighborhoods, the blame game of trying to ascribe the division to others must cease. At the same time, because of the imbalance of power, that is, the manner in which schools have government-sanctioned control of a neighborhood's children, it is also crucial that the role of school as institution be critically reexamined. My experience is that in spite of the negativity expressed toward teachers and principals, parents and residents are far more committed to their schools than schools are to their neighborhoods.

The Street: As Seen from the School

Three years ago I started supervising student teachers for the university and began to see the fortress mentality as an "insider," since my role as professor engaged me in the daily life of several schools. Based on this experience, I offer the following observations. It appears that those responsible for the fortress—school officials, principals, and teachers—often operate with a definition of school that does not include the surrounding neighborhood. Their definition suggests that schools function effectively without consideration for the forces and resources in the community. In other words, the successful schooling of the children is not dependent on an understanding of and acquaintance with the lives of the students outside of school.

In many cases, teachers and administrators seem to feel that the children's home environment is a hindrance to the overall purpose of the school. It is not uncommon to hear school faculty and staff speak with disdain of parents and the local neighborhood. A few minutes in the main office of the average school is likely to confirm this observation. Recently, for example, I was sitting outside a principal's office. The principal was rushing about, tending to multiple tasks. She glanced outside her door and saw several parents sitting in the waiting area. With little regard for those in earshot, she called to her secretary, "What are those parents doing in here? Don't they know I'm trying to run a school?" Although rarely stated so starkly, this sentiment reflects a far too common attitude among teachers and administrators. According to this viewpoint, parents and other community residents are generally regarded as a hindrance to the purpose of schools.

My experience is that principals and teachers sometimes function as though they have proprietary rights to other people's children. Some of this sense is rooted in the tremendous burden placed on school faculty to ensure children's safety. Feeling responsible for the children day in and day out contributes to this sense of ownership. However, this sense is also supported by a myth that pervades inner-city schools. The myth goes something like this: "Poor, inner-city kids have no one to raise them. Their home life is a shambles, their parents don't care or don't have adequate wherewithal to properly rear them. Our responsibility as educators is to rescue these children and to give them hope for a brighter future, a future that allows them the freedom to build a new life for themselves. Because conditions in this neighborhood are so bad, the future of these kids is to be outside of this community." With this myth in place, it's no wonder teachers and parents are often at odds with each other. Because the majority of principals and teachers are not residents of the neighborhood and are not historically or culturally tied to the community, this myth is especially entrenched and quite difficult to counteract.

This is not to say that most school folks don't talk the talk on parent involvement. Most educators today are sophisticated enough to know that parent participation is considered to be important, that research establishes the critical place of parents in learning. If nothing else, principals and teachers are aware that they need to demonstrate a relationship to the neighborhood if they are to satisfy the official regulators who are examining their practice on a regular basis. However, when it comes to actually involving parents and local community residents in the educational decisions that affect schoolchildren, teachers and principals do not really want "outsiders" in schools. They consider parents to be the folks they must deal with because the parents have legal custody over the children that society has commissioned them to raise. Educators consider their responsibility to begin when a child walks into the classroom.

Even teachers and principals who view home and neighborhood as relevant to the task of educating kids are unlikely to imagine the school as having much control or influence over community affairs. Because school personnel think they cannot influence what happens outside the school, they focus on their chief concern, that is, what goes on in the classroom. Unless it impacts directly on the safety of the children in the school, what's happening outside the walls of the school is not generally a major consideration.

Ironically, teachers and principals expend enormous amounts of energy trying to educate children day after day, often swimming upstream against the flow of social and cultural norms of the local neighborhood. Children understand better than most educators that their success on the streets is as important as their accomplishments in school. By creating a divide between schools and communities, educators split the hearts and minds of children, forcing them to live in two worlds. This splitting has enormous ramifications. For the children it means choosing between home and scholastic success. For parents, it means losing their kids, either to the dominant culture of the school or to the street, since the street rewards kids who are alienated from the academic process. For neighborhoods, the consequences are equally profound. The schoolchildren who do well tend to graduate out of the community, since their success requires an acquiescence to school's dominant culture, a culture alien to their home and neighborhood. Since the fortress is detached from the neighborhood, the highest-achieving students are urged to leave as they lose their cultural moorings.

In the end, the human resources of the neighborhood are depleted and, over time, conditions stagnate or worsen. The natural networks among people are further eroded, potential leadership is lost, and the talents of the young move elsewhere to benefit other segments of society. By remaining isolated from the community, schools help perpetuate this drain on the community and hinder the neighborhood's efforts to re-create itself. In this way schools preserve an unhealthy context for the children they hope to educate.

In October 1999, I attended a conversation on education reform held in the community where I work. Sponsored by a national nonprofit organization, the workshop, called "Improving Our Schools," brought together parents, principals, teachers, and administrators and, over the next three hours, prompted a dialogue on ways we could work together to better the education of local children. Because the topic concerned the local youth, the attendance from the community was excellent, standing room only in an auditorium seating over a hundred. Looking around the room, I was pleased to see so many parents present. Jacqueline was there, along with several of her friends. I counted four mothers in the room who had lost children to gun violence. I was also pleased to see so many school personnel. (I found out later that they had been pressured to attend by the district superintendent.)

After the introductions, the coordinators divided us into large discussion groups, placing parents with teachers and administrators. I noticed teachers and parents sat opposite each other. After watching a problem-posing video, the group facilitator opened the floor for discussion. What followed was, for me, a clear demonstration of the way educators support the divide between schools and communities. The teachers and principals were first to respond to the videotape. Sitting up in their seats and leaning forward slightly, several laced their sentences with education jargon, speaking of the challenges they faced trying to teach in this neighborhood, the problems they had getting parents to cooperate, the numbers of homeless children in their classrooms, the way the local children performed below standard, and so forth. It wasn't what they said that surprised me; they were articulate and clear. It was their tone. They spoke as outsiders, as though this was not their community. They blamed local residents for the problem. They spoke as though they knew more and were better than the parents. They spoke *about* the community, rather than *to* the community, almost as if no local residents were in the room. The teachers and principals functioned totally within their own cultural framework, demonstrated no awareness of a street perspective, and sent subtle nonverbal clues that positioned them as the authority on all things related to schools.

After the opening barrage from school folks, the facilitator never got the conversation back on track. Try as he might, he could hardly get the parents to respond. My observation was that the parents who were present did not feel confident to speak to their concerns in front of a roomful of education experts.

This event highlights the way schools and neighborhoods are divided, and the role educators often play in maintaining the chasm. It also raises questions about the preparation teachers and administrators receive in schools of education. It's safe to assume that virtually all of the teachers and principals at this event received training in a university-based education department. What might have happened on that October night if they had seen this as a golden opportunity to forge an alliance between themselves and local parents? What if the educators had had some sense of the community perspective, had been able to see the situation through eyes other than their own?

When teachers and principals engender isolation between schools and neighborhoods, they are simply functioning within the prevalent culture of public education. Public schooling, as an institution, promotes a disconnection between schools and local neighborhoods. This disconnect appears in all contexts, from wealthy suburban districts to poor inner-city ones; however, it is more pronounced in inner-city areas, where the detachment is further exacerbated by issues of race, culture, and class. Public schools, as institutions, are largely responsible for the gap because they control the community's children and choose to function in isolation from the neighborhood. The factors that foster this isolation are multifaceted and systemic, and are beyond the realm of personal accountability. Rather than discrediting hardworking and conscientious principals and teachers who support the isolation of schools, it seems more fitting to identify the cultural and systemic roots of the problem and suggest that in their undergraduate and graduate studies, educators be called to consciousness about the institution's tendency toward detachment and the need for collaboration between schools and neighborhoods.

To bridge the divide, those who prepare educators must revise the way they see the relationship between inner-city schools and their communities. My experience is that university teacher preparation programs tend to be cloistered in their own educational framework, which is entrenched in decades of institutional history. Rarely do university professors of education take to the streets and stand with residents of a low-income neighborhood. Seldom do the faculty of a school of education make it a priority to see schools with community eyes. This myopic vision handicaps urban schools of education in preparing educators who are able to broker a new relationship with neighborhoods. Because a new form of collaboration is sorely needed, schools of education would do well to locate concepts that provide insight into community development. One concept that is finding increasing acceptance among sociologists and political scientists is the concept of social capital. An understanding of social capital offers urban educators a way to reconstruct the dynamics between schools and communities. By integrating this concept into their philosophy and practice, schools of education are more likely to become the brokers I envision.

Urban Schools and Social Capital

To broker change in the way schools interface with communities, schools of education need a clearer vision of neighborhoods and how they work. They need insight into the nature of community development, especially the role that social capital plays in neighborhood revitalization. Since the mid-1960s, an increasingly significant body of research has suggested that in addition to financial and human resources, a neighborhood's overall quality of life can be measured in terms of social capital. Runyan, et al. (1998) describe social capital as the "benefits that accrue from social relationships within communities and families." Researchers studying social capital indicate that the interpersonal connections within a neighborhood are a resource, a form of capital, which provides a foundation for the neighborhood's health and prosperity. In other words, a neighborhood's strength and viability are influenced by the number and quality of relationships among local residents. Robert Putnam, whose extensive study on the subject is currently receiving widespread attention, demonstrates that the amount of social capital in a community can be a significant influence on its economic prosperity, productivity, safety, and health (Putnam, 2000, pp. 307–335).

In most low-income areas, numerous individuals and organizations are working to improve the community's quality of life. Community organizers are rallying local residents for various causes. Advocates are drawing attention to local needs and concerns. Community developers are forming alliances between corporate, governmental, and not-for-profit entities, attempting to bring new resources into a beleaguered area. Not-for-profit agencies are offering education, job training, youth initiatives, and a variety of social services. Religious leaders and their congregations offer numerous ministries to address community problems. In addition to the services these activities render, their primary contribution to the neighborhood is the network of relationships they engender. This intersection of relationships is a form of social capital.

Prior to the emergence of social capital as a concept, discussions of low-income neighborhoods often focused on the economic aspects of poverty, such as lack of capital investments, loss of employment opportunities, decline in home ownership, etc. For social capitalists, economics remains a central component of the conversation, although the economic foundations of poverty can be seen through an additional lens. Now the foundations can be analyzed in relation to the number and quality of networks among people in a neighborhood. While both economic and human resources are critical to development in a low-income neighborhood, the new research on social capital seems to suggest that a community's economic prosperity, human potential, and overall quality of life are built on a solid foundation of social networks.

Putnam proposes that there are two types of social capital, formal and informal (Putnam, 2000, pp. 93–115). In its formal permutation, social capital is evidenced by the civic groups and religious and grassroots organizations that bring people of a community together and activate them toward some collective action. The other type of social capital—informal social connections—is evidenced by small gatherings of people: folks dining together, playing cards together, etc. In the inner city, formal social capital is most evidenced by church and service organizations, e.g., Lions Clubs, Rotary Clubs, community-based not-for-profits, various youth initiatives such as scouting groups, after-school programs, and athletic leagues. Examples of informal social capital are also numerous and visible, from the door stoops where neighbors gather to occasional street parties and regular celebrations in homes and elsewhere.

To date, the research does not indicate a direct correlation between poverty and a lack of social capital. Putnam and others argue that the decline in social capital is a national trend that applies to a variety of urban, suburban, and rural contexts. The factors creating poverty are complex and, though they include the amount of social capital, they also include other factors, especially economic and political ones. At the same time, there are indications that many poor areas lack a strong social fabric, and as Putnam (2000) states, "precisely because poor people (by definition) have little economic capital and face formidable obstacles in acquiring human capital (that is, education), social capital is disproportionately important to their welfare" (p. 318).

My experience indicates that low-income communities face significant challenges in generating and maintaining social capital. These communities have been in transition since the 1950s. The residents with roots in the neighborhood moved to the suburbs in the 50s and 60s and since that time have been replaced by several waves of immigrant groups. In most cases, the residents who left were financially stable, owned their homes, and had established careers. They have been replaced by working-class families who are less well off, many of whom rented homes from those who had moved to the suburbs. These newer families have fewer historical ties to each other and, because they are often working long hours, have less time to establish new relationships. As working-class individuals often employed in low-paying jobs, fewer of their number are homeowners.

This results in a more transitory existence, moving from place to place, another fact that contributes to a difficulty in establishing social networks.

The sociological factors associated with poverty—especially crime, violence, and intense law enforcement—also detract from the creation of social capital in low-income neighborhoods. The sinister nature of the drug trade, the way it creates an atmosphere of distrust and fosters violent actions between young people and their families, diminishes the interaction among people that is needed to build social capital. In response to the drug trade, law enforcement officials use covert and sometimes brutal tactics that often maximize the level of distrust among people. Residents of high-crime areas tend to stay indoors after certain hours and keep their children inside, and can be hesitant to get involved in activities that require them to be out after dark. These factors directly influence initiatives to generate social capital. They are rarely acknowledged by principals and teachers as possible reasons for a lack of parent involvement in schools.

Many poor communities are hindered in creating social capital by a lack of public space. In one of the neighborhoods where I work, there is only one facility available for public use. The largest room in the building can hold no more than ninety people. Every classroom and office is occupied at all times, and the facility's director says that she is constantly turning down requests for meeting space. Meanwhile, there are two local schools with auditoriums and large areas that could accommodate several hundred. Since neither school is available for public use, local residents have no indoor place where large groups can gather and few places for smaller groups of residents.

Educators have at least two reasons to be interested in social capital. First, since social capital contributes to the overall economic and cultural stability of the community, it makes sense that social capital enhances the quality of life for schoolchildren and that children are more likely to perform well when they live in a stable, strong neighborhood. Second, the research seems to indicate that there is a possible link between social capital and academic achievement. Putnam (2000) suggests that social capital is a leading indicator in the academic performance of children (pp. 299–302). This idea is supported by Coleman and Hoffer (1987), whose study on high school students demonstrates a correlation between social capital and dropout rates. It is also confirmed by Runyan's study of high-risk preschoolers, in whom he shows a correlation between diminished social capital and behavioral problems (Runyan et al., 1998).

If social capital is critical to the overall development of a community and is important to the success of its educational attainments, then we are faced with the question of how urban schools can invest in the social capital of their communities. As indicated earlier, my experience is that schools are withdrawn from the neighborhood, isolated, operating as fortresses that bring children in and keep local residents out. Yet, of all the institutions in the neighborhood, the local school is most indigenously connected to the residents. The vast majority of the households in the area have (or have had) a relationship to the local school. The school is the natural hub of the community, the institution with the greatest potential to bring people together, to foster an environment where new relationships can flourish and preexisting ties can be strengthened. Because its mission is to nourish the neighborhood's most prized possession, its children, the school's potential to create social capital is clear. Imagine the possibilities if the schools shed their fortress mentality and became generators of social capital. What might happen if the school used its central position to bring residents together, helping them to construct human networks that support the neighborhood's development?

Cooperation is central to community development, and rebuilding an inner-city neighborhood, an area devastated by years of neglect and oppression, is a massive undertaking that cannot happen without the unity and support of everyone in the community. In light of this, it's no wonder that community organizers and local residents become frustrated at the posture often taken by their local schools. Having few resources and battling against extensive social problems, local residents are struggling to make things better, yet they receive little if any support from the one institution that, by its very nature, has connections to the most families in the community. Is it any wonder that so many inner-city residents speak in angry tones when talking about their local schools?

In the late 90s, I served on the board of a grassroots youth organization that was housed in the basement of a public housing project. The organization promoted academic excellence among local kids by sponsoring sports activities every afternoon and on weekends. The catch was: No child could play sports until that child could prove that he or she had completed his or her homework. The founder and director of the nonprofit organization was a local, semiretired man named Stanley who was totally devoted to the welfare of "his kids." He ran the organization on a shoestring and relied on the goodwill of local businesses and volunteers to pull him through. In the course of a month, Stanley and his volunteers worked with over three hundred kids.

Outside of his need for financial resources to run the program, the youth organization's main problem was space. The basement of the housing project out of which the program operated was no more than 28 feet by 15. Stanley had tutors willing to work with kids after school. He had scores of children eager to gain skills on computers. He needed classrooms, access to computers, and, during the winter months, access to a large enough indoor space for sports and games. As it happened, this dynamic youth organization was located directly across the street from an elementary school. The school housed over nine hundred children during the day and had a state-of-the-art computer lab and a gymnasium. The school was the only large facility in the neighborhood.

Stanley's requests for space in the school had received a cool reception from the principal. The principal was worried about the normal things administrators worry about: the security of the building, the safety of the property, hazard liability, and so forth. All of Stanley's requests had been rejected. In talking with Stan about his efforts, I was struck by the fact that he hadn't ever expected the school to be open to his request. He had asked because he desperately needed the space, even though he was fairly sure that the principal would not agree to help. I find that such expectations are quite common among inner-city residents. They have learned from experience that the schools are not really part of the community, and they don't foresee changes in schools' posture any time soon.

How might the result of this situation have been different if the school principal had understood herself to be a key player in the creation of social capital? What if, when approached by Stanley, the principal had seen an opportunity to further the network of relationships that builds a neighborhood? By allowing the local youth organization to use "her" facilities, the principal could have made a significant statement of support for the efforts of local residents to help their children. No doubt the principal would have faced obstacles in making such a collaboration work. The mundane considerations of security, insurance, and additional costs would have had to be addressed. But the point is that without a new vision of what a school can be in a neighborhood, the obstacles will always be too great.

Brokering Change through Learning Communities

The task of brokering change in the ways that schools interface with low-income neighborhoods begins with the formation of a triangular alliance among a school of education, an urban neighborhood, and the public school(s) in that neighborhood. A type of learning community, this alliance promotes educational reform through the formation of collaborative relationships between university faculty, school faculty, and the residents and organizations of the local neighborhood. Because of its credibility as an institution for higher learning, the school of education has potential to reach out to both parties—the schools and the neighborhood—and, by creating a space for dialogue, to foster change in the way they interface with each other. In what follows, I provide a conceptual framework for such an alliance and describe a learning community that is in its early stages. I also offer several reflections on how learning communities provide schools of education with a model for bridging the gap between neighborhoods and schools.

The term "learning community" is often applied to interdisciplinary learning in higher education. With roots in the experimental work of Meiklejohn in the 1920s, learning communities flourished throughout the 1970s and 1980s and today are found on college campuses across the country (Leigh Smith, 2001). Learning communities approach the academic curriculum in a thematic, interdisciplinary manner. These communities are often visible as paired or clustered courses in which faculty from a variety of disciplines engage students in an examination of a particular issue. Learning communities offer university students the opportunity to interface their studies with other academic departments. In this model, learning in such communities occurs exponentially, in terms of students learning from each other, students and professors learning together, and professors learning from other professors. The idea is that through the formation of community, the educational development of students (and their professors) expands beyond the traditional borders of highly specialized academic disciplines.

Because the learning community idea has historical roots in higher education, it makes sense that schools of education draw on the concept to shape an alliance between schools and neighborhoods. Instead of forming a learning community between a cluster of departments at a college, the learning community I envision brings together all the parties in a school and its surrounding neighborhood: children, parents, local leaders, local businesses, not-for-profits, teachers, principals, librarians, paraprofessionals, counselors, college professors, administrators, college students, student teachers, and others committed to the school. In keeping with the original concept, all parties contribute to the knowledge base of the learning community and learn from each other. With the local school serving as a hub, everyone invested in the success of the school becomes part of the learning community. The school of education plays a paracletic role, constantly advocating for the inclusion of all voices in the life of the learning community.

Since 2000, a small group of faculty have been leading the School of Education at Brooklyn College in the establishment of a learning community in one of our borough's poorest neighborhoods. The learning community is a collaboration between the School of Education, a cluster of three public schools (two elementary and one middle school), and the neighborhood where the schools are located. The learning community is situated in a densely populated area covering about twenty square blocks. The middle school is located near the center of the area, the elementary schools on opposite sides. Historically an area of European immigrant groups, since the 1960s the neighborhood has become home to African Americans, Puerto Ricans, Dominicans, and, more recently, a growing group of Bangladeshis.

During the past two years, the learning community has brought over two hundred university students and faculty into one of the three schools. Faculty supervise student teachers and fieldwork projects and conduct coursework in the schools. Student teachers involved in the learning community become a cohort, concentrating on urban education issues and practice, as they develop their skills in classrooms. In keeping with the spirit of the learning community, a reciprocal educational relationship is being established among the college, the schools, and the neighborhood.

College faculty are employed in the schools and, in exchange, teachers and administrators from the schools instruct preservice teachers, both on-site in the schools and on the college campus. In the second year of the learning community's existence, a third-grade teacher incorporated her knowledge, expertise, and experience into a graduate-level course that she taught at the college. Students who participate in the learning community are introduced to the neighborhood through interactive workshops with local residents and by completing research assignments that interface with nonprofits, after-school initiatives, and other programs in the vicinity. Three aspects of the learning community model make it especially useful in bridging the fissure between school and neighborhood and in helping schools become resources of social capital.

First, by participating in a learning community, the university establishes its presence in a low-income neighborhood and in the local schools, which is essential in effectively forging ties to local residents. It is also necessary to strengthen ties between the schools and the university. To build bridges between schools and communities, schools of education must stand in the gap, extend hands to both parties and, over time, bring them together. By committing itself to a neighborhood and its schools, a school of education is indicating its desire to build ties to all parties and an openness to form alliances that transcend historical tensions, tensions between schools and communities, and, more broadly speaking, tensions between segments of society.

From a neighborhood perspective, presence is especially important. Low-income neighborhoods are jaded by the comings and goings of organizations that have no grassroots base in the community. Lured by new funding streams, many organizations enter low-income neighborhoods, start programs, and then find, once the seed grants are used, that they have to close up shop. Because seed money is easier to secure than funding for ongoing expenses, the already transient nature of low-income neighborhoods is enhanced. Local residents are weary of seeing new initiatives come and go. They are tired of the disruptions caused by those who live outside the neighborhood who try to offer solutions that, no matter how well intentioned, are not grounded in the realities of the street.

Several years ago I was at a meeting to develop plans for a new adult education initiative in the homeless shelters of a low-income area. During the negotiations, one of the local religious leaders stopped the meeting and asked everyone present, "How many of you live in this neighborhood?" A sheepish look spread across a number of faces, including my own. Less than a quarter of the folks at the table were residents of the neighborhood where the initiative was to be launched. The minister's point was well taken: Why should those who live outside the neighborhood make decisions for those who live in it, especially when the perspectives of the local residents are more accurate and efficacious?

Because transience is a major obstacle in the creation of social capital in low-income localities, it is critical that the learning community's formation be accompanied by a serious, long-term commitment from the university. Poverty breeds transience. The comings and goings of not-for-profit and religious organizations, impermanence created by the transitory nature of funding streams, only add to the instability. The last thing a low-income neighborhood needs is for a school of education to launch a new effort without a commitment to remain in the community over the long haul. Building relationships that foster change requires years of effort. University educators should not be surprised if residents do not give their new initiative much credence at the outset, since, from their perspective, new initiatives are a dime a dozen. It's permanency and presence that count; schools of education must commit to maintaining their presence in a neighborhood over the long haul.

Second, the learning community model supports the creation of trust. Because learning communities are based on relationships, they offer a high level of human interaction and create an environment where trust becomes possible. The oppression experienced by many folks in low-income areas fosters fear and misgiving about institutions aligned with the dominant culture. This is evidenced by the way inner-city residents are regarded by many law enforcement officials. It is also visible in the anxiety and trepidation many carry toward their local school. The human, people-to-people dimensions of a learning community make it an ideal model to bridge this distrust.

The critical role of trust in university/school/neighborhood partnerships is highlighted by Smith and Kaltenbaugh (1996) in their description of the School Development Program's work at Southern University at New Orleans. As they indicate, the route to constructive reform in education is paved with relationships based on trust and mutual respect. Traditional authority/receiver roles hinder reform. This is why the formation of a learning community offers such potential by providing folks with a space to develop ties to one another that foster trust and breed dialogue. Principals can hear parents, parents can hear teachers, professors can listen to community leaders, preservice teachers can listen to principals, etc. In the formation of these relationships, new ideas and new ways of doing things can be born, because there is a belief that everyone is working together toward the same goal. Such a posture leads ultimately to trust, the most important component in influencing significant educational reform.

Last year one of my colleagues asked our student teachers to read Gloria Ladson-Billings's book *The Dreamkeepers: Successful Teachers of African American Children.* The ensuing discussions in our weekly tutorials were lively, some of the students disagreeing with the book's emphasis on cross-cultural teaching, others valuing Ladson-Billings's thoughts on the subject. Two weeks into the conversation, the principal called me into her office. She said she had some concerns, that she had heard we were promoting a book that said that only black teachers could teach black children. Several of her cooperating teachers (all white) were upset. The principal (also white) had never heard of the book and asked me what I believed on the subject. What followed was a positive, creative conversation. I bought the principal a copy of the book, and since that time, we have found greater openness with each other to explore issues of race, culture, and class as they affect her school. I also observe that the principal has broadened her perspective on the importance of hiring teachers of color to work with minority children.

The crisis around *Dreamkeepers* and the subsequent positive outcome would not have happened outside of the trusting working relationship created by a learning community context. Because the student teachers, cooperating teachers, administrators, local residents, and university faculty are in partnership with each other, we have a forum to process our differences, to challenge each other's perspectives and to be more progressive in our outlook.

Third, learning communities are ideally suited to help schools generate social capital because they are created organically. The institutional approach to bridging the gap between schools and neighborhoods would be to form a commission to research the problem, to allocate funds for the problem, and to develop programs to address the problem. By contrast, a learning community is an enterprise among people. Learning communities germinate when folks come together to share ideas and work toward a common vision. Although, technically speaking, the formation of a learning community can be thought of as a program, my experience is that a learning community's strength is its ability to bring stakeholders together, to create a context for the formation of relationships and to acknowledge the potential inherent in every situation. Because of its organic nature, the shape of the learning community is determined by the people involved and the available resources.

For example, in the learning community we are developing, there are two classroom teachers who grew up in the local neighborhood. Although such a small number of locally based teachers is nothing to be proud of, these teachers are a wellspring of information and insight. As we work to construct ties between the school and the neighborhood, they provide significant cultural insight and historical knowledge. They are able to involve parents and community leaders because they have such long-standing credibility in the neighborhood. Although the schools would be more effective if they had more teachers from the neighborhood, we are grateful for these two, and our community is being influenced by their participation.

Two of the professors involved in the learning community also bring their own uniqueness to the effort. One of the professors, an African American, grew up in the neighborhood. The academic resources he brings to the project are significant, and because of his history in the community, his capacity to build bridges to the local neighborhood is beyond what I can offer as a middle-class white man from the South. Another professor, an Irish American woman from Queens, brings significant experience from her doctoral work on the south side of Chicago. This work included empowering low-income mothers through a collective gardening project.

My point is that the shape of each learning community is determined by the identities, interests, and premonitions of those involved. It is also shaped by numerous environmental conditions and by the place it holds in the history of the participating institutions and individuals. The fluidity of a learning community's formation is, to my mind, a great strength in addressing the division between schools and neighborhoods and in creating schools that generate social capital.

Our learning community is in its initial stages. The relationships we are forming now are a foundation on which we can build a community that brings teachers, principals, parents, local leaders, college faculty, and students together to create schools that generate social capital in the neighborhood. Our vision is for the schools, as central institutions in the area, to foster new connections among local residents. We hope to see schools as spaces where residents can congregate to strategize on rebuilding their neighborhood. We hope to see the human and material resources of the schools made accessible to the neighborhood and to see its extensive resources integrated into the life of the schools. In multiple ways, we hope to see schools become generators and repositories of social capital.

Questions Raised for the School of Education

After two years of work on the learning community, I observe that the triangular alliance among university, school, and neighborhood is affecting our school of education in numerous ways. The experience is teaching me that commitment to a low-income neighborhood raises important questions for a university's teacher preparation program. The triangular alliance has the potential to challenge all the participating bodies to rethink their purpose and practice. Thus far in this chapter, I have offered thoughts on the effects of the learning community on schools and neighborhoods, the way the partnership helps schools generate social capital to enrich a neighborhood's quality of life. While the creation of social capital in low-income areas is the main thrust of this article, I think it is worth noting two of the most important questions surfacing in the school of education. Although these questions may be unique to our context, I suspect that, in one way or another, they give voice to issues that are raised in this type of collaborative.

The first question raised by the learning community is: How does the school of education's current curriculum prepare teachers and administrators to work in low-income urban contexts? Our ongoing intensive involvement in a low-income neighborhood is confronting us with the possibility that, even though we are located in the largest metropolis in the country, our curriculum is inadequate for the task of preparing educators to serve low-income urban kids, their families, and their neighborhoods. The learning community experience is asking us to consider a new level of inquiry. Does the curriculum challenge students to examine the tension between low-income urban neighborhoods and their schools? Are those relationships explored from the neighborhood perspective or from the vantage point of the institutionalized schooling? Does the curriculum prepare students to think and work cross-culturally? What fieldwork activities are students involved in that allow for interaction with parents, community leaders, and representatives of community organizations? Are education majors introduced to a conceptual framework that includes community development and the critical role of social capital?

Critical reflection on such questions is imperative. Unless the faculty has experiences with and commitments to urban education, the rationale for a neighborhood-based perspective is not always understood. The dialogue fostered by the learning community reveals that some of the faculty view public schools monolithically. For them, schools are schools, regardless of context, and the task of teacher education is to prepare teachers to function effectively in any school. The idea that teaching in inner-city classrooms requires a different set of skills challenges the way things are, particularly since few if any of us are prepared to pass those skills on to our students. The notion that all schools are the same simplifies the task and obscures the reality that educators in poor urban areas need a different quality of training. To acknowledge that teaching differs measurably from one school to another poses a threat to one of modern education's major tenets, that is, uniformity. The myth that all children in the system can and should receive the same instruction is entrenched, as is the presumption that any qualified educators can effectively teach any child.

Last year, at a faculty retreat, a colleague and I presented a videotape of three undergraduate students who had just completed their student teaching in a learning community school. Reflecting on their practice, the student teachers drew a sharp contrast between their student teaching experiences and the fieldwork they had completed in schools earlier in their program. Their fieldwork was in what many regard as the best public school in the borough. Located in an upper-middle-class neighborhood, the school has an active fund-raising mechanism and a significant track record of innovative practices. After completing fieldwork in this topflight school, the three students completed their student teaching in a learning community school, a school located in what many regard as a high-crime neighborhood. The videotape indicated that while the student teachers gained from both experiences, they valued teaching in the inner-city school for three reasons. First, they felt respected and appreciated by the local residents. Second, they liked the vibrancy and enthusiasm of the children, the way many of them seemed excited about learning. Third, they thought student teaching in this school exposed them to a context more consistent with their future job prospects.

The video prompted a controversial response among the faculty. Some expressed appreciation for the student teachers' comparisons, while others were critical, citing them as "simplistic" and "decontextualized." What struck me at the time was the strong reaction by a roomful of seasoned educators to these newly graduated, green teachers. The reaction seemed to center on the fact that these students had had an experience that identified one school as radically different from another. After thirty minutes of heated discussion, I realized that the debate was unfolding because the student teachers had identified their experience in the inner-city school as superior to the one they had had in the upper-middle-class school. The controversy centered on the idea that not all schools are the same. Several days after the retreat, a colleague summarized this position. "I've thought a lot about it," he said, "and I don't really buy it. I don't think it's helpful to give our students a sense that there's a real difference in teaching in an upper-middle-class school or in an inner-city one. Teaching is teaching and kids are kids."

Clarifying the uniqueness of urban schools is important if a school of education is to effectively broker the estrangement between schools and their neighborhoods. Yes, in many places around the country, urban and suburban, a gap exists between many public schools and the communities they serve. However, additional factors exacerbate the problem in the inner city. As Lois Weiner (1999) argues in *Urban Teaching*, important differences exist between urban schools and schools in other contexts, and effective educators would do well to constantly consider those differences in preparing to teach in urban situations.

A second question raised by our involvement in the learning community is: Where do our students come from? Although the Brooklyn

College School of Education is located in a multicultural setting, our work reveals the fact that most of our education majors are unfamiliar with the sociocultural context of a low-income neighborhood. By and large our undergraduate students are from first-generation, middle-class immigrant families. Few are familiar with the inner city. Few have ever been to a neighborhood like the one where the learning community is located. The most recent data suggest that less than 2 percent of our students in the School of Education live in the same zip code area as the learning community schools, even though the college is only two miles away.

Such low numbers of students from a particular section of the city is an obstacle in constructing an alliance between the higher-education institution, the schools, and the neighborhood. It also challenges the integrity of the School of Education's stated commitment to social justice. This contradiction, the fact that the School of Education claims a commitment to the neighborhood but has almost no students from there is problematic and must be changed if we are to secure the necessary credibility among the local population. Accessibility is a fundamental test of a college's relationship to any neighborhood or ethnic group.

My research into the causes of the exclusion is in preliminary stages. Anecdotally, I can identify some possibilities. When I worked in adult education in the neighborhood, I sometimes heard local folks discredit the university by saying that it was a place where people of color were not welcome. This sentiment probably stems from the college's history as a school with a student body of mostly white immigrant students. Whatever its history, the college is not helping to change its image when it fails to recruit students from low-income, minority neighborhoods. The network of alumni referring students to the college does not extend to this section of the borough because the college has few historical ties to the residents there. Whatever is at the root of the problem, a change is needed if the learning community is to help broker a new dynamic between the three schools and the neighborhood. The college's capacity to help schools generate social capital is based on its own ability to create social capital.

There is another reason to be interested in the college recruitment of the youth in this neighborhood. The learning community wants to create opportunities for youth from the area to become schoolteachers. Increasing the number of local schoolteachers is a fundamental way to broker new school/community relations and increase the school's potential to generate social capital. With that in view, I am hopeful that the recruitment of young people can become a priority for our learning community in the years ahead. One of the most radical steps a school of education can take in altering the dynamics between public schools and their neighborhoods is to have teachers in the schools be residents of the neighborhood. Teachers who are local residents understand the children, they communicate more effectively with parents, and they are committed to the development of the neighborhood. In short, teachers from the inner city inherently build bridges between the school and community because they live and work in both. They are in and of themselves generators of social capital.

Recently, I spoke with a teacher from a learning community school who grew up in the neighborhood of the children she now teaches. When I asked her to describe the contribution she made as an educator living in the neighborhood, she responded, "Several weeks ago I was walking down the aisle in the local supermarket when I heard a child whispering excitedly, 'Look Mom, she likes Lucky Charms.' When I looked in my basket and saw the box of cereal, I was reminded of how important it is for kids to see their teachers in other contexts than the classroom, for them to know that their teachers are real-life human beings."

Looking at inner-city neighborhoods through the lens of social capital offers insight into the advantages of having local teachers in schools. If the goal is for schools to become generators of social capital, then increasing the number of locally based teachers is entirely sensible. A teacher from the neighborhood has significant ties to the neighborhood that cannot be obtained by teachers from outside the community. This is not to suggest that all teachers cannot support the development of social capital. All teachers can strive to increase a neighborhood's social networks. The point is that, in this case, educators who are born and raised in the neighborhood are at a distinct advantage and should be actively sought after if schools are to become centers of social capital.

These two questions are but the first of many I expect to be raised by the university's participation in the learning community. The concrete realities of daily interaction with the inner city is bound to challenge the faculty to reflect on the effectiveness of their current practice. Already the learning community is prompting a new emphasis on urban education and a new way of thinking about our school of education's mission. The alliance that is taking shape is making tangible the need to bridge the gap between schools and neighborhoods. It is also laying the groundwork for additional work on the role of schools in the creation of social capital.

Conclusion

In this chapter I have argued that university/college schools of education are in a good position to help public schools break the pattern of isolation that besets them and redefine the role of public schools in low-income neighborhoods. After highlighting the divisions that currently exist between many schools and their surrounding communities, I articulated a way for educators to think about low-income areas: as contexts shaped by social capital. I also identified schools as generators of social capital, spaces where the available resources in a community can be invested through the strengthening of a neighborhood's social fabric. To accomplish this redefinition of schools, I suggest that schools of education form a dynamic alliance with a neighborhood and its local schools. The map I recommend for schools of education is not without challenges, as my final section indicated. It contains, however, a route that offers new possibilities for the education of poor children and increases the chances that the context in which they live will improve.

I am more convinced than ever that children and their families need schools to function as generators and repositories of social capital. The divide between schools and inner-city neighborhoods is destructive. It deeply affects the lives of children and their families and it inhibits the best efforts of a community to help itself. It supports the oppression of the poor and questions the fundamental purpose of schools. If, as I propose, university-based education programs are uniquely equipped to initiate partnerships that re-create the intersection between schools and neighborhoods, then those programs have a moral obligation to evaluate their present efforts in light of the potential to revitalize poor communities. The tragic history of Shawn and the thousands of boys and girls like him demand dramatic change in the way schools do business in the inner city. A tree in Brooklyn bears witness.

References

Cahill, M. (1996). *Schools and Communities: Working Papers*. Chicago: Cross City Campaign for Urban School Reform, p. 3.

Coleman, J. and Hoffer, T. (1987). *Public and Private High Schools: The Impact of Communities*. New York: Basic Books.

Leigh Smith, B. (2001). "The Challenge of Learning Communities as a Growing National Movement." *Peer Review, Association of American Colleges and Universities*, 3:1, pp. 1–3.

Putnam, R. (2000). *Bowling Alone: The Collapse and Revival of American Community*. New York: Simon and Schuster.

Runyan, D. K., Hunter, W. M., Socolar, R. R. S., et al. (1998). "Children Who Prosper in Unfavorable Environments: The Relationship to Social Capital." *Pediatrics*, 101:1, pp. 12–20.

Smith, D. B., and Kaltenbaugh, L. P. S. (1996). "University-School Partnership: Reforming Teacher Preparation." In Comer, Haynes, et al., eds., *Rallying the Whole Village: The Comer Process for Reforming Education* (p. 73). New York: Teachers College Press.

Weiner, L. (1999). *Urban Teaching: The Essentials*. New York: Teachers College Press, pp. 13–40.

Winters, W. G. (1993). *African American Mothers and Urban Schools: The Power of Participation*. New York: Lexington Books.

Chapter Four

Race and Education in New York City: A Dilemma

Haroon Kharem

I was standing in line at the bookstore on campus with another professor, waiting to pay for a book, thinking how good it was to be back home in New York City. When my turn came to pay for the book, the store manager asked me, "Are you faculty, student, or staff?" I responded that I was faculty; the store manager gave me one of those looks that some whites give when they question whether a black person is telling the truth; my response was, "Would you like to see my ID?" The store manager told me, "No, since you are with him [pointing to the other professor, who was white], there is no need." I looked at the manager as he was scanning the book—and decided not to buy the book. I asked him: "And if I were not with him—would I need to show my ID?" Before he could respond, I asked: "What does a professor look like? Are they all white? Do they all wear suits and ties?" My question caused the store manager to look surprised—he didn't know how to respond. He was stunned at my remark, said nothing—I left the book on the counter and left, mentioning to my colleague that the store would not get my business in the future. The bookstore manager in his consciousness of whiteness could see me only as a black man, with suspicion; when I confronted his whiteness, he had no response. My colleague expressed disbelief at the store manager's actions toward me and his revulsion over how people of color are continually treated in the city.

I walked into an elementary school in the East New York section of Brooklyn for a meeting with a principal and presented my ID at the entrance to the security personnel, who were somewhat surprised at me, as a professor, being there. Their surprise was obvious: Either they were not used to seeing black male professors coming into their schools or maybe they were not used to seeing black males as professors. I walked into the main office of the school noting the busyness of the various secretaries, teachers, and administrative staff moving around and through the office. After ten minutes at the front desk, with no one acknowledging my presence, Ralph Ellison's book *The Invisible Man* came to mind—I am invisible. Five more minutes, as they went about their daily routine, I still am not spoken to. They seem to notice me periodically. A white man in a suit walked in, people stopped what they were doing, and someone asked the man in the suit: "May I help you?" I began to smile; I had been ignored as I saw happen that very morning to parents who looked like me. I said: "No. You can help me, I have been standing here for fifteen minutes and not one of you has asked me if I need any help, though some of you looked at me." As I am talking out loud, I am also talking inside my head, asking myself, was it skin color? Did the office workers think I was a parent from the neighborhood? And if they did, what does that say about the relationship between the community and the school?

What message does this main office send to the parents of the children who attend this school? More importantly, it demonstrates that there is no working partnership between the community and the school. The school is a fortress where many suburban teachers come for maybe eight hours a day, into a section of the city they would normally avoid completely. What I found so sad was that some of the office workers were black females, women who have been so conditioned by societal norms to see a black male as someone to ignore, someone who is troublesome.

There have been times when I would sit on the school steps and watch drug dealing going on, across the street from the school, and wonder why there are no signs that declare "Drug free zone"—where are those signs? Why do I never see a police car drive past this school (with the police station only three blocks away)?

I don't believe these events are out of the ordinary. I could relate many more instances. In stores, I am watched more suspiciously than I have been watched in stores in the South. After traveling throughout the United States, I have seen how black and white people interact in different situations—I believe New York City is segregated. In this multiethnic city, many whites see blacks as inferior and are not reluctant to express this belief. I agree with Jonathan Kozol's (1991) assessment that the residential segregation here in New York City and its suburbs has a powerful effect on education and its resources. Kozol mentions that denial of "the means of competition" is perhaps the single most consistent outcome of the education offered to poor children in the schools of our large cities; and nowhere is this pattern of denial more explicit or more absolute than in the public schools of New York City (p. 83). What is peculiar is that I have not found any rebuttal by New York City's now-defunct Board of

Education to Kozol's indictments of the public school system. Kozol quoted a New York City Board of Education official who claimed that "there is no point in putting money into some poor districts . . . the poorer districts are beyond help . . . resources would be wasted on poor children" (pp. 98–99). I wonder if that official saw poor children as human beings worthy of the same education as his or her own children. Second, I wonder if that official would still want to keep it poor if his or her children attended the poorer district schools. But more importantly, the fact that this official believed that placing funds and resources into poorer districts was a waste is not benign neglect but a calculated strategy that leads to institutional racism or a belief in Social Darwinism and eugenics. Also, these opinions tell me that this Board of Ed official has no regard for the children he or she is paid as a public servant of the people of New York City to care for and needs to find a new profession. Unfortunately, newly appointed officials are modeling similar behaviors.

Growing up in Brooklyn in the early 1960s, I was bused to second grade from P.S. 287 in Fort Greene to P.S. 131 in Borough Park (at that time an all-white neighborhood). I remember getting off the school bus and being greeted by angry white parents who did not want any "niggers" in their school. I remember being escorted through a throng of furious parents to the school bus—rocks, bottles, and sticks were thrown at us— the white parents wanted to maintain racial segregation and keep their neighborhoods white. Remembering my experiences, I wonder what the white children thought of their parents as they watched them yell and throw things at us. Didn't those parents realize that we were the same age as their kids? I remember being scared, really scared, on the bus and angrily wondering why. Why were these white people trying to hurt us? I knew nothing about desegregation, but I learned quickly about being black, about race, racism, and its consequences. I learned that there were places in New York City that did not want me or anyone who looked like me. Schools in New York City haven't changed a lot, and, over thirty years later, I still see similar scenes, and get those same feelings, as I navigate my way across the city. I still see a segregated city where real estate is used as a powerful tool to maintain racial segregation, and thus is educational segregation in many ways preserved in New York City (Hacker, 1995; Massey and Denton, 1993).

All this leaves me with the conclusion that race is still a focal point in our society, and that race and class are in the forefront of the education system. Issues of race still facilitate decisions as to the kind of education children will receive. We thought we took concrete steps to eradicate racial segregation in schools with the landmark *Brown v. Board of Education* case of almost fifty years ago; however, Kozol noted in 1991 that he knew that "segregation was still common in the public schools" and went on to say, "I did not know how much it had intensified" (p. 3). Kozol clearly admits to the ever-present issue that we as a society still accept segregation in our schools, and that it is increasing. Today's code terms for keeping schools segregated are "choice" and "vouchers," policy initiatives that presume to give citizens a positive choice involving their children's education. However, the supporters of choice and vouchers never address the issue that only privileged children with savvy parents will know how to access the policies. In middle- and upper-middle-class families, the "choice" or privilege to choose what school a child attends is based upon the ability of the parents to either live in a certain neighborhood or transport their children to a school of "choice." Financial aid indicated for vouchers does not begin to pay tuition to private schools. Parents are expected to make up the difference. This restricts just who can make use of right-wing-sponsored proposals. After the courts ordered schools to desegregate in the 1970s, white flight went into full swing. I can only surmise that they were in flight from me and those who looked like me. As Donaldo Macedo (1994) describes:

> The very language of the reform movement, particularly the conservative proposals, points to an ideology that structures the education debate in terms of competition . . . and choice, which is a veiled proposal that makes us "unconsciously endorse the privatization and capitalization of every sphere of activity" within the education reform movements. The actual hidden curriculum of school choice consists of taking precious resources from poor schools that are on the verge of bankruptcy to support private or well-to-do schools. (pp. 165–166)

Macedo clearly states that we not only need to understand the acts of racism, but we must also recognize how the dominant culture hides behind a veil of language that is used to continually maintain the status quo so that there is no language clarity.

There is a need in higher education for professors to understand the power of language and discourse that excludes people from participating in the decision-making process. In turn, their students will hopefully become citizens who are not bamboozled into "stupidification" of fragmented knowledge; they will become citizens who will make connections with both what they learn in school and what they live outside the classroom, in the culture in which they live, and be able to analyze the relations of power and privilege in a society that hides oppression within slogans that chant "we live in a classless society," that proclaim "we are all the same, whether black, white, yellow, or red." We must ally ourselves with predominantly black and Hispanic communities, poor-white and Asian communities, with parents who do not have the "choice" or privilege to transport their children to a school of their liking but rather have to settle for the kinds of schools Kozol talks about. As bell hooks reminds us in *Where We Stand: Class Matters* (2000), "The poor are expected to live with less and are socialized to accept less . . . whereas the well-off are socialized to believe it is both a right and a necessity for us to have more" (p. 48).

Many would disagree with me and argue that class, not race, is the dominant source of social problems in contemporary America, that people of color, especially African Americans, have assimilated very well into American society. I would answer that while class and gender are definitely parts of the problems today, and while some African Americans and Hispanics have moved into the upper middle class and women are rapidly joining the ranks along with blacks in becoming poorer, blacks and Hispanics still experience a consistent pattern of racial segregation in the United States. I am reminded that Jim Crow, or what were called "Black Codes" in the early 1800s, was created in the Northeast, in cities like Boston, Philadelphia, New York, and Cincinnati, not in the South (Litwack, 1961). The legacy of racial enslavement and an American apartheid underscores the malevolent reality of the present racism in many of our well-established institutions (Feagin, 1991; Kozol, 1991; Massey and Denton, 1993; Omi and Winant, 1994). Scholars like Thomas Sowell, Nathan Glazer, Shelby Steele, Charles Murray, and others have succeeded in shifting the discussion of the conditions of black people from racism and discrimination to blaming the victim, much as scholars and public figures did in the early part of the twentieth century. The conversation has turned from the structural social relations of racism back to blaming black people for their lack of economic progress. Charles Murray claims in his "objective" research with Richard Herrnstein in *The Bell Curve* (1994) that blacks and Latinos are intellectually and morally inferior to whites. Murray and Herrnstein make the case that people of color are disproportionately on welfare and unsuccessful in bourgeois career paths because they do not have the intellect to achieve any higher. These thoughts take us back to the era of Social Darwinism in the late nineteenth and early twentieth centuries, when some scholars were openly claiming that blacks were inferior and did not have the ability to think abstractly.

I still hear people say that the reasons blacks have failed to integrate into American society is because of their culture and their lack of will to rise up out of poverty. Popular opinion is that poverty is black people's fault, that racism is not the cause of the persistent inequalities that blacks face today, and that they are in poverty due to their own proclivities— unfortunately, black people are beginning to believe in these pathological myths that it is their fault that they live in poverty, even though many scholarly works, like Alphonso Pinkney's *The Myth of Black Progress* (1984), Douglas G. Glasgow's *The Black Underclass* (1980), Jonathan Kozol's *Savage Inequalities* (1991), Douglas S. Massey and Nancy A. Denton's *American Apartheid* (1993), and Joe Kincheloe, Shirley Steinberg, and Aaron Gresson's *Measured Lies: The Bell Curve Examined* (1996), along with numerous others, have shown that race is very much responsible for the continuing poverty and inequality in society and its public school systems. I always find myself angry and saddened by the fact that the wealthiest nation on this planet cannot or refuses to change the inequities in its schools. A conversation with a human resources person with New York City's Board of Education revealed that most teachers want to work on Long Island—this forces the Board of Education to rely on special programs to bring teachers into the predominantly black and Hispanic schools. While I applaud and support any program that recruits people to the profession of teaching who will give inner-city children a chance to have a consistent teacher for a year, I wonder why someone who has majored in education would not want to go where the need is most? Why would education seniors here in New York City refuse to get their certification so that they do not have to go into predominantly black and Hispanic schools? I even wonder if some of the black education majors who have talked to me of their desires to teach in the suburbs also believe in the myths that black and Hispanic children do not want to learn, are prone to violence, and are inferior? There are education students who are terrified of going into nonwhite areas for their practicum. There are graduate students who refuse to do research or work in "those" areas. I wonder what kind of teachers they are.

Society has been trained well to think that "violence-obsessed" black and Latino students do not want to go to school and that they hate teachers. The movie industry has played a major role in maintaining the racial myths in its use of inner-city black and Latino characters as violent youth. Hollywood's image of these students has reinforced the interest of the dominant culture in films such as *The Substitute*, *Dangerous Minds*, *Lean on Me*, *The Principal*, and *187*. Images of violent black and Latino youth out of control—dealing drugs and battling it out in hallways with semiautomatic weapons—have been presented frequently to the American viewing public. The media's images of crime as an expression of black ethnicity have mobilized popular support not only for more police, but also for the militarization of our inner-city schools and the building of more prisons (Miller, 1996; Mauer, 1999). The demonization of black children by Hollywood has supported society's status-quo shibboleth of the "bad nigger" who needs to be put behind bars. Therefore, inner-city elementary schools become precursors of jails and prisons; the focus is on classroom management and obedient behavior rather than teaching and educating our children to compete and survive in a capitalist system that will otherwise relegate them to the margins of their own society (Delpit, 1995; Ferguson, 2000). In a conversation with an elementary school teacher in Brooklyn (who was not facing me as she closed the windows in her classroom), the teacher claimed that she did not expect much from her students and that they did not have the ability to learn. A white student told me in class that black children cannot learn, nor do they want to—this was an education student.

Society continues to believe the myths that have plagued us for centuries, that blacks cannot think abstractly or rationalize information, cannot learn as well as whites—which in turn facilitates the cry from society to not waste hard-earned tax dollars on them. As Jonathan Kozol and others have consistently argued, black and Hispanic children are relegated to mostly inner-city schools, and those schools continually fail or are just above the failing mark. And instead of being given an equal opportunity to succeed, these kids are either bused to predominantly white schools and then put in slow classes or left to languish and struggle through inferior conditions. Those teachers and/or educators who believe in the myths of black inferiority always claim the same argument that a member of an educational reform committee once made: "You just don't understand. We just want these black kids to learn how to learn" (Macedo, 1994, p. 137).

In the 1960s, many felt that if laws were passed to end racial segregation in such areas as housing and education, the problems would be solved. The federal government passed various Civil Rights Acts and Fair Housing Acts to integrate blacks into American society. However, even though some blacks have moved into the middle-class brackets, one can still look across the landscape of this nation and see the majority of black people living in communities and attending schools that are deteriorating. Scholars all over the nation have studied inner-city poverty, school busing, illiteracy, so-called racial quotas, welfare, black unemployment, etc., to try to understand how this inequitable segregation came to be and why it persists. Although the majority of the research conducted has concluded that "race" is the most defining factor and all have agreed that racial segregation still exists—that realtors still practice policies that maintain racial segregation of communities, that our schools remain for the most part racially segregated—we dare not talk about it openly (Massey and Denton, 1993; Omi and Winant, 1994).

We as educators forget sometimes that the children who are living in these segregated communities want to learn, they want to succeed just as badly as any other children, yet these kids may not know how to articulate how they feel, although they are well aware of and understand the dynamics of the segregation they are forced to live in (Kozol, 1991, 1995). More importantly, what some professors and teachers fail to understand is that these kids have the desire and know how to learn, but they just do not want to lose who they are and their cultural norms. Many forget that these kids have to negotiate and survive every day where death and drugs are a way of life, which takes an enormous amount of abstract and rational thinking. Also, even though most black and Hispanic students may never get to visit suburban schools or experience what they may offer, many of them can articulate very well what their schools lack, that their schools are segregated, and that the schools portrayed on television sitcoms are nothing like the schools they attend. They know very well and very articulately what they do not have. Educators continue to debate, write about, and discuss how our urban schools are continually overcrowded, understaffed, poorly maintained, and mismanaged. We as educators know that the school system, as Lois Weiner states in her book *Urban Teaching: The Essentials*, "constantly undermine[s]" the efforts of teachers who struggle hard to give students the opportunity to succeed in the midst of so much negativity and failure. As college educators, we are seen as the "experts" in education—no one listens to us if we advocate for social justice and equity, yet if we stand firm for standardized exams, no tolerance mandates, and quantitative Cartesian modes of research, policymakers will use our data to justify their unequal or racist policies. We know that these problems are more than pedagogical issues; we know that politics and race play a pivotal role in educational funding. We may even teach about the economic gaps between the privileged and the disenfranchised, but somehow we as a society allow politicians and school administrators to decide what school districts get enough funding, while the poorer districts continue to suffer from its lack.

Many predominantly black and Hispanic schools that I have visited beg the question: Is this a school or a detention center for children? The first person one sees upon entering a predominantly black and Hispanic school is the police officer—the servant of the community. However, these officers are not always necessarily "servants" to the people who live in the community. I have seen parents or guardians threatened by school police security when they had just come to the school to pick up their children. I once watched an elderly Asian woman who could hardly speak English being berated by a policeman for not understanding the rules when she came to get her grandchild. What made that situation even more heartbreaking was the fact that the police officer was Hispanic and another policeman watching was black—people who themselves are deemed inferior by the hegemonic society that employs them. A vision of black plantation overseers who themselves were slaves, who whipped other enslaved blacks for their white masters, comes to mind. Both Paulo Freire in *Pedagogy of the Oppressed* and Frantz Fanon in *The Wretched of the Earth* are correct when they talk about how the oppressed want to emulate their oppressors and oppress their own kind.

Schools of education produce thousands of new teachers every year, yet for some reason our inner-city schools are always in dire need of teachers. We need critical thinking, minds that question the status quo, people who want to be in these schools, who want to challenge society to take the next step toward a truly democratic way of life. Yet I wonder if the teaching profession is becoming like some of those in the health-care profession: Are we producing teachers who will learn how to teach curriculums that do not question the racial and economic inequalities? who do assessments that reinforce standards that are positivistic in nature? who are interested only in mammon and not in providing students with their human rights to speak their minds without punishment or with spaces in schools to resist the inequities they face everyday? Urban colleges of education can prepare teachers who want to become part of the struggle to end the inequities of inner-city schools. Urban schools are different—they are special. They need teachers who want to teach "those students" who, as the student mentioned above remarked to me, "do not have the ability to learn." What good is it to use Paulo Freire and other scholars whose concepts promote an emancipating, noncapitalist idea of education if our potential teachers believe the myths about children of color and are not prepared to struggle against the inequities that keep these students on the margins of society?

I believe that a good school of education will train future teachers to become reflective practitioners, social activists, scholars, mentors, community participants, and facilitators of knowledge who will encourage inner-city students to not become empty vessels waiting to be filled with certified and fragmented knowledge. A good school of education will train our teachers to become viable participants in making this nation a society in which all people have the opportunity to succeed. Hopefully, we can produce teachers who will want to commit themselves to urban schools and promote their students to become dynamic men and women who will construct and produce knowledge that will begin to change not just themselves, but their communities. I believe a good school of education can produce not only teachers who are aware of the hegemonic forces in society, but teachers who will in turn become activists for social justice within the communities they teach as allies with the people they serve. A good school of education, as Paulo Freire argued, produces teachers who understand the difference between a dominating/dehumanizing education and an education that liberates and humanizes the transference of knowledge.

Teachers are not in the classroom to domesticate students or treat them as empty receptacles. Teachers are in the classroom to challenge and encourage students to produce "new" forms of knowledge or re-create knowledge, and they are there to join with their students in the quest for knowledge that will liberate the mind of both the teacher and the student. A good school of education facilitates future teachers to avoid the dehumanizing ideology that prevents people from being reflective and active researchers and creative transformers of the world. A good school of education prepares teachers to become historically and politically involved with their students. They are trained to assist their students, who historically have had no voice as an oppressed group, to become prophets of social change and messengers of hope for the next generation (Freire, 1985; Macedo, 1994).

It is my hope that we as educators will prepare and guide future teachers into becoming revolutionaries in the struggle against oppression and the exploitation of all people and not give mere lip service to the struggle against the domestication of the minds of students. We as educators can prepare future teachers to strip away the layers of a capitalist, patriarchal society that supports the white supremacy of the dominant society. Teachers can also be prepared to not just identify but also actively resist the commodification, bureaucratization, homogenization, and standardization of our schools and the lives of students who attend them. It is my hope that we who teach in a good school of education will offer future teachers a possibility that directs or redirects their pedagogy and cultural practices toward true democracy and social justice.

References

Delpit, L. (1995). *Other People's Children: Cultural Conflict in the Classroom*. New York: The New Press.

Fanon, F. (1968). *The Wretched of the Earth*. Trans. Constance Farrington. New York: Grove Press. 1986.

Feagin, J. R. (1991). "The Continuing Significance of Race: Antiblack Discrimination in Public Places," *American Sociological Review*, 56, pp. 101–116.

Ferguson, A. A. (2000). *Bad Boys: Public Schools in the Making of Black Masculinity*. Ann Arbor: University of Michigan Press.

Freire, P. (1970). *Pedagogy of the Oppressed*. Trans. Myra Bergman Ramos. New York: Continuum Press. 2000.

Freire, P. (1985). *The Politics of Education: Culture, Power and Liberation*. South Hadley, MA: Bergin & Garvey Publishers.

Hacker, A. (1995). *Two Nations: Black and White, Separate, Hostile, Unequal*. New York: Ballantine Books.

Herrnstein, R. J., and Murray, C. (1994). *The Bell Curve: Intelligence and Class Structure in American Life*. New York: The Free Press.

hooks, b. (2000). *Where We Stand: Class Matters*. New York: Routledge.

Kozol, J. (1991). *Savage Inequalities: Children in America's Schools*. New York: Crown Publishers.

Kozol, J. (1995). *Amazing Grace: The Lives of Children and the Conscience of a Nation*. New York: Crown Publishers.

Litwack, L. (1961). *North of Slavery: The Negro in the Free States, 1790–1860*. Chicago: University of Chicago Press.

Macedo, D. P. (1994). *Literacies of Power: What Americans Are Not Allowed to Know*. Boulder, CO: Westview Press.

Massey, D. S., and Denton, N. A. (1993). *American Apartheid: Segregation and the Making of the Underclass*. Cambridge, MA: Harvard University Press.

Mauer, M. (1999). *Race to Incarcerate: The Sentencing Project*. New York: The New Press.

Miller, J. G. (1996). *Search and Destroy: African-American Males in the Criminal Justice System*. New York: Cambridge University Press.

Omi, M., and Winant, H. (1994). *Racial Formation in the United States: From the 1960s to the 1990s*. 2nd ed. New York: Routledge.

Weiner, L. (1999). *Urban Teacher*. New York: Teachers College Press.

Chapter Five

Who I Am Informs My Teaching

Alma Rubal-Lopez

As one of a few minority faculty members in the School of Education at Brooklyn College, and as one who has always reminded those around her that there are too few persons of color employed on all levels of the college, the invitation to write this chapter was met as both a challenge and an opportunity to be honest with myself and with our readers. More importantly, by taking on this task, my insistence on hiring more faculty of color based on the fact that they have much to contribute to any institution of higher education, in particular to a public urban college, is on the line. Unless I can justify my contribution to the college, my insistence on hiring more racial minorities will be unfounded.

I would like to think that my brilliance and infinite knowledge about the subjects I teach and the unique pedagogy I employ are the reasons why I should be teaching here. However, the truth of the matter is that I am not brilliant. Furthermore, my knowledge, although substantial, is not exhaustive of all to be known in my particular areas of scholarly inquiry (child development and sociolinguistics). Last, my methodology, which employs a very unique and personal approach, could be scrutinized and labeled as "unorthodox" and a deviation from what one might recognize as traditionally "acceptable" pedagogy.

I have reached the conclusion that the principal reason that I am at Brooklyn College and my contribution to the college are one and the same: my life experience as a New York Puerto Rican born and raised in the South Bronx. As a professor, I interface daily with students and other faculty members—this interaction answers why I do what I do. Who I am is not solely what I bring to the college, but is the reason why I was hired and the factor that distinguishes me from most of my colleagues. I am not ashamed to admit that being Puerto Rican was the reason I was hired, as this fact is more of an indictment of higher education than a reflection of my capabilities.

I acknowledge what affirmative action has done for me, I applaud it, and I thank those who came before me. As a person who has on many occasions been the "only one" or the "first," I know the loneliness, frustration, and complex of emotions that one has in such a situation. Although the downside of being a minority is that it can stand in the way of persons seeing anything beyond this, on the other hand it allows me to see things from a unique, nonmainstream perspective. I am someone who is looking in from the outside, and I have a unique analysis of what I see.

I was first hired as a counselor by SEEK (Search for Education, Elevation and Knowledge)—a program created in the 1960s to provide students from underprivileged backgrounds opportunities in higher education. Today, this program is housed in the SEEK Department at Brooklyn College, one of the few departments (ethnic studies not withstanding) whose members realize the importance of having minorities as colleagues.

Traditionally, a fairly significant number of faculty members in comparable departments throughout CUNY (the City University of New York) are persons of color, resulting in enclaves of minority hires located in similar departments and in ethnic studies. Without such departments, the numbers of nonwhite faculty would be even lower than they already are throughout most institutions of higher education. I would probably not be a teaching faculty member in a major school of education without first being hired in a "minority program" and entering my present department through the back door. Occasionally, other departments do articulate the need to diversify faculty; but when hiring new people, good intentions are often lost.

As a professor of future New York City teachers headed for schools with diverse populations that reflect those of our city and country, my identity is important and facilitates my primordial goal: to simultaneously stimulate my students' thinking and model effective pedagogy.

It would be impossible to meet my objectives without first engaging my students in a dialogue and process that is meaningful. Learning cannot take place without authentic student engagement. I must assist my students in their transformation as active participants. This objective is oftentimes difficult with students who have been passive observers and who have been rewarded for that role. Generally, such students have been recipients of the "banking" concept of education, in which the teacher issues communiqués and makes metaphorical deposits that the students patiently receive, memorize, and repeat. The scope of action permitted to the students extends only as far as receiving, filling, and storing the deposits (Freire, 1987, p. 58).

As a teaching approach, the banking method is inefficient because it presents information to be stored without being used, oftentimes resulting in inability to retrieve such information at a later date. Another consequence is the transformation of this material into inert knowledge that cannot be used in other domains. The information attained in high school foreign language classes is an example of inert learning. Despite years of high school foreign language instruction, few persons can carry on a conversation in that language because teaching has been conducted in the classroom without context (Slavin, 1997). The most tragic result of the banking method is that it leads to student disinterest in learning and, ultimately, a lack of vision regarding the importance of learning. An additional danger of employing this strategy is that we are merely feeding students rather than inspiring them (Macedo, 1994).

Student disengagement is a common phenomenon in the United States. In a study of 20,000 high school students, Laurence Steinberg (1996) found that a significant number of students were going through the process of completing high school without really being engaged in the process of becoming educated. The goal becomes the diploma rather than the acquisition of knowledge. For future teachers, this disengagement can be deadly; it can be instrumental in creating an ineffective and substandard educator. The engagement of education students is crucial in creating effective, lifelong professionals. I want my students to focus on internal rather than external reinforcements by having them find pleasure and satisfaction in the process of becoming a teacher—not an easy feat, but one worth pursuing. In this chapter, I want to discuss the ways that my identity facilitates student engagement in a process that could otherwise be another bank deposit. Who I am facilitates and strengthens this engagement.

The content of a course contributes to the selection of curriculum and to students becoming active participants. Naturally, much of this is influenced by the professor's life experience. The content of my class is no exception. Who I am is similar to who my students are—they are members of racial and/or linguistic minorities, children of immigrant blue-collar workers, poor, and uneducated. The class content often parallels their own interests as well.

Our commonality facilitates an honest dialogue about issues of equity, race, power, and gender discrimination. Such topics taken from students' lives are generative themes that arise at a point where the students' personal lives collide with the larger society (Kincheloe, Slattery, and Steinberg, 2000). Feelings of self-hate, shame, inferiority, anger, and despair, not often addressed and even less likely to be personally admitted to, are often discussed and reflected upon in a manner that enhances our knowledge of the origins of these emotions and their destructiveness in a learning environment. Thus, the stage is set for a discussion about child development and an opportunity to connect theory with practice. Without this link the class could become a mere cathartic exercise of feelings. This connection is not new. John Dewey (1904) recognized the importance of the use of a person's own direct and personal experience in teacher education and referred to it as the "greatest asset" the educator may possess. According to Dewey, failure to allow students to use their life experiences in light of theoretical constructs will produce the duplication of others' practices. The danger of this is a "mindless imitation of others' practice rather than a reflection on teaching as an interactive process—and it will leave teachers prime targets for any educational publisher's grand, new, state-of-the art magic potion" (Delpit, 1995, p. 125).

To my class I myself admit to having had the aforementioned negative feelings as a young child in an often hostile and racist system, and this admission sets the tone for a safe environment, in which students can become engaged without fear of embarrassment or ridicule. Such an environment allows critical thinking, knowledge production, and meaning making (Kincheloe et al., 2000) and recognizes the crucial role that emotions play in learning, an admission rarely made in a domain where logic and discrete variables are valued above all things.

Recent research regarding the interconnectedness of emotions, thinking, and learning recognize that there is no separation between mind and emotions. We must therefore uphold the importance and rightful and necessary inclusion of emotions in learning and in schools (Jensen, 1998). Such research recognizes that emotions give us a more activated and chemically stimulated brain, which helps us recall information better. Not surprisingly, the recognition and focus on students' lives, which in turn activates and acknowledges students' emotions, will ultimately enhance and facilitate learning.

As a Puerto Rican woman who speaks about a childhood in public housing projects, poverty, biculturalism, bilingualism, racism, marginalization, a sense of not fitting in, machismo, religion, and many other aspects of an experience similar to that of my students, I encourage them to use their lives as vehicles to understand and, if necessary, reject theory. By allowing them to know who I really am, I too reveal my own lack of "institutional fit." This truth allows for the demystification of my role as a college professor and a continuing dialogue.

Another by-product of the demystification process is that it provides hope. Frequently, many of my students are the first in their family to go to college. Unrealistic notions about what is necessary to attain a degree and the fear of failing often result in viewing such a goal as unattainable. Such beliefs lead to a lack of motivation and the emergence of an external locus of control that focuses blame for failure on everything but one's own fear of failure. By dethroning my role, I permit students to see career possibilities, so that students who enter my class thinking that they cannot hopefully leave with the realization that they can.

The importance of encouraging students to develop an internal locus of control is that it forces them to take responsibility for their lives. Research findings reveal that after ability, one's locus of control is the best predictor of academic success (Slavin, 1997). For racial minorities this is important. Although racism is an undeniable evil of American society, students must see beyond this and not use this societal demon as an excuse for not achieving their desired goals.

The chief advantage of exposing my education class to the importance of engaging students through their teachers' own lives is in the applicability of this approach in their future classrooms. On the topic of classroom management, notions in behavioral psychology focus on why and when it is appropriate to use reinforcement and punishment in order to maintain class orderliness, and little if any attention is given to the root causes of the unruliness. The consequences of such disengagement, i.e., student unrest, anger, and frustration, are rarely part of the classroom management discourse. In such instances, teachers need to capitalize on the antagonistic cultural elements produced in subordinate students' acts of resistance and create a pedagogy that would enable students to comprehend their world so that they can read it, act upon it, and, if necessary, transform it (Macedo, 1995, p. 54). The purpose, as proposed by Kincheloe in chapter 1 of this book, is for students to "begin to understand that pedagogical methods and classroom management techniques are not isolated, rule-driven, universal procedures, but parts of larger articulations of educational purposes."

As future teachers, students who have completed my class will hopefully have a better understanding of children and adolescents and more insight regarding their own childhoods and how their past experiences have contributed to forming their perceptions about the young. The nature of the courses I teach in child development and human development address many theories reflecting the human condition. I can only hope that students would look at these theories with a critical eye rather than merely accepting them as textbook truth.

Since education is an applied science, I repeatedly use theory and connect it to my own experience and encourage students to also apply this knowledge to their lives and to the classroom setting. Thus, students become creators and contributors of knowledge rather than recipients of the gift of knowledge bestowed by those who consider themselves knowledgeable and donors of this information to those they consider to know nothing (Freire, 1987, p. 58). Students not only develop an understanding of who they are, but realize that they have something to contribute to a dialogue that is often centered around theoretical notions of human behavior without much applicability, in a setting that can oftentimes be intimidating. The classroom discourse now becomes an exchange between students who know and educators who also know (Macedo, 1994). Issues of power regarding teacher/student interaction enacted in the classroom, and addressed by Delpit (1995), are to some extent lessened by using such a strategy.

This approach discourages talking about reality as if it were motionless, static, compartmentalized, and predictable (Freire, 1987, p. 57). It prevents the expounding of issues that are alien to the students' experience. Frequently, students' cultures and backgrounds are not taken into account when curriculum is designed, resulting in the invalidation of the students' experiences. The ramifications of such an omission of a person's life are great. This frequently leads to students' being muffled, feeling as if they shouldn't contribute to a discussion or say anything. This silencing repeatedly goes unnoticed. As cited in Kincheloe et al. (2000), when one lives in the mainstream, one is less likely to notice the way outsiders are silenced by enforced conformity to unfamiliar norms and discourse. Magda Lewis (1995, p. 36) refers to this experience as the "double-cross-reversal," which she defines as the privilege of the dominant to talk at great length about that which is not and to stay silent about and ignore that which is. For such groups, possibility is defined through denial, freedom is reinterpreted through constraint, violence is justified as protection, and in schools, contrary to the belief that it is a place where knowledge is shared, knowledge withheld articulates the curriculum. We are silenced because of our personal histories, and our social identities are cross-cut not only by who we are but as well by the ceaseless reinforcement of who we are not.

Said practices result in the disengagement of students and their eventual failure in school. If one does not see a reason for attending, then there is no reason to continue. This phenomenon might to some degree help to explain the significantly high secondary school dropout rates for African Americans, even higher rates for Hispanics, and subsequently the drastically low representation of such students in the domain of higher education.

By using one's own experiences to examine theory, one can say that truth or the approximation to truth is heightened because now a theory can be scrutinized by someone from a different culture, socioeconomic level, or religious perspective than that of the theorist. This allows for the generalizability and validity of such an idea to be tested. Oftentimes, Piaget, Kohlberg, Freud, etc., are met with hesitancy and skepticism by students whose reality is different from those of the theorists being studied, resulting in the questioning, dissecting, discarding, and reformulation of the knowledge presented. The sacred cows of developmental theory are now replaced by questions coming from budding theorists.

The importance of this is the change in the thinking process that students go through, from a mindset of knowledge acquisition through acceptance to a mindset of knowledge creation and deconstructing of existing knowledge. This approach attempts to avoid what Kincheloe in chapter 1 of this volume refers to as the "positivistic, technicist tendency in teacher education to take unproblematized universal truths, transform them into fixed pedagogical procedures and pass them along to students."

Students become critics of what has been traditionally accepted as truth in academia. This allows students to connect theory to their own reality and, by doing so, to subject the traditional canon to scrutiny. It also validates students' lives, experiences, cultures, and beliefs. It allows them to reflect on their own patterns of behavior and to question the value and validity of these norms, resulting in the scrutiny of their own sacred cows. For urban students who are often not part of the mainstream, this approach permits them to be the focus and, by doing so, allows them to realize that they are not alone in not having the correct "institutional fit." They also should recognize that what they bring to the classroom is important and necessary for teaching in an urban setting.

For students with life experiences closer to that of the mainstream population of the United States (a population less likely to be found in my classes), this approach enhances their knowledge of those from other backgrounds and hopefully instills a sensibility for those who are not from their group. They too, by looking at their own reality, can bring into question the validity of their own beliefs and values.

Although my impact on students is my most important reason for being a college professor, it is also crucial for me to be a faculty member at Brooklyn College for policymaking—this is manifested in my interactions with colleagues. As a member of various changing committees, I am often the voice of the minorities. In committees that enforce student academic policies, I have had to remind members that financial inability, familial responsibility, and other life circumstances must be taken into consideration when making punitive judgments that can impact negatively upon the lives of students. I often remind my colleagues that adhering solely to official policy is not good enough. One must understand the circumstances and the factors leading to whatever situation we are considering. This stance is often met with hostility toward me as a "bleeding heart." I answer that I am trying to make a difficult playing field more equal.

When I sit on selection committees for new hires, I am repeatedly looking for someone who can bring to the college an understanding of how to teach our students. If the search is one for an administrative position, I focus on whether diversity and the needs of the community are of importance to the candidate. The university's mission, which states that we must be responsive to the community, is an issue that must be brought forth. Another reminder is the profile of the CUNY student who is very often poor, the first in his/her family to go to college, and a member of a linguistic and/or racial minority. Oftentimes committee members are very much impressed by prestigious credentials in the academic world and overlook the gap in the life experiences between our students and the prospective administrator or faculty member.

If the vacant position requires the creation and implementation of policy, then the distance between who the candidate is and the student population should be as narrow as possible. As in the case of teaching, a candidate's life experience will determine his/her approach and perception of students. My presence or the presence of other persons with similar views on a search committee does not guarantee the hiring of such a person. However, it can invite someone for an interview who might be considered an unlikely candidate by those whose interests lie in maintaining the status quo. If such a person is not hired, the institution at the very least must respond to the issue of why the candidate was not hired.

Who I am—a Puerto Rican woman with origins in the South Bronx—is why I must be at Brooklyn College. My worldview is formed by my ethnicity, race, socioeconomic status, linguistic repertoire, and gender. These descriptors define who I am in a society often marked by exclusion, elitism, racism, and resistance to change. Without a doubt this is the most valuable and unique commodity that I bring to the college. Who I am brings with it a message of value for who my students are, and it brings hope for who they wish to become.

References

Delpit, L. (1995). *Other People's Children: Cultural Conflict in the Classroom*. New York: The New Press.

Dewey, J. (1904). "The Relation of Theory to Practice in Education." In M. L. Borrowman, ed., *Teacher Education in America: A Documentary History*. New York: Teachers College Press, 1965.

Freire, P. (1987). *Pedagogy of the Oppressed*. New York: Continuum.

Kincheloe, J., Slattery, P., and Steinberg S. (2000). *Contextualizing Teaching: Introduction to Education and Educational Foundations*. New York: Longman.

Jensen, E. (1998). *Teaching with the Brain in Mind*. Alexandria, VA: Association for Supervision and Curriculum Development.

Lewis, M. (1995). "Power and Education: Who Decides the Forms Schools Have Taken, and Who Should Decide?" In J. Kincheloe and S. Steinberg, eds., *Thirteen Questions: Reframing Education's Conversation*. New York: Peter Lang.

Macedo, D. (1994). *Literacies of Power: What Americans Are Not Allowed to Know*. Boulder, CO: Westview.

Slavin, R. (1997). *Educational Psychology*. Boston: Allyn & Bacon.

Steinberg, L. (1996). *Beyond the Classroom*. New York: Simon & Schuster.

Chapter Six

Community Knowledge–Centered Teacher Education: A Paradigm for Socially Just Educational Transformation

Nora E. Hyland and Shuaib Meacham

How many preservice teacher education students are committed to teaching in communities that have been historically marginalized by race, class, language, or religion? That is, how many preservice teachers are enthusiastic about spending their teaching careers in schools located in economically poor, predominantly African American, Latino, or otherwise educationally underserved communities? Unfortunately, very few. As teacher educators, we have noted that our students are anxious to practice, teach, and spend their education careers in predominantly white, Christian, economically affluent areas. Many of our student teachers are fearful and angry when they are placed in economically poor neighborhoods and neighborhoods of color because most of them have decided that they will not ultimately teach in such communities. They make this decision not based on personal knowledge of the neighborhoods but rather on the pervasive deficit ideology that such neighborhoods are dangerous and populated with uncaring, incompetent families who have produced difficult-to-manage children who are dysfunctional learners, and that the schools serving these communities are situated in urban school districts marked by overwhelming political bureaucratization, marginal funding, and rigid standardized curricula. In spite of this, given the competition for jobs in affluent, white communities, some of our students go on to teach in the same neighborhoods that they regard with fear and disdain. Are these preservice teachers prepared to teach in neighborhoods that they have overwhelmingly chosen not to be in? Are teachers better prepared simply because they have student-taught in a neighborhood school with similar demographics and bureaucratic structures?

Consider the relatively few preservice teachers who are committed to working in racially, ethnically, and economically marginalized urban communities: How well prepared are these teachers? Does choosing to teach in such a community automatically make one effective there? The commitment of young teachers to teach in marginalized communities is often driven by a missionary zeal characterized by a desire to save or help students who are perceived to have very few personal, familial, or neighborhood resources. Might such assumptions serve to reify the marginalization of students and their families? Even preservice teachers who are from communities of color and/or low income, who may not hold deficit assumptions, will likely work in a school culture in which the prevailing ethos is one of distance from the community and is marked by contempt for, or mandates against, pedagogical practices that emphasize the authentic cultural knowledge of students' home communities. Few teachers are prepared to function in the bureaucratic milieu of urban schools serving historically marginalized populations. Their options are to either quit (which they do in large numbers), learn not to get involved, mind their own business and thereby contribute to maintaining the urban educational machine (which most of them do), or organize with students and parents to fight the injustices that define urban schooling (which few teachers do, and even fewer do successfully).

These are perhaps the definitive challenges for teacher educators who aim to prepare teachers to be agents of change in culturally and economically diverse urban schools and communities. The challenges are complex and multilayered, comprising such factors as the largely homogeneous preservice teacher population; the bureaucratic structures of urban schools; the deficit ideology that characterizes the teaching culture of most urban schools; the current traditions of teacher educators and teacher education; and the dominant American ideology about race, class, and urban containment. In this chapter, we attempt to identify some of the key challenges in preparing teachers for urban communities of color and low income, examine some of the ways that teacher educators are tackling these challenges, and offer a model centered on community knowledge with which we might approach the preparation of teachers and generate a new model of urban schooling.

The Challenges

Dominant teaching practices in urban settings are marked by what Haberman (1991) refers to as a "pedagogy of poverty," characterized by activities focused on control and basic skills instruction rather than education and critical thinking. These practices are supported by urban educational reforms that embrace high-stakes testing, scripted curricula, extensive test preparation, and increased social control of students. None of these practices build upon, or even acknowledge, the social, intellectual, cultural, or political capital of students and their families. These dominant practices function to further isolate and marginalize communities that have already been contained by urban segregation. The results of these institutional arrangements include a reification of deficit ideology about students of color and economically poor students, as well as an adversarial relationship between teachers and parents.

The deficit assumptions held by teachers and student teachers who find themselves working with historically underserved populations can serve to alienate students from school and perpetuate the cycle by re-inforcing social distance between teachers and families. A major challenge to the educational achievement of many children of color from low-income communities is that of alienation from school. That is, students are often torn between school and their home lives. This alienation is due, at least in part, to pervasive deficit ideologies in society and among school personnel, which emphasize the ways in which poor students and students of color and their communities are deficient in the areas of intelligence and language and learning capability, as well as the shortcomings of African American and Latino communities in their effort to support their children's education. Baugh (1994) found that negative dispositions toward the cultures and languages of people of color were particularly prevalent among teachers. This is particularly problematic, as Fine (1991) contends that when teachers convey deficit beliefs about the learning potential and capabilities of low-income students of color and their com-munities, students often distance themselves from school and thus com-promise their ability to achieve.

This problem of alienation becomes more challenging when one con-siders that students of color, especially in urban areas, come from back-grounds that are very different from teachers and student teachers. As of 1995, 87% of elementary and secondary public school teachers were white, and 80% of students enrolled in teacher education programs were white. At the same time, in many urban centers throughout the United States, a majority of the students were students of color. This mismatch between the demographic composition of urban school students and that of teachers and student teachers constitutes a major challenge facing teacher educators who prepare preservice teachers to be successful in cul-turally diverse urban communities. Demographic differences based on class, religion, learning style, and language accompany ethnic differences.

Educational research indicates that a common characteristic among effective teachers of low-income students of color is a respect for, knowledge of, and relationship with the home communities of the students. Yet very few urban schools, or individual teachers within them, have established such relationships with local community members. More often than not, teachers in such communities view the families and home communities of their students as the primary obstacles to their students' success and therefore maintain a striking social distance from families and community members, supported by the curricular practices that assume deficiencies in urban students of color. Urban school educational cultures are often marked by a disrespect for parents and students, and a tendency for teachers to absolve themselves of responsibility for student failure or disruption. In-service teachers in these schools are therefore unable to provide preservice teachers with needed models for the kinds of community engagement and cultural relevance that is characteristic of successful teachers of children of color. Feiman-Nemser and Floden (1986) have pointed out that the educational cultures of schools in which teachers work have a far greater influence on teachers and their teaching than does preservice teacher training. By placing preservice teachers in schools in historically marginalized neighborhoods without considering the in-house cultures of such schools, the dominant teaching practices, and the pervasive ideology among the mentor teachers, we are likely (re)producing teachers who conform to the social distance and deficit thinking that have historically proven so destructive for students in communities of color and low income.

Therefore, to combat school alienation and the continued miseducation among students from historically marginalized racial, ethnic, and economic groups, it is imperative that we teacher educators interrogate our own practices. Traditionally teacher education has rested on the assumption that the key ingredients to learning to teach lie in particular teaching methodologies and subject-area content. Therefore, we emphasize pedagogical knowledge in our methods classes and content knowledge in the liberal arts core requirements. The field-based and student teaching requirements are opportunities for students to practice utilizing their content knowledge in the context of pedagogy or their pedagogical content knowledge.

Typically, teacher education students have one or two required multicultural education courses in which they are asked to consider the kinds of pedagogical knowledge they may need to teach racially, ethnically, or economically diverse students. Multicultural education requirements such as these are typically taught in isolation from other courses, and the content and perspectives represented in them are rarely reinforced in other required teacher education courses. Rarely are education students asked to examine the very notion of knowledge and how our definitions of what counts as knowledge produce hierarchies of power that have both real and symbolic effects on people's lives. For example, we rarely ask our students to consider a "radical redefinition of school knowledge from the hetero-geneous perspectives and identities of racially disadvantaged groups—a process that goes beyond the language of 'inclusivity' and emphasizes relationality and multivocality as the central intellectual forces in the pro-duction of knowledge." This kind of critical pedagogy, in which students examine knowledge in relationship to power and consider the effects of subjugating or reauthoring the knowledge of certain groups, is infre-quently included in teacher education curricula; when it is included, it is often disconnected from the core of the teacher education experience. Because these issues are rarely addressed in teacher education, there is almost no opportunity for students to consider ways to understand, value, and develop pedagogy grounded in the subjugated knowledge of margin-alized groups.

Likewise, our teacher education students are not taught to navigate the terrain of urban educational systems. Even if historically subjugated cul-tural and political knowledge is centered in a teacher education program, to what extent are committed preservice teachers prepared to work in a system that is unlikely to value such forms of knowledge and, in fact, is a primary means by which such knowledge has been subjugated? Navigating the political topography of urban schools is one reason why so many for-merly dedicated teachers leave the system or become complacent.

If we are to truly educate future teachers to become agents of educa-tional justice, teacher education must be radically reconfigured to allow students to consider subjugated knowledge and then to learn to use it in the transformation of classrooms and schools. It is not enough to place white and middle-class preservice teachers in schools in historically mar-ginalized communities; teacher educators must create new learning expe-riences that challenge traditional understandings of knowledge, introduce subjugated knowledge, and transform pedagogical interpretations of knowledge and learning.

Many teacher educators have developed curricula and programs to transform the preservice experience and prepare teachers to effectively engage and teach students from racially, culturally, and economically diverse urban populations. The following section will examine these efforts and draw from their lessons. The final section will offer a description of an approach to teacher education centered on community knowledge that offers what we believe is a culturally rooted and potentially transformative model for teacher education.

Models of Teacher Education Aimed at Preparing Teachers for Diversity

Postsecondary efforts to effectively prepare preservice teachers for successful urban educational experiences have traditionally encompassed three categories:

STRUCTURAL—features changes in the relationship between teacher education programs and the public schools, often supported by the establishment of professional development schools (PDSs)

CURRICULAR—emphasizes knowledge derived from the intellectual, cultural, and literary scholarship on nonmainstream cultural populations, often coupled with teaching strategies that complement diverse cultural learning styles

EXPERIENTIAL—features practical experiences in nonmainstream community settings as a means of obtaining comfort within those communities as well as knowledge about urban students and families.

These three categories, while distinctly identified, often interconnect in actual programs. However, the labels have been constructed as a means of identifying primary approaches to prepare teachers for urban, culturally diverse, and historically marginalized student populations.

Structural Approach

Structural efforts to improve the preparation of teachers for urban school environments emphasize change in the relationship between college/university-based teacher education programs and the public schools. The Holmes Group, a consortium of school of education programs, recognized that university-based teacher education programs and teacher education faculty were disconnected from the practical realities of the public school environment. The member institutions and committees of the group came up with the PDS model (Holmes Group, 1995) so that schools might create relationships between schools and teacher education programs similar to those between hospitals and medical programs. Specifically, the PDS model allows successful practicing teachers to have a more prominent role in the training of future teachers while also fostering more intellectually rigorous, research-based teaching approaches. Initially, this structural reform in the relationship between important teacher education constituencies was to include communities within which schools were situated (Holmes Group, 1995). However, that component was not realized in practice.

In the area of culturally diverse and urban teacher preparation, teacher education programs have sought to take advantage of the PDS structure by having preservice teachers spend more time in urban schools throughout their teacher education program. As part of that practical experience, preservice teachers would also receive instruction from expert or mentor teachers, often serving in the role of "clinical faculty," who would team-teach university courses with regular school of education faculty members. In this way, the theoretical and conceptual knowledge promoted in the university would be complemented by the experiential insight of an expert, practicing teacher. These courses often take place in the schools to provide more connection between theoretical concepts and practical application and to provide university faculty with more of a presence in the schools.

The strengths of the structural approaches to urban teacher preparation lie in the increased experience in urban schools that preservice teachers receive. Preservice teachers are often exposed to a variety of urban schools representing many different cultural communities. Additionally, preservice teachers not only learn research-based, intellectually sound curricular and instructional approaches, but they see how these approaches must be modified in the context of complex urban classroom environments.

The shortcomings of the PDS model lie in the almost exclusive focus on school-oriented knowledge and competencies. Knowledge that is authentic to the communities served by these schools does not appear to have a prominent role in PDS programs. Since neither schools nor universities have been places inclusive of historically subjugated community knowledge, collaboration between the two does not represent, in itself, progress for those students and communities that are alienated from schools. In fact, this "tighter coupling" of universities and schools has reinforced status and power differentials between school professionals and parents. Programs often incorporated into the PDS model, like family literacy, teach parents school competencies rather than integrate parent and community learning competencies into the culture of the school. Finally, PDS programs, while situated in urban schools, may not necessarily include curricular changes that inform preservice teachers regarding the cultures, languages, and learning styles of urban students and how these insights may be used to instructional advantages. In fact, PDS programs that employ materials emphasizing urban student learning difficulty may reinforce deficit conceptions about students and their home communities.

Curricular Approach

By far the most prominent postsecondary approaches aimed at improving preservice teacher effectiveness in culturally diverse urban classrooms are those that modify the curricula of teacher education courses. The prominence of curricular modifications reflects an emphasis not so much on the relationships between universities and public schools but on the knowledge deficits of predominantly white middle-class preservice teachers, especially as it relates to the lives of non-mainstream students. Gloria Ladson-Billings refers to this deficit as the "multicultural illiteracy" of preservice teachers, emphasizing as well that preservice teachers of color often do not know basic information about cultures beyond their own group. Given this deficit, prominent researchers such as Banks and Banks (1997), Nieto (1996), Grant and Sleeter (1989), and Cummins (1996) have constructed curricular rubrics and basic frameworks for culturally diverse content knowledge to be taught to both students and preservice teachers. These rubrics, or curricular typologies, suggest that culturally diverse curricula should move from knowledge acquisition of culturally diverse content information to action regarding the social issues and challenges faced by culturally diverse learners and their communities. Researchers such as Au and Jordan (1981), Foster (1997), and Philips (1972), while emphasizing the importance of information, have demonstrated the manner in which communicative competencies, culturally based teaching strategies, and styles of learning, all supported by students' homes and communities, can increase the achievement of students of color. Curricular modifications based on this research attempt to help teachers build on the culturally based learning strengths of students rather than emphasizing learning deficiencies.

The strengths of curricular modifications as an approach to preservice teacher education lies in their ability to intellectually challenge the prevailing assumptions and comfort levels of preservice teachers in a manner that can lead to changes in attitudes and ultimately teaching practice. A comprehensive approach to reforming the teacher education curriculum is clearly essential to generate cultural understanding, cross-cultural competence, and potential cultural emancipation that emphasizes the history and culture of historically marginalized groups. However, Ladson-

Billings cautions that the curriculum reform model is truly effective only when accompanied by comprehensive program redesign and commitment to the objectives of culturally diverse urban teacher education. When curricular modifications are mere add-ons to a traditional teacher education structure, students rarely address such approaches with the necessary degree of integrity. When the program design is sufficiently comprehensive, the curricular modification approach helps teachers in the following areas:

- identifying and adjusting instruction to accommodate an array of learning styles and multiple intelligences in the classroom

- seeing beyond cultural deficits to see students in terms of cultural strengths and learning potential

- helping students to gain an awareness of the educational impact of the social and economic challenges faced by families and students in urban contexts

- helping preservice teachers to identify and reflect upon their own cultural identity and social privilege in productive ways

Although this model makes it more likely that preservice teachers will have a greater understanding of historically marginalized knowledge and cultural styles, they are left with few answers as to how to live this knowledge in a way that could be transformative for schools and classrooms. Alverman et al. (1997), in particular, emphasize the problem of teacher attrition, which can occur when innovative and socially conscious instruction meets with student resistance and professional risk. This approach does not address the realities of the school cultures in which preservice teachers will ultimately teach. The most profound weaknesses of the curricular modification approach lies in its overreliance upon attitudinal change through reading and reflection. McCarthy (1993) points out that this approach depends on individual teachers changing their attitudes and techniques, but the basic structure of the educational system is left intact; the approach fails to address schools as sites of power that are fundamentally designed to maintain an unjust status quo. In most cases, the practical relationship between the school and the community is unchanged; community people, institutions, and issues continue to remain outside of the teaching and learning experience.

Experiential Approach

The experiential approach in the preparation of preservice teachers for urban school settings often aims to provide students with experiences outside of school contexts as a means of gaining insights about culturally diverse children and urban communities. This approach is frequently applied at the beginning of the preservice teachers' entry into the education program and emphasizes some kind of service learning. Teacher education programs that employ this approach often assign preservice teachers to community centers and after-school programs where they engage in tutoring, mentoring, and other service practices. The logic informing the experiential approach is that learning occurs in areas of children's lives outside of school and that insights regarding the learning experienced by children in such settings can be meaningfully applied to the classroom. Preservice teachers may also observe aspects of students' talents and personalities that may not be evident in classroom activities but may emerge more directly in a setting where the classroom contingencies are not as prominent. Finally, in some cases, teacher education students are encouraged to engage in service to the students and their communities as part of a movement toward addressing social injustice.

A different yet prominent version of the experiential is found in the work of Luis Moll. Unlike models that feature tutoring or some other kind of service learning, Moll's work with in-service teachers emphasizes the importance of doing research on community practices so that students can learn about the knowledge resources possessed by lower-income urban communities. Moll and colleagues refer to these knowledge resources as "funds of knowledge" (Moll et al., 1992). Rooted in the economic survival strategies of working-class Chicanos in the Southwest, the concept of funds of knowledge suggests that each family has a set of skills that it is able to share with others in the community. Moll has trained teachers to conduct research wherein they identify these funds of knowledge and provide opportunities for Chicano parents to share their community knowledge in the classroom. With this model, not only do teachers learn, but the school becomes a more functional member of the community. The model, however, has not been integrated into an undergraduate teacher education program.

The best part about the experiential approach is that it has the potential to bring preservice teachers into meaningful relationships with educationally relevant adults in children's lives as a means of expanding their teaching capabilities. Preservice teachers have seen children outside of school and realize that in contrast to the kind of boredom or disruption they may evidence in class, these children do have important talents and interests that may be engaged for their own benefit.

When implemented comprehensively, the experiential approach can help preservice teachers to identify important educationally relevant competencies within cultural populations usually associated with cultural deficit. That is, prospective teachers can identify authentic forms of historically subjugated knowledge rooted in the community and in practices they encounter in their field experience.

The shortcomings of this approach lie in its complexity and difficulty of implementation. The experiential approach requires levels of coordination and management that may not be within the comfort levels of many teacher education faculty. For example, this approach must be accompanied by the kinds of comprehensive curricular reforms described previously. Also, without any emphasis on the ways that preservice teachers can work with community members toward school transformation, these community-based experiences function, at their best, to change attitudes of individual teachers, yet they still leave the basic structure and inner workings of the school system as they are. At worst, and frequently, the emphasis on service that often accompanies the experiential approach can actually reinforce deficit beliefs and reify the idea that teachers in historically marginalized communities are missionaries deployed to save and fix children from dysfunctional communities. Communities and children who have historically been marginalized are thus further marginalized, by being exclusively defined in terms of their "issues," shortcomings, and challenges and having their identities inscribed within the traditional deficit model.

An Important Shortcoming of the Models

A significant shortcoming common to all of the above approaches to teacher education reform is the shortage if not absolute dearth of classroom teachers and schools that model effective ways to use subjugated community knowledge as an empowering educational tool. This poses a significant challenge in the education of preservice teachers, who need such models from which to learn. This particular difficulty suggests that the effective preparation of preservice teachers for culturally diverse school contexts cannot be separated from simultaneous professional development for practicing in-service teaching professionals as well as school-reform initiatives aimed at local bureaucracies.

A Community Knowledge–Centered Model

In the final section of this chapter, we describe a model for teacher education that we have begun to develop and implement in small but significant ways. The community knowledge-centered (CKC) model builds on each of the models previously discussed; however, it requires a significant paradigm shift for the field of university-based teacher educators, for schools, and for communities. It is based on the assumption that colleges of education have an ethical responsibility to systematically work toward educational justice and take a lead in this effort. As teacher educators, we have a corner on the market for teacher preparation, yet we are failing to produce teachers equipped to teach in historically marginalized communities. Teacher educators are often critical of alternative-route programs to teacher certification and defend the primary role of the university, yet we have taken little responsibility for the current state of urban education, nor have we altered our own practices to significantly influence change in these school settings. The model we present here requires teacher educators to reconceptualize their roles by becoming accountable to communities for which they prepare teachers. Colleges of education engage in numerous acts of self-preservation; we argue that the best way to preserve ourselves is to dramatically change our practices.

The primary innovation of the CKC approach is that colleges of education acknowledge the community voice that has been absent from school and teacher education reform and take an explicitly political role in organizing and fighting for policy change. It presupposes that colleges of education will model for students and teachers how to organize collectively to incorporate subjugated knowledge and marginalized community perspectives in their own practice. Our model assumes the radical position that education is eminently more important than maintaining institutional arrangements.

In the following sections, we outline the philosophical orientation of the CKC approach, followed by the specific structural aspects of the model that build upon the various existing models of teacher education reform described above.

Philosophical Underpinnings

A primary teaching method that informs the CKC process is that of a pedagogy of instructional relationships. Preservice teachers, colleges of education, schools and teachers, and members of historically marginalized communities will have instructional relationships with each other. That is, each will become a teacher for the other. Through these relationships, members from each group are engaged in a process of curriculum development, instruction, and political action, which calls for them to center community knowledge in creative and innovative ways. Kincheloe (1993) offers a rich description of centered African American community knowledge:

> A practice grounded on an understanding of a history of subjugated black knowledge would be aware of the way schools are structured around particular silences and omissions. Teachers would thus seek to incorporate subjugated black knowledge by forging links with the black community—not just the dominant culture's definition of the "successful" elements of that community but a variety of groups and subgroups in the black community. The diverse resources to be found in the community open the school to a variety of community traditions, histories, and cultures discredited within the culture of the school. The stories, the worldviews, the music, the politics, the humor, the art of the black community become a central part of everyday school life, never viewed in isolation or as supplements to the "real work" of the school but always viewed in the context of the general curriculum. (p. 258)

In Kincheloe's description, it is clear that the perspectives and knowledge of historically marginalized groups form the basis of the curriculum, which necessitates building relationships between teachers and community members. The nature of these relationships turns the traditional deficit-ideology paradigm on its head. In the traditional curriculum and instruction model, outcomes relate primarily to learning goals produced by instruction informed by the curriculum design. As suggested above, most urban teacher education models that bother to connect to communities do so through instructional experiences such as tutoring and "family literacy" programs. While such programs are important and necessary, they, like most schools and classrooms, also engage the urban community from the perspective of what it is lacking, i.e., adequate learning outcomes.

In the CKC model, community members possess important and vital knowledge, and educators learn from them. The important knowledge is owned by each member of the community, not just those who are deemed "successful" by dominant standards. For example, in our practice, we have found that the knowledge of grandmothers with limited formal education but a penchant for gardening as well as young people of color engaged in hip-hop poetry have engaged in educationally meaningful relationships with teachers and schools.

Therefore a central assumption of the CKC approach is that historically marginalized communities are resource rich and have the power to create change. Effective community development principles compel us to engage the community from the perspective of resources. In other words, instead of beginning with a notion of deficit, effective community development begins by building on resources that the community itself possesses to address its needs. For this project, all factors of the program are defined in terms of resources, of which community participants make up a distinct form. In other words, university preservice teachers and faculty, public school teachers and students, community experts, parents, and organizations are all considered to be resources that are applied to the task of urban teacher education.

A critical benefit to this perspective lies in the manner in which community development perspectives enable us to identify and evaluate the presence of relational processes underlying effective learning that are not visible through an exclusive focus on outcomes. Most programs fail because of a "weak associational sector" or weak connections between resources and components of the program. From this perspective, we can see that the failure to achieve outcomes may not relate so much to faulty learning theories or instructional practices as to faulty connections or relationships between important community-based factors and the classroom learning experience. Connections are most effectively utilized when people in communities become coproducers of resources and engage in the analysis. Thus, we have devised a model that includes community resources, or areas of community capacity, to address the model's needs and realize its visions.

A key aspect of realizing a coproduced vision lies in combating the educational political status quo that dominates so many urban schools. Urban schools have been constructed as fortresses against the communities they are commissioned to serve. They are marked by incredible bureaucracy, limited resources, restrictive policies and curricula, an emphasis on testing and control, and an ethos of complacency and fingerpointing. These conditions present real challenges to centering community knowledge in the curriculum and preparing teachers for schools. By creating communities of stakeholders committed to educational transformation, CKC presents the possibility of real change in urban education. By creating opportunities for teachers, community members, teacher educators, and preservice teachers to build a sense of community, "perceptions of the environment, social relations, and perceived empowerment within the community" can be catalyzed. This sense of empowerment can create opportunities for teachers, community members, and university teacher educators to exert influence on the educational system, thereby working in unity with rather than, as they have historically operated, at odds with each other. Chavis and Wandersman (1990) posit that

[a] community development process stimulates opportunities for membership, influence, [meeting of] mutual needs, and shared emotional ties and support. The stronger the sense of community, the more influence the members will feel they have on their immediate environment. . . . The relationship between a sense of community and community competence (its problem-solving ability) through collective effort is reciprocal. (pp. 56–57)

Being a part of such a community is critical to preservice teacher development because to become a successful urban teacher requires more than just learning how to teach students of color effectively. It requires a critical consciousness about how to effect change in the broader social and political contexts of urban schools and communities.

These philosophical tenets of centering historically subjugated community knowledge, seeing urban communities as resources, building complex instructional relationships, generating new collaborative knowledge, and collaboratively challenging and opposing dominant structures of urban schooling have informed the structural components of the CKC model we present in the following sections.

Organizational Structures of the CKC Model

In an effort to meet the goals stated in the preceding paragraph, the CKC design relies on the participation and collaboration of many stakeholders and the careful, deliberate planning of various levels of curriculum (university and school) through such collaboration. The program design features three major components with nine supporting structures. The three major components are:

1. an integrated preservice teacher education program for teacher education students emphasizing community resources in the teaching process,

2. professional development for teachers in partner schools, which create classroom-based models for using community resources, and

3. community-based events and organizing that support teaching activities.

The nine supporting structures are:

i. the developmental identification and establishment of neighborhood clusters consisting of geographically linked partner schools, community members, community organizations, and faith-based organizations;

    ii. ongoing monthly university/school/ neighborhood knowledge circles for building relationships and introducing knowledge;

    iii. an advisory board for each cluster made up of community members, university faculty, and teachers;

    iv. professional development opportunities for participating in-service teachers and community members to develop and discuss curriculum and supporting community events;

    v. integrated preservice teacher education classes;

    vi. a coordinated preservice curriculum;

    vii. ongoing community-based practicum experience for preservice teachers;

    viii. classroom-based practica for preservice teachers with participating teachers in CKC partnership schools; and

    ix. ongoing program evaluation.

Building on the Structural Model

By bringing together university faculty, preservice education students, elementary and middle school teachers and students, community leaders, community organization staff, community experts (from arts, activism, business, and faith-based sectors), and parents in a collaborative teacher education program, we transform the PDS model, which privileges "professional" knowledge. The community professional development schools (CPDSs) that we envision are rooted in neighborhood clusters that can identify and work with local community members. This notion of neighborhood clusters is essential because it centers a school as part of a neighborhood, as an institution of local neighborhood control in neighborhoods in which many community members are typically rendered powerless in the political process.

Central to these CPDS clusters are the knowledge circles. It is in these forums that community knowledge can begin to be privileged and discussions about curriculum and community organizing can occur. The knowledge circles will serve three major functions. First, they will create a context for people from various sectors to come together to share ideas and build relationships. Second, they will provide opportunities to generate resources in the community. For example, a teacher may be working on a play with a class and would like to enlist a role model from the community who is affiliated with theater production, or gain a community perspective on the content of the play. Other resources may include workshops in which one teacher or community member shares his/her specific knowledge, or the group may decide that it wants to hear from an expert on some topic. The main idea is that knowledge circles are a shared space in which knowledge is collectively generated and community perspectives privileged. Finally, knowledge circles are a place for action research. Participants will generate and share knowledge and then translate that knowledge into classroom practice. They may use knowledge-circle time to generate curriculum or to plan next steps or conference presentations.

Schools of education must also work to create professional development opportunities that bring teachers and community members together to do the real work of curriculum development. Historically, the PDS model has found ways to make intensive forms of professional development beneficial to teachers through college credit or in-service credit. We must search for ways to ensure that community members also benefit from this kind of intensive work. Through the structures of knowledge circles and professional development courses, all stakeholders will have opportunities to work together to generate a sense of community and work for transformation. Through participation in these structures and fieldwork within these clusters, preservice teachers will see models of how schools and communities can organize for change.

In order for neighborhood clusters and CPD schools to operate successfully, a critical mass of teachers from the school must be committed, along with significant numbers of community members. Faculty from schools of education must be active in generating this enthusiasm and spend time getting to know teachers and community members. There must also be strong curricular links established with a community organization and community members. The neighborhood clusters and CPD schools will be generated in part by school and community interest and the ongoing facilitation of partnerships.

Building on the Curricular Model

Fundamentally, the CKC program aims to create multiple contexts in which the various stakeholders can come together to generate knowledge and create positive educational experiences for children. The knowledge and pedagogical strategies that are generated will lead to specific outcomes for preservice teachers, elementary and middle school students, teachers and schools, community members, and university faculty. It is critical that university faculty examine their courses to try to understand how to create coursework that supports the CKC model. This means that university faculty must reexamine some of their programs and perhaps yield some of their intellectual territory to create a CKC model that privileges the historically subjugated knowledge of community groups. This can happen in a variety of ways—for example, during the 2000–2001 school year, while both authors were on the faculty at the University of Delaware, we met weekly with a group of colleagues who were all involved in teaching the "methods" courses to preservice teachers; together, we wanted to find a way to create teacher education curricula that focused on urban community knowledge and development. In an effort to integrate the curriculum for each of the courses, we searched for areas of overlap, met with community members, devised an innovative schedule for coursework, identified community projects and practica that could be required across classes, and designed the basis for the model described herein.

We found that central to this collective work was the development of interdisciplinary curricula and projects aimed at bringing community resources and issues to the fore of the teacher education courses. This means that the university faculty involved in teaching preservice teachers had to meet with one another, become educated about urban issues, examine their own beliefs and ideologies, and learn to center their own coursework around subjugated knowledge as well. Additionally, specific faculty should be associated with particular clusters, so that true partnerships can form.

Core faculty must meet with teachers, school personnel, and community members from their clusters in knowledge circles and professional development courses. They can thus integrate their work with the students' community and school practica, allowing all stakeholders to make and see explicit links between university classes, community-based experiences, and classroom teaching. They will also be better able to assist students.

Building on the Experiential Model

A community knowledge-centered model of teacher education builds on the strengths of the structural and curricular approaches with a particular emphasis on further developing the experiential approach in preservice

teacher education. This can create impressive levels of academic engagement on the part of the students as their community becomes an educationally productive part of the learning environment. It is our contention
that experiential modifications in preservice teacher education, in combi-
nation with curricular and structural changes, hold the most promise for
preparing preservice teachers to effectively engage the problem of deficit
ideologies, hegemonic knowledge sources, and the pervasive problem of
student alienation.

In order for teacher education students to understand the life experiences and authentic knowledge, as well as the multiple people resources,
in historically marginalized communities, it is important that they have
opportunities to work alongside community-based people on community
issues. By providing opportunities for preservice teachers to engage as
part of a political struggle with members of historically marginalized
communities, they will have opportunities to build both relationships and
a knowledge base. Therefore, in the CKC model, preservice teacher education students have an ongoing community practicum experience within
their CPDS neighborhood cluster. These practica are conceptualized
slightly differently than the ones outlined previously as being part of the
experiential approach. They will still allow for teacher education students
to see community children in other contexts and build community relationships, but their primary function will be for preservice teachers to
learn from community members and develop an understanding of the
political struggles of historically marginalized communities. Therefore,
community practica should be developed within grassroots community
organizations in which community members are leaders and that are
fueled by community knowledge and engender community empowerment. These kinds of organizations (which may be quite informal) can be
identified within the knowledge circles. An important outcome of these
practica are for preservice teachers to see themselves as part of a common
political struggle with members of communities of color or low income.

An additional innovation lies in the idea of "community faculty" who
will supervise students in their community-based practica. The term itself
emerges from the idea that community members, based on their life experience and their personal commitment to positive social change and the
education of young people, will play a profound role in the teaching experiences of preservice teachers. This level of specificity regarding the role
and integration of community experts and their knowledge into the preservice teacher curriculum to the point of curriculum development represents a central level of community engagement.

By creating community and school practica that are geographically and programmatically linked, we aim to help teacher education students build relationships with particular neighborhoods over time. These relationships will also build a self-sustaining structure for ongoing school, community, and university partnerships. The primary area of innovation for the CKC model in preparing preservice teachers to be effective in urban school settings, especially in light of the problem of alienation, resides in the area of experiential modification. This model takes the step of making community placements for preservice teachers part of their professional development. While this alone is not innovative, the fact that preservice teachers will have a classroom placement in the course of the same semester represents an unprecedented opportunity for them to experience multiple forms and styles of teaching and to reflect on the comparative benefits and challenges represented by both. Not only will preservice teachers be working with classroom teachers, they will be working with classroom teachers who will also be integrating community expertise into their classrooms. This creates a necessary innovation and modification of the idea of preservice teacher placement. The preservice teacher is placed in the cooperating teacher's classroom not only for the purpose of practical application under the supervision of a more experienced professional, but to assist the cooperating teacher in the implementation of instruction that incorporates the knowledge and expertise of the aforementioned community faculty.

This model takes advantage of the strengths of the structural, curricular, and experiential approaches to urban teacher preparation and builds on their shortcomings. In the context of creating curricula, students will be learning about community issues from knowledgeable community members, challenging preconceptions at the level of idea and experience. Additionally, faculty develop integrated community-based curricula rooted in connecting community strength and issues to the fabric of learning to teach. Structurally, the model is designed to move toward an enhanced PDS model that integrates community, school, and university in the partnership, creating a CPDS through the use of neighborhood clusters.

Conclusion

We envision CKC as a potential national model for teacher education built on true community/school/university partnerships aimed at educational transformation for social justice. Central to this model is our unwavering belief that historically marginalized communities have the resources that teachers and universities are sorely lacking. By bringing together these stakeholders in systematic and organized ways, we have the potential to create just classrooms, schools, and teachers. It is clear that such a model requires an enormous commitment from faculty, teachers, and community members; however, we have found that people in each of these walks of life are eager to participate and do so enthusiastically. Therefore, it is essential that we continue such work, modify and invent new ways of conceptualizing teaching and learning on all levels, share models and ideas, and ultimately collect data on our experiences with implementing potentially transformative models.

References

Alverman, D. E., Commeyras, M., Young, J. P., Randall, S., and Hinson, D. (1997). "Interrupting Gendered Discursive Practices in Classroom Talk about Texts: Easy to Think About, Difficult to Do." *Journal of Literacy Research*, 29, 73–104.

Au, K. H.-P., and Jordan, C. (1981). "Teaching Reading to Hawaiian Children: Finding a Culturally Appropriate Solution." In H. T. Trueba, G. P. Guthrie, and K. H.-P. Au, eds., *Culture and the Bilingual Classroom: Studies in Classroom Ethnography* (pp. 139–152). Rowley, MA: Newbury House Publisher.

Banks, J. A., and Banks, C. M., eds. (1997). *Multicultural Education: Issues and Perspectives*. 3rd ed. Boston: Allyn & Bacon.

Baugh, J. (1994). "New and Prevailing Misconceptions of African American English for Logic and Mathematics." In E. R. Hollins, J. E. King, and W. C. Hayman, eds., *Teaching Diverse Populations: Formulating a Knowledge Base* (pp. 191–208). Albany: SUNY Press.

Chavis, D. M., and Wandersman, A. (1990). "Sense of Community in the Urban Environment: A Catalyst for Participation and Community Development." *American Journal of Community Psychology*, 18:1, pp. 55–81.

Cummins, J. (1996). "Empowering Minority Students: A Framework for Intervention." In T. Beauboeuf-Lafontant and D. S. Augustine, eds., *Facing Racism in Education* (pp. 349–368). Cambridge, MA: Harvard Educational Review.

Feiman-Nemser, S., and Floden, R. (1986). "The Cultures of Teaching." In M. C. Wittrock, ed., *Handbook of Research on Teaching* (pp. 505–526). New York: Macmillan.

Fine, M. (1991). *Framing Dropouts: Notes on the Politics of an Urban Public High School*. Albany: SUNY Press.

Foster, M. (1997). *Black Teachers on Teaching*. New York: The New Press.

Grant, C. A., and Sleeter, C. E. (1989). *Turning on Learning: Five Approaches for Multicultural Teaching Plans for Race, Class, Gender, and Disability*. Columbus, OH: Merrill Publishing.

Haberman, M. (1991). "The Pedagogy of Poverty versus Good Teaching," *Phi Delta Kappan*, 73, pp. 290–294.

Holmes Group (1995). *Tomorrow's Schools of Education*. East Lansing, MI: Author.

Kincheloe, J. L. (1993). "The Politics of Race, History, and Curriculum." In L. A. Castenell and W. F. Pinar, eds., *Understanding Curriculum as Racial Text:*

Representations of Identity and Difference in Education (pp. 249–262). Albany: SUNY Press.

Ladson-Billings, G. (1992). "Liberatory Consequences of Literacy: A Case of Culturally Relevant Instruction for African American Students." *Journal of Negro Education*, 61:3, pp. 378–391.

Ladson-Billings, G. (1994). *The Dreamkeepers: Successful Teachers of African American Children*. San Francisco: Jossey-Bass.

Ladson-Billings, G. (1995). "But That's Just Good Teaching! The Case for Culturally Relevant Pedagogy." *Theory into Practice*, 34:3, pp. 159–165.

McCarthy, C. (1993). "After the Canon: Knowledge and Ideological Representation in the Multicultural Discourse on Curriculum Reform." In C. McCarthy and W. Crichlow, eds., *Race, Identity, and Representation in Education* (pp. 289–305). New York: Routledge.

Moll, L., Amanti, C., Neff, D., and Gonzalez, N. (1992). "Funds of Knowledge for Teaching: Using a Qualitative Approach to Connect Homes and Classrooms." *Theory into Practice*, 31:2, pp. 132–141.

Nieto, S. (1996). *Affirming Diversity: The Sociopolitical Context of Multicultural Education.* 2nd ed. White Plains, NY: Longman.

Philips, S. U. (1972). "Participant Structures and Communicative Competence: Warm Springs Children in Community and Classroom." In C. B. Cazden, V. P. John, and D. Hymes, eds., *Functions of Language in the Classroom* (pp. 370–394). New York: Teachers College Press.

Chapter Seven

Special Education, Urban Schools, and the Uncertain Path to Social Justice

Alberto Bursztyn

Special education departments/programs in colleges of education occupy an ambiguous space between areas of the academic unit that deal with pedagogy and those that concern themselves with foundations of education—namely philosophy and history of education, and educational psychology. Representing a unique specialization that focuses on students' limitations, special education faculty generally do not readily identify themselves with "mainstream" colleagues in curriculum and instruction; the interests of the two rarely overlap. Among the latter, special educators are often seen as a special-interest group with a narrow agenda. A relationship between theory and practice is occasionally noted; foundations faculty engage in theory building or research, while teacher educators concern themselves primarily with methods and application. Special educators are a separate case of teacher education; their focus is on learners' deficiencies and on curriculum adaptations to address those deficiencies rather than curriculum content.

Not surprisingly, in most universities, the special education program/department has a separate administrative structure that affords it some measure of independence, but that arrangement also inhibits collaboration with other education faculty. Being on the periphery of the education project leads to a sense of professional defensiveness and displacement, which is echoed in the way that special education programs are constructed in public schools. Our graduates working in poor, urban schools are generically allotted the most undesirable workspaces and resources. In the pecking order of administrative priorities, special education comes last.

Recently, teaching a graduate course in special education, I was assigned a basement classroom with a deafeningly loud cooling vent. I explained to the class that the room assignment was partly my fault, since I had requested a change in the original schedule at a late date. My students accepted the explanation and we set out to find a quieter space; but all of them laughed when someone noted that this was expected treatment for a special education class.

Curious about the extent of spatial marginalization in schools, I asked my students to describe their work settings. Some worked in small, crowded spaces such as converted bathrooms and supply closets; those who were coteaching felt like guests in the regular education teacher's space. A few worked in self-contained schools for children with severe disabilities that were located in poor, high-crime areas of the city. The most extreme case was that of an itinerant special educator serving two schools—in one school, she had access to two shelves in a bookcase; at the other site, all her materials were stored in a milk crate. She met with children for resource room services in the cafeteria, or in stairwells if lunch was being served.

Of course it is the children served under this system who most acutely experience marginalization, but the teachers and teacher educators are not immune to the stigmatizing effects of disability. One teacher reported that her mainstream colleagues would exclude her from curriculum meetings and viewed her work primarily as "baby-sitting." Others in my class concurred that their professional work is misunderstood and/or ignored by other teachers and administrators.

Historically, people with disabilities have encountered prejudice and the cruelest forms of discrimination. For example, state policies have supported sterilization programs, involuntary commitment to horrific institutions, and denial of public education to persons with cognitive challenges and other disabilities; these policies were in effect well into the twentieth century. The legacy of abuse and oppression has been slow to fade (Safford and Safford, 1996).

Since the enactment in 1975 of Public Law 94-142 (the Education for All Handicapped Children Act), which guaranteed children with disabilities access to public education and to a least restrictive environment (LRE) for learning, there has been a concomitant acceptance of individuals with disabilities in society at large. Yet programs for the disabled have not eliminated oppression and marginalization (Losen and Orfield, 2002). In fact, some of the programs that were created to integrate children with disabilities into schools have become instruments of segregation in their own right (Erevelles, 2000; Lipsky and Gartner, 1996).

In this chapter I will describe how special education has become an oppressive force in urban communities despite teachers' good intentions and extensive bureaucratic and legal safeguards. I will also suggest possible ways to question and transform current practices in teacher education that may promote integration and learning and support social justice for children with a wide range of abilities and disabilities.

Visiting Special Education Classrooms

Walking into P.S. 601 to observe a newly assigned student teacher, I was struck by the high sheen on the granite floors and bright luster of the white marble details. The school, built during the Depression years, was the most imposing building in a neighborhood of rundown tenements, abandoned buildings, and cracked and dirty sidewalks. A long-abandoned and graffiti-covered car stood across from the school steps as a sign that the municipal sanitation department does not pay much attention to this part of the city.

Yet, once inside, the school was clean, orderly, and strangely quiet. My student, Ms. King, had been assigned to Ms. Marconi's class, a group of third graders classified as severely emotionally and behaviorally disturbed (EBD). The classroom was located on the fourth floor, sharing space with the fourth and fifth grades. The mainstream third graders were on the floor below and kept different lunch hours from their special ed counterparts. The classroom was impressively large, with only eight little desks arranged in two parallel rows. Only five students were present, and there were five adults milling about them, including Ms. King. The students were all black or Latino males. The teacher, Ms. Marconi, and my student were white; the paraprofessionals were all black females and significantly older than the teacher. The classroom had Thanksgiving decor: hand-traced turkey cutouts, pictures of Pilgrims and Native Americans, and cardboard pumpkins. The students were required to copy a form letter to an imaginary friend describing Thanksgiving. The five-line letter was written on the board and each child was told to add "What am I thankful for" on the single blank space in the last sentence.

Every adult noted my presence; after brief introductions, they each assumed a position behind a child and proceeded to monitor his work. The children were insecure and tentative in their writing, since every alphabetical letter they formed was commented on ("Nice 'T'!" "Make the tail of that 'p' longer"). There were remarks about leaving spaces after periods, and other instantaneous corrections; most were nonthreatening but insistent in tone. The coaching was so intrusive that the children worked at a snail's pace and in absolute silence.

I questioned Ms. Marconi about her didactic approach, and she told me that she was recognized as an expert on direct instruction among the special education staff. This approach, she said, "is highly structured and uses repetition until the child achieves mastery."

I asked if the children got bored or restless with this teaching method. She explained that since the children had major behavior "challenges," most were assigned a behavior management para(professional) and that she kept the students on task with the paras' help. One child was an English Language Learner (ELL) and was assigned a bilingual para who translated for the child and also helped him "focus." Ms. Marconi lamented that the parents were not in favor of medicating the children to help them with their impulsivity and concentration. She was therefore careful to eliminate distractions in the classroom and had to be very "regimented" to help the children maintain attention on the classwork.

At a middle school in another poor neighborhood, I visited an inclusion program in which one of my students was the special educator. The school was a large, bland, square building, typical of 1970s institutional architecture. Inside the building was a chaotic stream of children and teachers trying to reach their classrooms during the four-minute "passing" before the second bell. Although the principal pointed out with pride that all the special education students in his school were included in regular classes, I had already heard from my graduate student, Mr. Gregory, that the school's model of inclusion was to "throw all the students in the same space" and distribute the special education staff across classrooms. In fact, I saw that the special education students in one of Mr. Gregory's classes were seated within a cluster and were expected to complete all assignments. Mr. Gregory's role was to individualize instruction for each of the eighteen special education students in every subject in his two assigned classrooms and complete all paperwork related to individualized education plans (IEP). In the classroom, I observed that the children in special education were mostly busy with one another while the teacher struggled to make the whole class attend to his social studies lecture. The group was quite diverse, but there were no white students among those classified as needing special education. I did not observe any interaction between the "included" children and their mainstream classmates during the lesson or after the bell rang and the class left the room. Despite the principal's sunny description of the program, all staff I interviewed were resentful and dissatisfied. Special educators were particularly concerned that IEP goals would not be met and that they would be held responsible.

At a very large secondary school in a residential area where most white homeowners were "fleeing" and a wave of Caribbean immigrants were settling in, I had to go through the metal detectors before I reached the front desk. The special education wing was located on the third floor above the library: a semisecluded set of small classrooms, informally known among staff and students as "the Zoo." Most of the students were black and male; most teachers were white and female. A student, confronted by a teacher about "roaming the halls," responded in a threatening way, and the teacher proceeded to call school security. The school had a multiscreen closed-circuit TV security system. Security guards communicated via walkie-talkies. A heavyset security guard soon arrived and the youngster ran in the opposite direction.

In the cafeteria, one of the male teachers lamented how the school had gone "down the tubes" and how he was counting the days until retirement. The special education supervisor sitting at the same table proudly told me that she was teaching a graduate course on classroom management at a private college and suggested that she could also teach it in our program. Ms. Paisley, a student in my research class teaching ninth-grade English to mainstream and special education self-contained classes, related privately to me how her special education students pleaded with her to allow them to leave the classroom a few minutes before the bell so that their peers would not see them coming from the Zoo. She was disturbed by the uninhibited contempt that some of her colleagues in both regular and special education held for the new immigrant children and those with disabilities.

While presenting these brief glimpses into special education contexts, I am aware that they may not be entirely representative and that they are skewed by my intent to illustrate how the services intended to help children with disabilities can further impair their growth and education. Yet these problematic educational attitudes, approaches, and practices are commonplace in our urban schools; we abdicate our role as educators if we pretend that they are isolated or unusual cases. The weight of being perceived as defective, the overcontrolled environments, and the stifling curriculum all contribute to a massive exodus of minority special education children from public schools (Sleeter and McLaren, 1995).

Figures published in national studies substantiate the claim of many advocates that urban minority children are disproportionately identified as needing special education and receive inferior services once they enter the system. The Office for Civil Rights (OCR) of the U.S. Department of Education, which considers inappropriate special education placements for minority children a form of discrimination, has taken up this matter. Throughout the country, OCR has placed numerous school districts under corrective action to reform their special education identification and placement practices (Artiles and Zamora-Duran, 1997).

About a million and a half minority children are classified as exhibiting mental retardation, emotional disturbance, or specific learning disabilities. African American children are three times more likely than white children to be labeled "mentally retarded." While rates of identification in the category of EBD (Emotional/Behavioural Disorder) vary geographically, rates are higher in the Northeast. Cohen and Osher (1994) found that the lower the percentage of African American children in a school, the higher the likelihood that these students would be labeled EBD. The EBD designation is associated with dire consequences for minority children. Researchers demonstrated a relationship between minority children's high representation in the "emotional disturbance" category and disproportionate rates of the same children as dropouts and among inmates in the corrections system (Osher, Woodroof, and Sims, 2002). The high number of incarcerated youths may be the most disturbing measure of how poorly the education system serves minority children and specifically black boys. Twice as many African American students with EBD drop out of school as similarly labeled white classmates. Of those African American boys with EBD who drop out, 73 percent are arrested within three to five years of leaving school.

The fact that these dismal education outcomes are absent in the vaunted discourse on educational standards and the rhetoric of No Child Left Behind only highlights the powerlessness of minority group members to call attention to a different reality and to effect real change in the education of their children. Since more than two-thirds of the minority children in special education have no visible signs of disability, their identification is based on school failure and subsequent testing by assessment professionals. Advocates and researchers have questioned the validity of an assessment process that is decontextualized and that seeks answers to school failure by examining the child without addressing the nature of instruction and social relations in school (Cummins, 1986; Figueroa, 1995).

The plight of minority and poor urban children in special education is not only generally ignored by mainstream educators and policymakers; it is also minimized in the professional special education discourse. Special education organizations tend to downplay the centrality of racial, class, and linguistic issues in schools. Within those organizations, individuals who call attention to the potentially damaging effects of special education placements and services are a frequently marginalized minority themselves. Because the profession promotes itself as benevolent and beneficial to disabled children and families, it has limited capacity to reflect on its potentially negative impact on a segment of the population. Consequently, dissenting voices are silenced within the profession by being relegated to powerless interest groups and dead-end committees.

Professional special education has concerned itself with how persons who are considered disabled, or "special" in current euphemistic language, fit into society and with developing techniques and practices for "dealing with," managing, and providing for them. Professionals working with this client population are seen as enacting humanitarian practices that are good for the recipients. Thus, professional practice, grounded in a functionalist approach, views the clients of special education as constituting a social problem that can be dealt with by professional teamwork and access to the right resources. This perspective emerges from a consensus on the deviancy of special education clients. Deviancy, in turn, effectively impedes the validation of the views of these clients and prepares the families and schools to accept the notion that professionals really know best (Safford and Safford, 1996; Skrtic, 1995). Prescriptions to address lack of progress or negative impact of services typically involve more of the same services. This is justified on the basis of the belief that empirically validated practices are the best available treatments. When these practices fail to bring about the desired results, professionals explain that interventions have to be applied more carefully or more intensively (Cummins, 1989).

Change of direction is usually needed to work toward client self-sufficiency and integration, yet the professional approach generally suggests staying the course, i.e., continue to adapt the regular curriculum through the atomization of tasks and encouragement of the use of external means of behavior control. This attitude contrasts sharply with views by persons with disabilities engaged in self-advocacy and through disability studies in academic circles (Erevelles, 2000; Middleton, Rollins, and Harley, 1999).

Within the profession it is difficult to recognize the failure of accepted practices, particularly when applied to minority communities. This difficulty stems from a deep commitment to an empiricist, positivistic model of scientific research. To clarify this statement, we need to consider the emergence of special education within a particular tradition in the social sciences and the role it plays in relation to the larger educational system.

In the Beginning There Was a Wild Boy

Special education sprang out of convergent, but distinct, social forces and reflects contested historical and cultural assumptions about individuals with disabilities. In recent years, the evolution of approaches to educating exceptional children paralleled the broader discourse on the purposes of education and civil rights for individuals with disabilities. However, traditional pedagogy and its claim to legitimacy for teaching children with disabilities are rooted in the work of Jean-Marc-Gaspard Itard (1775–1838).

Dr. Itard was a young French physician during the intellectual ferment of the Enlightenment who sought to rehabilitate the "wild boy of Aveyron." The child had emerged from the woods naked, grunting, and scarred, unable to speak at all. There were questions in the scientific community of the day whether this child—wild, mute, and animal-like—was indeed a human being. Itard took on the challenge to transform the child for a life in polite society. His approach, novel at the time, was to break down complicated instructional tasks into their smallest segments and use tangible rewards as the child achieved the intended learning objectives. Task analysis, direct instruction, behavior modification, and intensive record keeping, all currently pillars of special education pedagogy, are rooted in Itard's carefully documented method of breaking tasks into their smallest components, teaching systematically and gradually, and offering rewards (Safford and Safford, 1996).

The boy, eventually named Victor, was never completely rehabilitated despite years of intensive work; he acquired limited language and social skills and died poor and forgotten. Nevertheless, Itard achieved wide recognition for his instructional method. In the twentieth century, Watson, Thorndyke, and Skinner, among others, elaborated his didactic approaches into behavioral theories and interventions that eventually found fertile ground in special education classrooms in the United States and other Western countries.

The behavior-shaping traditions introduced by Itard spring from assumptions about children with disabilities that may be summarized as follows: Due to diagnosed deficits, students with disabilities lack the capacity to succeed in the standard curriculum; therefore, pedagogy and curriculum must be modified to suit their learning capabilities. Diagnostic procedures are required to ascertain the nature and extent of the child's limitations; the role of professional special educators is to develop specific adaptations to assist these learners. This model of practice is well suited to quantitative study and monitoring, since students' responses can be charted and changes may be noted in response to reward schedules.

Of all areas of education, special education is the most closely associated with behavior modification and all its permutations. Perhaps because exceptional children, like Victor, are understood to lack understanding, constructive initiative, and capacity to reflect on experience, external control is a treatment choice. The child is believed to be helpless without professional intervention; social and academic learning is understood to be contingent on reactions to structured external demands. In this paradigm, professionals silence their clients and assume a caretaking role.

Sorting Children

The practice of psychological evaluation in schools also originated in France. But intelligence testing grew stronger roots in the New World, leading eventually to a veritable "testing movement" between the two world wars. In the early 1900s, industrializing countries were beginning to recognize the need for a literate workforce to operate and maintain increasingly sophisticated machinery and to function as clerks for growing civic institutions. Consequently, nations began to offer free public education to their citizens. The government of France commissioned Dr. Alfred Binet to develop a method to be used to screen out children with cognitive delays, who were thought to be unable to and would not profit from regular public school instruction. Binet sought to identify children with mental retardation via a medico-pedagogical test, institute special classes or schools, and develop a curriculum to improve the learning outcomes for these children. A pilot program in a local school would be used as a prototype for this instruction. Dr. Binet developed the precursor of the IQ test, which proved to be an efficient tool to achieve the first objective. Unfortunately, neither Dr. Binet nor his colleague, Dr. Théodore Simon, succeeded in addressing the second and third parts of their commission: implementation of a pilot project and formulation of an effective pedagogy for the children (Safford and Safford, 1996).

Special education in its modern form emulates a medical model by combining the traditions of psychological assessment and behavior modification. The child, who generally does not have a visible disability, is initially diagnosed with a disorder, and a behavioral program is prescribed as treatment. In other words, special education builds on a quasi-medical paradigm by which the children are constructed as suffering from specific pathologies (some deviance from normal functioning), which require specialized services with varying degrees of intensity (from minor curriculum modifications to segregated schools or hospitalization). The symptom of the disease is school failure; a professional multidisciplinary evaluation establishes the nature and severity of the disease—e.g., emotional disturbance, learning disability, mental retardation—and the interventions that professionals must provide (Skrtic, 1995).

Once formally established as an entity within education, special education led to the proliferation of assessment and instructional specialists trained to focus on the learning characteristics of children with various diagnosed conditions. Since the enactment of Public Law 94-142 in 1975, the proportion of children served under special education has grown to approximately 12 percent of all children in American public schools; most of these children have no visible disabilities or serious medical conditions. Some conditions, like learning disabilities, have no uniform standard for diagnosis, and, not surprisingly, identification rates vary dramatically across states, counties, and schools (Artiles and Zamora-Duran, 1997).

Despite the legal requirement that children identified as having disabilities be served in the "least restrictive environment," the reality of practice for minority children suggests otherwise. Most of these children are separated from their peers for part of the school day; many are served in segregated classrooms or schools where they don't have access to the regular curriculum. Minority children who enter the system not only suffer the consequences of the double stigma, they also receive inferior services (Bursztyn, 2002; Milofsky, 1989).

Curriculum Crisis in Special Education

Periodic revolts by parents and advocates have forced the system to address the practice of segregating students with disabilities, to account for the meager graduation rates of special education students, and to justify the disproportional representation of children from linguistic, cultural, and racial minorities in its programs. Critics have noted that the system achieved the goal of universal access to public education but failed catastrophically to improve educational outcomes for identified children, despite enormous cost. Special education is in a state of crisis, but within the profession there is little incentive to abandon the established paradigm for research, organization, and practice.

Critiquing special education practices and pedagogy requires that we examine the assumptions underlying the system and question their claim to validity. How is that accomplished? There are currently two approaches to inquiry in the social sciences that are relevant to this project. The first is the traditional approach, which aims to study and justify social practices and institutions as true representations of the social world. This is the dominant paradigm in special education. The second approach, which will be elaborated here, aims to deconstruct and reconstruct social practices and institutions in order to reconcile them with desirable social ideals, i.e., equity and democracy. The latter approach is consistent with critical pragmatism, building on the American philosophical approaches of William James and John Dewey, and as more recently exemplified by Richard Bernstein (Skrtic, 1995).

The model of science embraced by the special education establishment is consistent with those in traditional social science research, derived from the natural sciences. It claims that the nature and needs of people with disabilities, and the best educational approaches to serve them, are knowable through systematic experimentation. This type of research approach is expected to reveal foundations of knowledge that reflect, with increasing accuracy, the real world. The flow of knowledge is unidirectional and hierarchical. As scientists uncover the foundations of behavior in controlled or laboratory settings, they share their findings with professionals and programs that prepare practitioners. For example, if individuals grouped by specific diagnoses respond well to experimental treatments under controlled conditions, those treatments are expected to be effective when administered by practitioners in field settings. Researchers communicate their findings in peer-reviewed journals read by teacher educators, who in turn transmit the new knowledge to teachers through teacher education preservice and in-service programs.

In recent years there has been a major shift in the social sciences, as researchers have increasingly begun to question the underlying assumptions in the social sciences described above. This crisis is rooted in the understanding that human behavior and development are governed by, and respond to, complex contextual forces. Efforts to isolate and study those variables out of context do not yield knowledge that mirrors the real world. Instead, they foster a reductive view of human nature that inevitably leads to the establishment of sorting systems for identification and service of "clients" (Kincheloe, Steinberg, and Hinchey, 1999). Thus despite decades of study on treatment and instruction for diagnostic categories such as specific learning disabilities, mild mental retardation, and emotional disturbance, the services and outcomes for these students have been essentially the same: disappointing. The lack of success in the application of scientific methods is tacitly recognized; school districts increasingly pay less attention to the diagnostic entities and instead group students by staffing formulas, focusing attention on practical matters such as the intensity of service, e.g., teacher/student ratios.

Presently, the expectation that a diagnostic-prescriptive approach would be the answer to integrating children with mild disabilities into the mainstream has been largely abandoned in the field, despite a continuing stream of empirically validated research and supporting literature. Parents, skeptical of specialized programs, are increasingly demanding regular classroom placements for their children with a range of disabilities (Lipsky and Gartner, 1996; Thomas and Loxley, 2001).

While curriculum approaches tailored to specific disabilities have lost credibility among parents and teachers, the provision of support services continues to be central to the special education enterprise. When a multidisciplinary team for special education services evaluates children, students are typically found to have specific areas of functional deficit. Those areas are the province of various support professionals who are charged, through the IEP process, to provide remediation or therapy.

This multidisciplinary approach to evaluation and treatment has led to fragmentation of care. It is not unusual for children to be pulled out of various classes during the day to receive personal counseling, speech therapy, occupational therapy, and resource room and other services. Related service providers rarely speak with one another or with classroom teachers. Consequently, specialists attend assiduously to their respective areas of functioning as if they were independent of one another, disregarding the child's capacity to participate as a full member of the class or the child's need for continuity of instruction and peer relations. As children get pulled out for specialized services, they lose instructional time, further hampering their ability to make sense of the curriculum. When children are partially mainstreamed, as is the case when they join a regular class for specific subjects, they in turn tend to lose the thread of instruction in their special education class.

Ms. Powell, an experienced special education teacher in a middle school, expressed her frustration this way: "Some of my kids are mainstreamed in some subjects. When Derek and Shavone get regular music in the third period, I'm teaching math and they miss out on that subject. I've got five kids mainstreamed in other subjects during the day. They have to catch up on reading, social studies, or whatever I did with the rest of the class when they were gone. On top of that, I've got kids leaving the class for speech, ESL, or counseling during the day—not when they have lunch or gym, but when the counselors or therapists are around. It has to fit their schedule! Some of [the kids] don't want to go, but it's in their IEPs."

The reliance on multiple professionals to develop an IEP for each child has led to the often unmanageable proposition that all services be provided at once, without attending to the disruption that the interventions will cause in the child's life. As a result of constructing the learner as a collection of deficient and disconnected parts, the system contributes to the systemic disempowerment and marginalization of its "clientele."

In underfunded urban schools, the dysfunctionalism of the system is due to lapses in parental oversight and uncertified and/or inexperienced service providers. Mindful of special education monitors, administrators tend to focus their attention on issues of compliance, rather than on the quality of services. Teachers and parents then complain that there is greater attention paid to the child's file than to the child—a consequence of a paper-driven, legalistic, and bureaucratic approach to education (Harry, 1992).

Reconciling Special Education and Social Justice

Special education in urban schools can strive to be a path to social justice rather than an instrument of oppression by reassessing its role in the control and marginalization of those deemed pathological by virtue of school failure. The problem of school failure is at the root of contemporary special education dysfunctionalism. Simply stated, special education allows general education the illusion of fairness and efficiency by compartmentalizing and isolating those who fail to meet its expectations. The deficiencies are thought to lie in the individuals, not in the regular pedagogy or curriculum. Skrtic (1995) noted that the institutional practice of special education is an artifact of the functionalist quest for rationality, order, and certainty in public education.

Yet the beliefs about the necessity of special education services are buried so deep in our culture that we accept their precepts without question. Teachers and related-service support staff refer to students' classifications as if they were part of the natural order of life, and therefore indisputable. For example, informal statements like "Jordan is a real EBD kid, he'll need a one-to-one para" are easily translated into IEP language without questioning the nature of the phrase "real EBD kid" and the verb "need." In the coded language of classification, the child is a "real" manifestation of an uncontested social construction. The rationale for the treatment is, likewise, beyond doubt.

Once children acquire a label in the system, they become closely identified with the diagnosis or intervention program, making it practically impossible for them to separate themselves from the assigned category. It is noteworthy, however, that minority parents are often at odds with the classification language of school and occasionally resist the special education language, culture, and structure. But nevertheless they are generally unable to change the child's fate in school (Bursztyn, 2002; Harry, 1992).

Special educators have not examined their role; instead they have approached the persistent general education curriculum dilemma from a child deficit perspective: Fix the child, fix the instruction, and offer basic skills instruction rather than fix the curriculum (Pugash and Warger, 1996).

Special education's relation to anticipated or actual failure is consistent with the medical model of disability; difficulties to be overcome reside in the individual, not in the curriculum or the school. Therefore, special education is concerned with access to the curriculum through the modification of instructional approaches (Nolet and Tindal, 1993), along with task analysis to ensure participation in specific activities. This implies that special educators are uncritically supportive of a curriculum designed and implemented by regular education (Pugash and Warger, 1996). The medical metaphor, however, breaks down once we recognize that the increasingly standardized and prescribed curriculum in the schools is a major disabling agent for large numbers of students. School is not equivalent to life and the curriculum is not the path to opportunity it claims to be.

Pugash and Warger (1996) noted that no work in curricular reform can ignore the fact that without being identified as disabled, many students are placed at risk by curricular demands. A sociocultural rather than individual deficit perspective may be more pertinent for reframing special education, particularly when poor, minority, and ELL (English Language Learner) children are labeled as having mild disabilities. Special education perpetuates the perception of children with disabilities as defective individuals in relation to a curriculum that they may not master. It deflects responsibility from schools to provide flexibility for differentiated learning and instruction in mainstream curriculum.

Colleges of education are the natural cradles for nurturing an emancipatory approach to education that embraces all students and validates their dignity and humanity. This assertion implies the rejection of reified categories of learners as well as procedures for sorting children by those categories. I do not suggest that schools should be blind to children's disabilities and other needs. On the contrary, the emancipatory approach I envision means that each child would be understood and educated by teachers who strive to be cognizant of children's needs and develop class-room practices that support the dignity, curiosity, creativity, and cognitive development of their charges. Instead of separating out children who cannot meet the expectations of the standard curriculum, the curriculum and its associated pedagogy should be modified accordingly. A metaphor may be useful here: In recent years many cities have acquired "kneeling" buses in order to conform to the requirements of the Americans with Disabilities Act. These buses can lower a retractable ramp that allows persons using wheelchairs to board the vehicle. Applying this concept to education, we note that the bus—the curriculum and pedagogy—does not kneel. Instead the child is picked up by a van that does not follow the bus's route and is oblivious to the wishes of the rider. The child ends up stranded in the wrong part of town after the buses have stopped running. In school, the child is placed on an educational track or in a program that often leads to dropping out or warehousing.

Current efforts by advocates and parents to reform special education have sought to do away with segregated programs by demanding inclusion of children with disabilities in regular classrooms (Thomas and Loxley, 2001). These efforts have found some support within the profession, but many special educators are wary of the implication that special education programs have little intrinsic value. Administrators, however, have moved in the direction of enforcing inclusion because of new federal requirements demanding that more services to classified children be delivered in the regular classroom.

Although this seems to be a promising approach, in poor and minority districts the implementation of this policy is problematic. In underfunded schools, many of the regular education children fail to attain minimum scores on standardized tests, consequently the "included" children are prone to be neglected by teachers who are under pressure to raise the test scores of the children who "count" in their classroom statistics. In other words, the bus stops in front of the kid with disabilities, but the ramp is not functioning. And the van doesn't show up either; the child stays at the curb waiting for the next bus while his more academically able classmates wave goodbye.

However, in the process of reimagining special education, we cannot afford the fantasy of wishing away disabilities. Such an approach would be akin to pretending that race, class, culture, gender, and other aspects of identity are of little consequence to instruction and learning. For children who have pronounced disabilities and the teachers who work with them, the emerging rhetoric of disability as social construction leaves deeply puzzling questions unanswered. Tomlinson's (1982) clarification regarding disabilities is an appropriate starting point in understanding the difference between categories of disability that are relatively incontrovertible and those that fit more readily in the frame of cultural construction. Tomlinson argued that normative disabilities are those that professionals and laypeople would not dispute, given these conditions' historical and biological roots. Examples may be blindness, deafness, physical disabilities, and severe cognitive challenges; these forms of disability exist in all classes, cultures, and racial groups in similar proportions. Nonnormative disabilities are those that tend to be of lesser severity, hinge on subjective measures, and may be contested on the basis of contextual circumstances.

It is in the area of normative disabilities that special education has historically been most effective in adapting curriculum and pedagogy. For example, few would argue against the benefits of American Sign Language, Braille, assistive technologies, and person-centered planning. These are approaches that should not be swept aside in the interest of maximizing exposure to the standard curriculum or socialization. On the contrary, they are valuable assets for maximum participation in society. Moreover, there is growing recognition of cultures and subcultures associated with sensory deficits and disabilities, e.g., deaf culture. As one colleague who is blind explained about his own relations with other blind people: "You don't need to explain, teach, or feel different with another blind person. You can share jokes and simply relax, be yourself." There is a danger in adhering to an extreme ideological posture that suppresses the existence of normative disabilities. That view, if translated into policy, may not only deprive individuals of contact with those who share similar challenges and experiences, but may also delegitimize an important aspect of their identity.

Discussion: Reimagining Special Education

Historically, educational policies have promoted segregation and stigmatization of children with disabilities and of racial minorities; reform efforts in the last fifty years have sought to counteract that legacy but have been derailed. Racial segregation is still pronounced despite replacement of busing with "magnet programs." Special education has become the equivalent of the lowest academic tracks in older schools where children of immigrants, the poor, and racial minorities find their crowded classrooms (Erevelles, 2000; Ogbu, 1995). Considering the stability of social stratification, the path to emancipatory school reform should take into account students' uniqueness and group identities, such as language, culture, gender, sexual orientation, and disability (Waters, 1996). Contemporary teacher education cannot afford to ignore the contextual nature of school, the political purposes of the curriculum, and the braided identities of students and communities (Apple, 1990; Banks, 1996; Bursztyn, 1999; Freire and Macedo, 1995). Teacher educators need to address the unfulfilled promise of Public Law 94-142. In that landmark legislation and subsequent reauthorizations, there is a mandate that the public schools tailor instruction to the unique needs of individual learners. Regrettably, the policies that flowed from the legislation, as implemented in urban schools, led too often to conditions of increased segregation and control, cumbersome legal requirements, and atomized instruction. Breaking that pattern of oppression and marginalization requires teachers who are capable of engaging in reflective practice and critical pedagogy.

Rodriguez (1999) notes that the work of Giroux, Grumet, Kincheloe, Pinar, and others has exposed the political nature of the curriculum. In their interpretations, curriculum is not the innocent provider of social opportunities but the embodiment of discourses that shape social relations and identities in relation to power. Rodriguez questions special education's uncritical work in adapting curriculum for children with special needs. Recognizing that curriculum embodies the ideology of dominant groups, curriculum modifications and adaptations for labeled minority children perpetuate their marginalization.

Banks and Banks (1995, 2002) offered a framework for creating school culture designed to respond to student diversity by incorporating transformative scholarship into curriculum and pedagogy. They envision five interrelated aspects in this project: content integration, the knowledge construction process, prejudice reduction, and an empowering school culture and social structure. This framework seeks to counteract the damaging effects of a hegemonic curriculum on minority children and children with a wide range of challenges and disabilities.

Content integration refers to efforts by teachers to develop an inclusive curriculum in subject areas and disciplines. In the multicultural project, this entails incorporating examples and content from a variety of cultures and groups to illustrate key concepts, principles, generalizations, and theories in subject areas or disciplines. This approach, extended to include children with disabilities, requires integrating the experience and knowledge of people with disabilities in the course of instruction (Nieto, 1999).

The knowledge construction process pertains to teachers helping students understand, investigate, and determine how biases, frames of reference, and perspectives within a discipline influence knowledge as constructed. Access to knowledge and research is thereby demystified, and students and teachers are empowered to create knowledge themselves. This is consistent with Joe Kincheloe's approach to teacher research (Kincheloe et al., 1999, and this volume). This aspect of the curriculum is particularly relevant to students with disabilities because it opens the door to exploring the dynamics of labeling and sorting students in relation to various personal and contextual factors (Thomas and Loxley, 2001).

Under the rubric of prejudice reduction, Banks and Banks (2002) propose that teachers engage students in learning activities that promote knowledge of and respect for members of diverse racial and cultural groups. This is necessary to counteract the stereotypes and prejudices that children bring to school and that erode the confidence and self-image of children belonging to disparaged groups. The application of this concept to include children with disabilities is clear; children should learn to appreciate and respect their classmates across socially constructed barriers that have historically isolated and demeaned individuals (Hoffman, 1996; Korn, 1997).

The fourth element in transformative multicultural education is equity pedagogy, an approach to instruction that takes into account the particular learning needs and styles of children from diverse cultural groups. For example, cooperative learning approaches are more consistent with Native American cultures, since competition among learners is generally discouraged by those groups. This dimension of pedagogy is key to appropriate practice in special education and is an aspect of the enterprise worth preserving. Children with special needs benefit from pedagogical approaches that take into account their learning strengths and difficulties. For instance, the use of assistive technologies to facilitate communication in children with autism or with severe speech impediments facilitates their capacity for meaningful learning (Miramontes, Nadeau, and Commins, 1996; Robinson-Zanartu, 1996).

Finally, this framework addresses school cultures and school structures. Educational quality and cultural empowerment are possible only if the entire school commits to systemic reform to achieve these purposes. To arrive at an empowering school culture, the organization must examine and change grouping practices, the social climate, assessment practices, extracurricular programs, staff expectations, and responses to student diversity. A reconceptualized school needs to consider its approach to students with diverse aptitudes and challenges so that they too become empowered and fully engaged in learning. In this regard, teachers need to be particularly conscious of the potential marginalization of children who belong to one or more oppressed groups, such as children who are members of nonwhite groups and are also disabled, and/or ELL children (Beckum and Zimmy,1991; Trueba, 1993).

Banks and Banks's (2002) framework represents a blueprint for teacher educators who strive to prepare teachers for ethical and democratic schools. I believe the framework needs to be complemented by an additional component, one that links schools and communities, teachers and parents. I will refer to that dimension as *building trust*. Although not commonly addressed in the education literature, trust is an essential link between people that permits and encourages learning and, at the institutional level, meaningful reform. Before trust develops, teachers and schools need to recognize its centrality and work to form the requisite relationships with students, parents, and communities. In the rule-bound, bureaucratic system of urban schooling, trust is in short supply. Urban public schools have yet to uphold many of the values they purport to represent, such as access, excellence, equity, and opportunity. In fact, poor public schools are known to parents of "at-risk" and diagnosed children as formidable institutions, where they cannot be heard and where their children are too often deprived of dignity and opportunity. Parental disengagement, unfortunately, is often misinterpreted as lack of concern (Harry, Kalyanpur, and Day, 1999), thus compounding teachers' reluctance to extend themselves. Yet without building bridges of trust with parents and communities, schools will continue to fail their students and fail as institutions.

All too often we encounter the argument that we need to prepare teachers for schools as they are, so that teachers will have an easier time adjusting to the harsh realities of urban education. That stance, not uncommon in staff development programs led by seasoned teachers, is welcomed by novice teachers eager to acquire survival techniques in order to bind their anxiety about being in charge. These teachers are hungry for a script, a ready-made approach to teaching that, once deployed, can minimize their self-doubt and help them steer clear of bumps. Unfortunately, many teachers become so fixated on the mechanics of teaching that they lose sight of the greater goals they set for themselves when they entered the profession. The danger to children is that "what works" tends to be a narrowly focused set of behavior control skills, which may be deployed at the expense of meaningful instruction.

I believe we should have the courage in teacher preparation to sustain and support teachers' idealism and work with schools toward a more equitable path to educate the next generation rather than perpetuate the injustices and suffering that are disproportionately borne by urban and minority children. Special education teachers in particular can and should be in the forefront of educational change. Since special education has been repeatedly distorted and has betrayed the most vulnerable children and parents in contemporary society, it is in this field that the need for reform is most urgent. Although, in the past, schools have promised access and support, they often delivered marginalization and control in the form of special programs and designations. The survival of public education may hinge on their capacity to evolve and deliver on their promise of access and equity for all children, particularly the most vulnerable among them.

References

Apple, M. (1990). *Ideology and Curriculum*. 2nd ed. New York: Routledge.

Artiles, A., and Zamora-Duran, G. (1997). *Reducing Disproportionate Representation of Culturally Diverse Students in Special and Gifted Education*. Reston, VA: Council for Exceptional Children.

Banks, J. A. (1996). "Multicultural Education and Curriculum Transformation." *Journal of Negro Education*, 64, pp. 390–399.

Banks, J. A., and Banks, C. M., eds. (1995). *Handbook of Research on Multicultural Education*. New York: Macmillan.

Banks J. A., and Banks, C. M., eds. (2002). *Multicultural Education: Issues and Perspectives*. 4th ed. New York: John Wiley & Sons.

Beckum, L. C., and Zimmy, A. (1991). "School Culture in Multicultural Settings." In N. B. Wyner, ed., *Current Perspectives on the Culture of Schools*. Brookline, MA: Brookline Books.

Bourdieu, P. (1976). "Les conditions sociales de la production sociologue; sociologie coloniale et decolonisation de la sociologie." In H. Moniot, ed. *Le Mal de Voir*. Paris: Union General d'Edition.

Burke, P. J., (1996). "Educational Change in the United States and its Potential Impact on Children with Disabilities." In L. Florian and M. Rouse, eds., *School Reform and Special Educational Needs: Anglo-American Perspectives*. Cambridge, UK: University of Cambridge Institute of Education.

Bursztyn, A. (1999). "Psychological Vistas on Prereferral Interventions for CLD Students." In M. Lupi and G. Rivera, eds., *A Monograph on Prereferral Intervention Strategies for Linguistically and Culturally Diverse Students* (pp. 36–58). New York: Hunter College–CUNY and New York State Vocational and Educational Services for Individuals with Disabilities (NYS VESID).

Bursztyn, A. (2002). "The Path to Academic Disability: Javier's School Experience." In C. Korn and A. Bursztyn, eds., *Rethinking Multicultural Education: Case Studies in Cultural Transition* (pp. 160–183). Westport, CT: Bergin & Garvey.

Cohen, J., and Osher, D. (1994). *Race and SED Identification: An Analysis of OCR Data.* Technical paper prepared for Division of Innovation and Development, Office of Special Education Programs, U.S. Department of Education.

Cummins, J. (1986). "Psychological Assessment of Minority Students: Out of Context, Out of Control?" *Journal of Reading, Writing and Learning Disabilities International,* 2, pp. 1–8.

Cummins, J. (1989). *Empowering Minority Students.* Sacramento: California Association for Bilingual Education.

Demetrion, G. (2001). "Discerning the contexts of adult literacy education: Theoretical reflections and practical applications." *Canadian Journal for the Study of Adult Education,* 15,(2), pp. 104–127.

Erevelles, N. (2000). "Educating Unruly Bodies: Critical Pedagogy, Disability Studies, and the Politics of Schooling." *Educational Theory,* 50:1, pp. 25–47.

Figueroa, R. A. (1995). "When Minority Concerns Become Majority Imperatives: A California Case Study." *Educational Record,* 76:2–3, pp. 72–81.

Freire, P., and Macedo, D. (1995). "A Dialogue: Culture, Language and Race." *Harvard Educational Review,* 65, pp. 377–402.

Greene, M. (1996) "Plurality, diversity, and the public space." In A. Oldenquisted, ed., *Can Democracy be Taught?* Bloomington: Phi Delta Kappa Educational Foundation.

Harry, B. (1992). *Cultural Diversity, Families, and the Special Education System.* New York: Teachers College Press.

Harry, B., Kalyanpur, M., and Day, M. (1999). *Building Cultural Reciprocity with Families: Case Studies in Special Education.* Baltimore: P. H. Brookes Publishing.

Hoffman, D. (1996). "Culture and Self in Multicultural Education: Reflections on Discourse, Text, and Practice." *American Educational Research Journal,* 33:3, pp. 545–569.

Kincheloe, J., Steinberg, S., and Hinchey, P. (1999). *The Postformal Reader: Cognition and Education.* New York: Falmer Press.

Korn, C. (1997). "Translating Stories across Cultures." *Education and Culture: The Journal of the John Dewey Society,* 41:1, pp. 18–23.

Lipsky, D., and Gartner, A. (1996). "Equality Requires Inclusion: The Future for All Students with Disabilities." In C. Christensen and F. Rizvi, eds., *Disabilities and the Dilemmas of Education and Justice* (pp. 145–155). Buckingham, UK: Open University Press.

Losen, D. L., and Orfield, G., eds. (2002). *Racial Inequity and Special Education.* Cambridge, MA: The Civil Rights Project at Harvard University and Harvard Education Press.

Middleton, R. A., Rollins, C. W., and Harley, D. A. (1999). "The Historical and Political Context of the Civil Rights of Persons with Disabilities: A Multicultural Perspective for Counselors." *Journal of Multicultural Counseling and Development,* 27:2, pp. 105–121.

Milofsky, C. (1989). *Testers and Testing: The Sociology of School Psychology.* New Brunswick, NJ: Rutgers University Press.

Miramontes, O. B., Nadeau, A., and Commins, N. L. (1996). *Restructuring Schools for Linguistic Diversity: Linking Decision Making to Effective Programs.* New York: Teachers College Press.

Nieto, S. (1999). *The Light in Their Eyes: Creating Multicultural Learning Communities.* New York: Teachers College Press.

Nolet, V., and Tindal, G. (1993). "Special Education in Content Area Classes: Development of a Model and Practical Procedures." *Remedial and Special Education*, 14:1, pp. 36–48.

Ogbu, J. U. (1995). "Understanding Cultural Diversity and Learning." In J. A. Banks and C. A. McGee-Banks, eds., *Handbook of Research on Multicultural Education* (pp. 582–593). New York: Macmillan.

Osher, D., Woodruff, D., and Sims, A. E. (2002). "Schools Make a Difference: The Overrepresentation of African American Youth in Special Education and the Juvenile Justice System." In D. L. Losen and G. Orfield, eds., *Racial Inequity and Special Education*. Cambridge, MA: The Civil Rights Project at Harvard University and Harvard Education Press.

Pugash, M., and Warger, C., eds. (1996). *Curriculum Trends, Special Education, and Reform*. New York: Teachers College Press.

Rodriguez, E. (1999). "Intelligence, Special Education, and Post-formal Thinking: Constructing an Alternative to Educational Psychology." In J. L. Kincheloe, S. Steinberg, and P. H. Hinchey, eds., *The Post-formal Reader: Cognition and Education* (pp. 391–408). New York: Falmer Press.

Robinson-Zanartu, C. (1996). "Serving Native American Children and Families: Considering Cultural Variables." *Language, Speech, and Hearing Services in Schools*, 27:4, pp. 373–384.

Safford, P., and Safford, E. (1996). *A History of Childhood and Disability*. New York: Teachers College Press.

Skrtic, T. M., ed. (1995). *Disability and Democracy: Reconstructing (Special) Education for Postmodernity*. New York: Teachers College Press.

Sleeter, C. E., and McLaren, P. L. (1995). *Multicultural Education, Critical Pedagogy, and the Politics of Difference*. Albany: SUNY Press.

Thomas, G., and Loxley, A. (2001). *Deconstructing Special Education and Constructing Inclusion*. Buckingham, UK: Open University Press.

Tomlinson, S. (1982). *A Sociology of Special Education*. London: Routledge and Kegan Paul.

Trueba, H. T. (1993). "Cultural Diversity and Conflict: The Role of Educational Anthropology in Healing Multicultural America." In P. Phelan and A. L. Davidson, eds., *Renegotiating Cultural Diversity in American Schools* (pp. 195–215). New York: Teachers College Press.

Waters, M. C. (1996). "The Intersection of Gender, Race, and Ethnicity in Identity Development of Caribbean American Teens." In B. J. Ross Leadbeater and N. Way, eds., *Urban Girls: Resisting Stereotypes, Creating Identities* (pp. 65–81). New York: New York University Press.

Chapter Eight

Run Jane Run: Researching Early Childhood Teacher Practice Frame by Frame

Carol Korn-Bursztyn

Early childhood education has traditionally privileged the invisible developmental line, the trajectory through time and space that children are assumed to travel. In this vein, optimal development assumes a coherence and continuity between different contexts, especially home and school. Such coherence is viewed as optimal to the well-being of children and as especially indispensable to long-term academic achievement. Early childhood education, viewed as laying the foundation for further educational attainment, aims for an uninterrupted flow between the contexts in which children live. Seamlessness between domains is presented as an ideal—a virtual, if not always real, possibility. Early childhood teachers are expected to create bridges across these multiple domains, especially those of home and school. When fissures appear between the real, multiple contexts in which children live, teachers are expected to minimize these, all without missing a curricular beat.

In striving to attain the pedagogical ideal of a seamless, easy flow between borderless contexts, some contexts are inevitably privileged, while others are nudged to the rear, only to jut out in real, unexpected, and often unwelcome ways. When such disjunctures emerge, they are typically met with teacher reactions that range from a hardened and defensive "It's not my job" to dismay and even despair at efforts to repair such breaches. In this paper, I describe early childhood teacher praxis as one of negotiating the varied, often competing contexts in which children grow and in which teachers teach. I will refer to these contexts as "frames"—now visible, now hidden from view; now intersecting, now obscured.

When teachers research their own classrooms and reflect upon their practice, the frames that constitute their work and their children's lives become increasingly apparent. The virtual world of seamless edges falls away to reveal the real presence of multiple frames, notably the curricular, affective, familial, cultural, and organizational. The process of teacher research further clarifies how these frames are positioned and how they operate. They may be positioned one behind the other, stacked so that only the frame that is up front is visible; they may be aligned, or they might even jostle for space. Greater clarity of vision brings necessary complications; the steady, reflective gaze of the teacher leads to greater awareness of the frames that constitute early childhood settings and opens up real possibilities for teachers as they work to create classroom environments. Clearer vision gives rise, too, to reassessment of expectations for seamless transitions, revealing the at times virtual nature of teacher expectations, and the real experience of creating thriving early childhood classrooms.

Teacher research, conducted by early childhood teachers, advanced graduate students in early childhood education at Brooklyn College, is presented. The contexts in which these research projects were conducted, notably place and cultural and educational zeitgeist, are explored for their impact upon educational practice. The teacher research stories reviewed here reveal the curricular, affective, familial, cultural, and organizational frames in which teaching and learning in a major urban setting take place. In gaining greater understanding of how multiple frames operate in the classroom, teachers gain critical awareness of their own classroom-based choices and actions and the impact of these on the children they teach. Teaching young children is redescribed as a performative act in which pedagogical choices and decisions are informed by close study of the frames that surround and impact on early childhood teacher praxis.

Discussion of teacher research in a highly diverse, urban setting precedes the research vignettes presented. This work extends the growing body of literature on teacher research (Clandinin and Connelly, 1991; Connelley and Clandinin, 1988; Goodson, 1992; Jalongo and Isenberg, 1995; Kincheloe, 1991; Schön, 1983, 1987), demonstrating how teachers negotiate diverse frames in their classrooms, even as these bump against each other. The teachers' stories of their own practice in New York City early childhood classrooms underscore the complex role responsibilities of teachers as they gain growing understanding of how the curricular, affective, familial, cultural, and organizational frames that constitute classroom life operate in their own rooms.

Each frame will be taken up by category according to its prominence within the selected vignettes. This organization is for purposes of clarity only and is not meant to imply that these frames operate in discrete categories. On the contrary, a close reading of these vignettes will reveal considerable overlap between frames. Finally, discussion of the role of colleges or schools of education in integrating comprehensive understanding of early childhood education theory and practice with an approach to critical early childhood pedagogy will follow.

Teacher Research in New York City

In recent years, the historical nature of early childhood education as a protected, self-contained environment has been challenged by the contemporary trend to push down curriculum and to reconfigure early childhood education as preparation for the rigors ahead. The architecture of New York City public schools has implicitly followed this lead: gone are the separate entrances with KINDERGARTEN etched in the stone lintels that were a fixture of public schools during the earlier part of the twentieth century. Four- and five-year-olds are expected to enter and exit through the same doorways and travel the same academic pathways as their older elementary school counterparts. Long gone are the gardens that occupied a corner of the paved schoolyard. Playgrounds are quickly becoming an historical footnote as schools are renovated to accommodate greater numbers of children and the demand for increased time devoted to skill development and institutional fear of personal injury litigation rises.

Contemporary revision of curricular practices in early childhood education focuses on skill development in discrete content areas. This is a significant departure from early childhood professional practice of integrated curriculum inclusive of children's affective and developmental needs. In the early childhood classroom, this has meant an increased emphasis on a fairly narrow range of academic skills acquisition—primarily literacy, then numeracy. Many New York City school districts, for example, call for extended blocks of time devoted exclusively to literacy and mathematics skills development; teachers report that they must scramble to find time for mandated social studies and science lessons. This trend is accompanied by a concurrent decrease in emphasis on social skills development and play and creative endeavor, including the arts. It is not unusual to find that, when offered, the creative arts are squeezed in between bathroom/wash-up and lunch times. Even kindergarten has been reconfigured as preparation for the lengthy regimens of skill development instituted in first grade. Prekindergarten, or what was referred to in more leisurely times as nursery school, serves the purpose of preparing children for kindergarten. Child care, public and nonpublic, unsurprisingly becomes prep school for prekindergarten.

The social pressures that drive these recent trends and their negative effects on children have been noted for more than two decades (Elkind, 1981; Postman, 1982). The phenomenon of testing two-, three-, and four-year-old children for admission to selective schools and programs within both the private and public sectors has given rise to acute parental anxiety regarding their children's academic and, by extension, social and economic futures. This common parental anxiety figures, ironically, as a bridge across the social, economic, racial, and ethnic divides that distinguish the forms of schooling available to children in New York City. The contemporary social pressures—in which expectations for achievement are high, childhood is hurried, and time is always short—are consistent with the zeitgeist of "busy-ness" that Adam Gopnik identifies in his recent essay, "Bumping into Mr. Ravioli" (2002). In this piece, Gopnik draws upon his two-year-old daugh-ter's relationship with her imaginary friend, Charlie Ravioli, conducted through imaginary cell phone conversations, unanswered messages on answering machines, taxis hopped into, and lunches "grabbed" on the run:

> "I bumped into Charlie Ravioli," she announces at dinner. . . . "We had coffee, but then he had to run." She sighs, sometimes, at her inability to make their schedules mesh, but she accepts it as inevitable, just the way life is. "I bumped into Charlie Ravioli today," she says. "He was working." Then she adds brightly, "But we hopped into a taxi." What happened then? we ask. "We grabbed lunch," she says. (p. 80)

Gopnik traces what he refers to as the "constant, exhausting, no-time-to-meet-your-friends Charlie Ravioli-style busyness" (p. 81) as a modern affliction, a busyness that is isolating and, finally, far less productive than its predecessor, business. Observing that when the institutions of bour-geois life were being built in the seventeenth and eighteenth centuries, the people who were building the institutions left no record of complaint that they were too busy, he comments:

> Samuel Pepys, who had a Navy to refloat and a burned London to rebuild, often uses the word "busy" but never complains of busyness. For him, the word "busy" is a synonym for "happy," not for "stressed." Not once in his diary does Pepys cancel lunch or struggle to fit someone in for coffee at four-thirty. Pepys works, makes love, and goes to bed, but he does not bump and he does not have to run. Ben Franklin, a half century later, boasts of his industriousness, but he, too, never complains about being busy, and always has time to publish a newspaper or come up with a maxim or swim in the ocean or invent the lightning rod. (p. 82)

Gopnik differentiates between the "work" of the bourgeoisie and the "labor" of the working class (who he noted were too busy to be busy) during the seventeenth through the early twentieth centuries and by extension identifies contemporary busyness as a bourgeois phenomenon. Busyness, I argue, together with hurried childhood and curricula that are driven downward, has resulted in a common early childhood experience that cuts across socioeconomic strata. Early childhood teachers in both the public and private sectors are thrust into the vanguard of change, as unwilling participants in a process over which they have little control and are unwitting players. The busyness that suffuses the particular New York City zeitgeist that Gopnik describes has already struck deep roots in its schools. Teachers are today's laborers, too busy to be busy, trying to meet the demands for a busyness whose hallmarks are voluminous paperwork and pressure to cover a broader curriculum, in less time, and with younger children.

Unsurprisingly, when called upon to conduct research in their own classrooms, early childhood teachers/advanced graduate students often choose to develop and study curriculum. In identifying a question to research, many candidates begin with classroom-based problems, often centered on how to more effectively develop specific academic skills. Responding to the pressures they face teaching within New York City's public and private schools, and mirroring current trends in education, the teacher impulse is to privilege the narrowly curricular. Faced with the pressured environments in which they teach, and the academic demands of the teacher research sequence, many candidates lapse into student survival mode. They envision simply preparing lesson plans that can be useful in the classroom, save limited preparation time, garner critical approval from school administration, and complete the requirements for their master's degree in early childhood education. The process of conducting close study of their own teacher practice, and of shaping and reshaping their research projects, leads to the uncovering of frames previously hidden from view. These frames increasingly come to inform their everyday work with children and shape how they come to view their own development as teachers.

The teacher research project, the focus of the yearlong capstone sequence in teacher research that I teach, leads to and includes preparation of the Independent Project in Early Childhood Education. This project is designed to further an inquiry-based approach to teaching and learning. It centers on asking questions and investigating teacher praxis and children's experience and, following the qualitative research convention of triangulation, calls for multiple means of investigating the question(s) posed (Lincoln and Guba, 1985). Triangulation, for example, might involve instituting a regular schedule of classroom observations, interviews with teachers, administrators, and family members, and survey methodology. Hewing to conventions of educational research, multiple means of investigation or triangulation enhances validity through the use of at least three different measures of investigation. Drawing on multiple measures, rather than relying on a single measure, reduces the risk of skewed results.

Triangulation serves another, more subtle purpose: It pushes teacher thinking toward a more nuanced and critical understanding of teacher praxis, children's learning, and classroom dynamics. The emphasis on triangulation, common to the teacher research projects presented (and to others too numerous to be presented here), serves to implicitly guide teacher thinking in the direction of encountering different perspectives and confronting frames that diverge from those they typically privilege in their everyday work with children. As the field of early childhood education redefines itself in response to the zeitgeist of time, place, and cultural phenomena, teachers need to be able to identify the frames that operate within their classrooms and that undergird their practice. This understanding is critical to teachers' capacity to articulate a leadership role for themselves and for their profession.

The self-contained and protected early childhood classroom of the early twentieth century, encoded in the separate entranceways for kindergartners, has given way to a more permeable space, marked by such contemporary phenomena as busyness and achievement anxiety, and buttressed by the academic trend of high-stakes testing. If the early childhood classroom is no stranger to curriculum wars and the standards movement, it is also no stranger to an appreciation for how family, culture, and community seep into the classroom, with or without invitation, ready or not. These contexts, redescribed as frames that provide a focal point through which to examine classroom practice, are examined in the case vignettes that follow.

Exploration of the curricular frame suggests how the implicit presence of multiple frames impacts upon what is initially conceived of as a straightforward task of curriculum development. Detailed examination of this frame underlines the significance of the curricular frame to early childhood education and to teacher education. How teachers organize classroom environments and what they actually do in the classroom are in the end what distinguish exemplary from indifferent teaching. Subsequent vignettes from student research projects demonstrate how teacher focus on the affective, cultural, and organizational frames inevitably calls up multiple frames of reference, impacting on the intellectual, cultural, and emotional tenor of the classroom. Finally, the role of colleges and schools of education in preparing teachers to recognize and work with the multiple frames that constitute children's experience is discussed.

Framing the Curricular

Deceptively titled "How Can I Improve Children's Comprehension and Writing Skills by Using Graphic Organizers in an At-Risk School?" this first case vignette involves a research project that was submitted for filing under a pseudonym, giving a hint of how dramatically the scope of the project extends beyond the narrow curricular focus implied by its awkward title. The writer, a first-grade teacher in an economically depressed, high-crime Brooklyn neighborhood, teaches in a school she describes as recently removed from the New York State list of Schools under Registration Review (SURR), though only 23.8% of all students in grades 3 through 5 evidence a minimal level of English language arts proficiency. The school's population is largely minority: 65% of the students are African American, 34% are Hispanic, and 1% is "Other."

The teacher, Ms. Hernandez, is deeply committed to the children she teaches. She hopes to provide her class with the academic skills they will need in the upper grades and wishes to avoid the blame for the later academic failure often attributed to teachers of early childhood (here defined as preschool years through grade 2) by their upper-grade elementary school colleagues. An unintentional by-product of the recognition of the critical nature of the early childhood years is the way that responsibility, blame, and defensiveness circulate among teachers in underperforming schools, themselves under close scrutiny. Children's achievement is typically viewed through a number of alternate, competing frames. When the curricular frame is invoked, teachers are held responsible for their students' learning. Following the logic of this frame, early childhood teachers are responsible for the subsequent failure of children who have passed through their classroom doors. Failure to read by third grade, for example, will often be informally attributed to failure of first- and second-grade teachers to teach reading. (Kindergarten teachers, in turn, are often suspect when children have difficulty learning to read in first grade.)

Ms. Hernandez's concern that she be perceived as a good teacher, whose children learn to read, reflects the power of the curricular frame to not only structure how curriculum is described in the classroom, but how teachers assess themselves and how they are assessed by their peers and supervisors. Ms. Hernandez began her second year of teaching for the New York City public schools with determination to make good use of what she had learned in teacher development workshops. She was impressed with the connections between children's ability to talk about stories they heard and the development of reading comprehension skills and was eager to try some new strategies with her students. It was critical to Ms. Hernandez that she demonstrate to her colleagues and supervisors that her children were capable of learning and, thanks to her efforts, would be well prepared for the next grade's work.

Taking her cues from these schoolwide workshops, in which the ability to retell stories was presented as key to, and synonymous with, conversation about stories, Ms. Hernandez planned a program of developing story-retelling skills. She planned to draw on graphic organizers, such as diagrams, charts, and other visual displays, to illustrate story ideas in order to help the children recall key information. Parent involvement was important to this project, and Ms. Hernandez planned to keep parents informed of their children's progress and to elicit their help in strengthening the children's skills. A warm and organized teacher, Ms. Hernandez anticipated little difficulty in implementing her curriculum development project and was confident that with carefully prepared lessons and a program of parent outreach, her children would make steady progress.

The first clue to Ms. Hernandez that her well-intentioned beliefs would be challenged by her applied research in the field came with her first set of informal interviews with children in her class about their experiences with, and attitudes toward, reading. John remarked, "Mrs. Hernandez, I don't need to learn how to read." Further conversation revealed that most of the children's parents did not read to them; some children shared books with their younger or older siblings. A common refrain was, "My mommy doesn't read to me—she's really busy, so I read to my baby sister/ brother" or "I read with my older brother/sister."

The time seemed ripe for bringing the hidden frame of family into view, codified in educationspeak as "parent involvement." Ms. Hernandez telephoned her students' parents to explain the literacy project she was beginning in her classroom and to ask for their cooperation and assistance. Of the 23 families she contacted, only 9 agreed to speak with her. Near tears, Ms. Hernandez reported that some parents slammed the phone down; others excused themselves before hanging up. Only a few parents came to the parent-teacher conference later that month. She comments:

In all my years of teaching day care, I never experienced the frustration of non-parental involvement. However, since working for the Board of Education, I have had to learn to deal with it on a regular basis. When I began my phone interviews with my parents, I noticed something disturbing. As I introduced myself to the parent, I would suddenly hear a dial tone.

Ms. Hernandez later learned that six of her students were in foster care; a seventh was removed from her mother's care and placed in foster care early in the year. Expanding the scope of her curriculum development project, she arranged to speak with the caseworker of a new student, Ann, who had entered the school midyear and was also in foster care. Ms. Hernandez was distressed when the foster parent dismissed her requests that she, the parent, assist Ann with schoolwork and was taken aback by the foster parent's insistence that Ann be promoted to the next grade because "It's not her fault." The caseworker helpfully explained to Ms. Hernandez the process by which a child enters foster care, but balked at her questions regarding monitoring of the foster home. Explaining her busyness, the caseworker observed:

We should visit the foster home at least three times a month, but in all honesty I have a huge case load and at times I find myself just calling some of the parents and talking to them on the phone. The foster parents I do talk to have been in the foster care system for a long time, and I know them very well.

Ms. Hernandez mused aloud as to whether the caseworker's relationship with the foster parents had become too friendly or her caseload too unwieldy. She wondered about how this affected the caseworker's ability to monitor the children. The caseworker stood up, effectively ending the conversation, and observed, "I have a lot of cases and not enough time. You have to look at it this way, the child is safe." In interviews with her early childhood colleagues, Ms. Hernandez heard experiences that echoed her own. She heard of deliberate turning away from the familial frame, a dangerous matching of a perceived parental attitude of unconcern with the teachers' own brand of toxic cynicism. Ms. Hernandez writes:

I have spoken to my colleagues and found that I wasn't the only one in this situation. They also are faced with a lack of parent involvement. However, their attitudes towards this problem are completely different than mine. One teacher stated, "If the parent doesn't care, then I don't care." Another colleague said, "Why do you worry about it, just teach what you have to teach. Whoever gets it, gets it and whoever doesn't, doesn't." When I object, they look at me like I'm crazy.

The familial frame, centered here on inadequate "parent involvement," occludes teacher responsibility for the curricular frame, that is, for creating a lively, intellectually stimulating, and emotionally responsive classroom environment. Lack of parent support is demoralizing to teachers; the shared emotional investment in the child-rearing project, of which teaching is part, suffers. Viewing parents as uncaring—toward both the children and the school/teacher—presents a danger as teachers begin to set greater emotional distance between themselves and the children they teach and between their own sense of self-worth and their professional role. Shared consensus of the impossibility of bringing the familial frame into focus—and the parents to school—serves another survival function for teachers working in difficult circumstances. It deflects attention from the curricular frame and from teacher responsibility for maintaining a focus on teaching children.

Like the caseworker, the teachers Ms. Hernandez interviewed pleaded excessive "busyness" as justification for lack of curricular innovation. Like Mr. Ravioli, they too were too rushed, too busy—and finally, like the elusive Mr. Ravioli, had little to show for so much busyness. Ms. Hernandez was surprised by the curious absence of graphic organizers on her colleagues' classroom walls despite their participation in the school's in-service workshops. They pleaded, "That's too much work," or "Too much writing for me," or "What's the use, after all that work some of them still won't understand." Irked with her colleagues, Ms. Hernandez writes:

> And, the most famous line, "I don't have enough time." When I asked what strategies they used to help children better understand the story, one teacher said, "You have to look at it this way. If they don't get it this year, they will get it next year." That statement really stood out.

Yet, she understands them too. No stranger to teacher despair, Ms. Hernandez is also vulnerable to that particularly virulent strain in which a teacher's sense of personal and professional efficacy becomes undone by the difficulties faced by the children she teaches. The despair of parents and children resonates within, mixing with her own growing self-doubt about her worth as a teacher and, by extension, choice of profession. Writing about parent involvement primarily from the perspective of the accrued benefits to children, Ms. Hernandez alludes to its ambiguous impact on self-confidence and achievement—for children, but perhaps, for teachers, too:

> This year, I have found myself becoming frustrated as a teacher. At times I feel helpless, I just don't feel as if I am doing enough for my students. My attitude has always been, if a student fails, then I failed. My feelings of frustration have a lot to do with parents not being involved in their children's education. In order

for a child to succeed, a teacher needs support from the home. The extra push, for the child, can make all the difference. I can understand the attitudes of my colleagues, and without parental support I feel their attitudes will never change. That is what scares me. What would happen to children if we all take that "I don't care" attitude? I know parent involvement equals self-confidence and achievement.

The curricular frame tends to be constructed of simple binaries: One succeeds or fails; classrooms are perfect or not; strategies work or are discarded. The contexts in which teaching and learning take place are excluded; alternate frames are hidden behind the curricular, creating a deceptively smooth and glossy exterior. Revisiting the teaching videotapes that so impressed her with the promise of graphic organizers, Ms. Hernandez reflects upon the virtual reality of the videotapes and the real space of her classroom.

When I attend workshops and see videos that demonstrate a strategy to be used in the classroom, I get very discouraged. These videos usually show a perfect teacher with her perfect students sitting around her and raising their hands. I often wonder what medication do they give these students to make them behave so well? These videos don't show the teacher in the real classroom, where some students shout out without raising their hands—and then you have the ones that you have to keep close to you for fear of what they will do next.

Ms. Hernandez comments on how the scope of her project changed over time and how she came to make room for the multiple frames that constitute classroom life and the children's out-of-school lives as well. She is pleased with her work with graphic organizers, and notes a general improvement in the children's ability to talk about stories they have read, the evidence of which she posts publicly on the hallway bulletin board:

My project has metamorphosed. I had believed that I was going to walk into my classroom with this one goal in mind, perfect results from my children using graphic organizers. I went into my classroom with a perception of how my project was supposed to work out. Instead of a smooth ride, my students confronted me with reality. It was not easy; some of my students got the concept, while others just could not. . . . In addition, by displaying my students' work in and outside of my classroom, I have involved the rest of the teachers in my grade in the use of graphic organizers. They come into my room to ask for copies, and to discuss how much more my students are writing. Their attitudes are still the same, but I could see that they have noticed a positive change in my students and they obviously want the same for their students.

The story, though, does not end with graphic organizers—not for the children, and not for their teacher, either. The familial and broader social frames that form children's lives remain a constant presence, a reminder that the curricular frame can never obliterate the presence of other, real frames. Ms. Hernandez muses about Ben, whose mother removed him from his foster home and disappeared. The school attendance officer comments, "It feels like the caseworker is waiting for the school to track Ben down. Nobody knows where Ben is, and until he readmits to school, nobody will ever know." "Here's a child," Ms. Hernandez observes, "who is actually lost in the system. Every day that I take attendance and look at Ben's name is a reminder of the struggles some of my students face outside of school." She ends her project with a simple plea to parents, a counterpoint to the curriculum strategies that circulate in her school and that assume the major focus of her project and of her work as a teacher. "I'm not asking for parents to become teachers, all I want them to do is talk to their children."

The intrusion of the outside world, the insistence with which unbidden frames breach the secure entrances to school, creates a haunting presence for early childhood teachers. Of these, the affective frame, constructed of family and social contexts, is especially difficult to negotiate, as teachers work to maintain a focus on the curricular frame and on their role responsibility to teach the children in their charge. The brief case vignette that follows illustrates how early childhood teachers acknowledge and address the extracurricular struggles of their students, even as these are nominally unrelated to the technology of teaching in the content areas, as exemplified by such strategies as graphic organizers.

Framing the Affective

George was sitting like a pretzel in the library when Peter came over, snatched the book out of his hands, and sat down. George got up and marched over to Peter, who pretended to look at the book, while keeping an eye on George. George threw himself on a third child, Brandon, who wrapped his arms around George's neck and began to choke him.

So begins Ms. Gregory's account of her mixed-age class of 22 children, ages four through six, that she teaches in a homeless shelter. Identifying her young students' twin inarticulateness and impulsivity, Ms. Gregory embarks on an intensive program of storybook reading, selecting stories that portray conflict and strong emotion, and their resolution. She valiantly plows ahead with her curriculum, reading to the children, giving them plenty of paper and crayons to draw with, and encouraging them to talk about their feelings. Having read the stories of conflict to the children, Ms. Gregory begins to listen more closely for the emotional storms that color their stories. She recalls how after hugging Sam, he is throttled by a jealous child, and how she needs to intervene when the pampered grandson of a colleague is promptly ostracized by his peers. With each storybook, Ms. Gregory becomes more and more aware of the emotional reality in which her students live and in which she teaches. She describes her setting:

> In my classroom, I can often smell marijuana. Although there is security, the shelter is large and attracts a wide range of people in desperate situations, which makes it a breeding ground for crime. Several weeks ago, we had a rapid dismissal because of a gang dispute. Albert, a child at the center, walked in saying, "The Bloods are coming to shoot up the block." In the house area, children often play cops and robbers. Nobody wants to be the cop. Their play seems so real it is scary.
>
> After the World Trade Center attack, I took them to the police station, and the children were terrified of the police officers. When an officer offered the children a chance to climb into his police car, one child threw his arms around my leg. Numerous times, children have told me about witnessing sexual activity. When children are subjected to this environment it affects more than their language development.

Keeping her pulse on the emotional climate of her classroom, Ms. Gregory makes room for the affective frame, and positions this alongside the curricular frame, as represented by her storytelling and deliberate efforts to address children individually, engaging them in conversation or, with uncommunicative youngsters, modeling language practices. The children's language skills develop, predictably, at different rates and with varying degrees of proficiency. Intermittent demands on the part of the director of the child-care center at the homeless shelter are an added source of tension for Ms. Gregory. She complains of pressures to eliminate playtime in the mornings and naptime after lunch and to assign homework daily for all of the children in this mixed-age classroom, but does not seem unduly troubled by this. Mirroring the haphazard nature of child rearing in this homeless shelter, administrative demands are similarly inconsistent and are treated by Ms. Gregory and her colleagues as inconsequential flurries of activity, a busyness unlikely to bear results, either desired or otherwise.

The local culture of school typically reflects the social and cultural contexts in which children live and that frame their development (Bursztyn, 2002). In the case vignette presented above, Ms. Gregory attempts to order her early childhood classroom as a bulwark against the random and unpredictable nature of the children's everyday lives, and also against her own sense of an unpredictable administration at the homeless shelter. In the vignette that follows, the classroom or curricular frame is made consciously permeable to the surrounding cultural contexts. Alternate cultural frames are invited forward; others, though, are deliberately set aside, privileging the curricular frame of school.

Framing the Cultural

A Haitian boy, Jean, arrived at school dressed neatly in a long-sleeved shirt and pants, despite the warm weather. He looked out of place in a preschool environment designed for play and exploration. Children were expected to paint, play in sand and water, and get a little messy. Jean didn't seem ready for this kind of play. He had a serious expression on his face that seemed to match the facial expression of his parents. I welcomed them to my class and they stood stiffly at the door watching the other children playing. His father frowned at their play, but said nothing.

This opening scene from a year in the life of a diverse Head Start classroom, where the families are predominantly of Haitian, Hispanic, and Caribbean background, sets the stage for the delicate work of drawing connections between the frames of the cultures of home and school, even as these bump against each other. In her research project, Ms. Santiago, an experienced Head Start teacher, sets out to explore the experience of transition from home to school and from school to home from the perspectives of families, children, and early childhood teachers. The Head Start program, she notes, is heavily family oriented and by policy invites parents to volunteer in the classroom, join policy committees, and become paid employees of the program (Zigler and Muenchow, 1992).

As she conducts home visits, observes the children and parents in her class, and interviews parents, children, and colleagues, Ms. Santiago uncovers fundamental tensions between the frames of the cultures of home and of school/curriculum. Each frame creates boundaries around the assumptions and expectations of school, including socialization into specific cultural norms and practices. Gender emerges as a hidden frame, with more mothers than fathers open to adoption of new cultural frames and ways of being. It should be noted that in most early childhood settings, more mothers than fathers are involved in Head Start activities; they are also more likely to seek and find employment at Head Start, which often leads to a career in early childhood education.

For the young boys for whom the cultural frame of home discourages or even forbids such activity, play with dolls and the accoutrements of homemaking takes on the delight of the forbidden. In the example above, the father's stern and disapproving demeanor was matched by his son Jean's serious and reserved manner when the father accompanied him to school in the morning. Once his father left, Ms. Santiago reported, Jean "loosened up, ran around, and played with dolls in the house area." She writes:

> [Through my] interviews I discovered conflicts between cultural beliefs about children's education and Head Start's principles of appropriate practices for preschool children. . . . Often there are cultural conflicts or struggles within the immediate family. Usually once the philosophy of Head Start is explained to the mother, she accepts it; the father will disagree and refuse to change his attitudes and beliefs about their culture. Usually children are directly affected by these struggles.
>
> A good example of this cultural conflict occurred with a Hispanic mother and her husband. She shared this experience with me: "When my son was just three, he entered Head Start. My husband and I walked into the class with my son. My son wanted to play in the house area with a doll. My husband glared at me and said, 'Do something.' I told him it was okay, but he became angry, walked over to his son, and took the doll away from him. He brought a car to play with. Later, at home, he told me, 'I don't want my son playing with girl toys.'"

Expressing some satisfaction at her child's socialization to what she experienced as the cultural frame of school, his mother proudly observes that her now grown son washes dishes, cooks, and cleans the house—and is unabashedly nurturing and affectionate. Ms. Santiago is clearly aligned with what emerges as the feminine perspective on adaptation to the new beliefs that make up the frame of the common culture and that are reflected in nonsexist early childhood practice. She observes that Head Start's goal is "to help children become independent and creative thinkers" and is clearly comfortable with the dominance of the early childhood curricular frame rooted in contemporary understanding of gender roles, as reflected in her Head Start classroom.

Ms. Santiago observes philosophically that change is a part of our lives, affecting both families and schools. She observes that she has learned much from speaking with parents and colleagues about cultural frames and would like parents to speak openly about their perspectives. An invitation to speak about family perspectives, however, does not imply significantly altering the curricular frame of her classroom to meet the culturally rooted expectations of the children's immigrant families. Ms. Santiago recognizes and speaks to the tension between the cultural expectation for quiet seatwork, as well as rigid gender role definitions in school, and early childhood practice as supported by writers in the field and codified by the National Association for the Education of Young Children (NAEYC) in their guidelines for developmentally appropriate practice in early childhood settings (Bredekamp and Copple, 1997; Gregory, 1997; Keats, 1997; Lynch and Hanson, 1992).

Her stance is unwavering; she explains the curricular frame to families and invites families to share aspects of their cultural lives within her classroom. Ms. Santiago speaks to the need for Head Start programs to increase communication with families around cultural expectations and differences and resolves to increase such time-honored multicultural activities in her classroom as singing, cooking, and storytelling. She does not consider abandoning or significantly altering the developmentally appropriate curricular practices that provide the dominant curricular frame in her Head Start classroom.

The organizational and philosophical frame of Head Start informs the research project in the vignette described above. The curricular, cultural, and familial frames are juxtaposed, sometimes in uneasy proximity to each other. In the brief vignette that follows, the organizational frame alluded to earlier moves to the front. The organizational context in which teacher, children, and families come together becomes the organizing frame for the interactions that unfold.

The Organizational Frame

I had three years of classroom experience as a teacher before accepting a position at Red Book Store [New York City]. This store is nestled in SoHo, where the streets are bustling with tourists, workers, residents, and vendors. As you walk through the door, you are greeted with 6,100 square feet of floor space under a fifteen-foot ceiling. Within this space, the bookshelves and display towers are heavily stocked with attractive books, games, plush dolls, and animals for sale. Midway through the store is the ten-foot activity circle, surrounded by shelves and displays of attractive items available for purchase. Twice a week, for approximately twenty-five minutes, between twelve and forty guests gather in or around the activity circle. Adult listeners (generally nannies) tend to sit outside the circle, on benches, while the children sit inside the circle on the carpeted floor, directly in front of me. I face the audience, seated on a foam block or rocking chair. For each Story Time event, I select four to five storybooks—two to three different stories in addition to those I plan to retell. As I sit before the audience of listeners, I once again become a teacher.

As she begins to consider her new job, Ms. Long puzzles over whether the children are enjoying her selection of stories and muses about her new identity as storyteller. She comments:

If not for my inner teacher, would I have chosen to retell favorite stories in a commercial setting? Probably not. My job responsibility was to ensure customer enjoyment and satisfaction (and to increase sales). My innate sense of responsibility to the audience, specifically the children, extended beyond offering an enjoyable, complimentary event. I sought to encourage book enjoyment and contribute to literacy development, albeit a miniscule contribution.

Soon she feels that she is no longer a teacher, but an entertainer, though the role of teacher is not one she willingly leaves behind:

> I was now an entertainer. Nevertheless, I did not entirely fight my teacher's instincts. As an entertainer, my role as a supervisor is limited, practically nonexistent. As I became more of an entertainer and less of a teacher, no longer did I ask myself, "What do the listeners need?" This conflict between the teacher inside me and the role as a storyteller in a commercial environment gnawed at me.

Ms. Long begins her project planning to focus on children's responses to story retelling, based on her work in the bookstore. As she observes the children more closely and tracks her own reactions to these seemingly simple storytelling events, the organizational frame becomes increasingly prominent, edging out the curricular frame she initially privileged and assumed could be maintained in this new setting. The commercial context has rendered her an entertainer, at odds with her teacher identity, or what she refers to as "the teacher within."

In an effort to transfer the classroom frame to a radically different setting, Ms. Long continues to doggedly track the listening interests of two three-year-old regulars at her storytelling sessions at the bookstore. Like many of her early childhood teacher colleagues, "disruptions" and "behavior problems" repeatedly distract her as she attempts to single-mindedly pursue her curricular aim. A second, unplanned storyline emerges, that of Ms. Long's questionable authority and ambiguous role, an ambiguity that is echoed in the disconnect between the children and their caregivers. As the children subtly test her authority, she reconsiders how the organizational frame of the commercial setting defines her role and erodes her sense of teacher authority.

> Today, a girl, Beanie, begins to engage in a progression of footsie antics while I am reading to the audience. First she slides the top of her foot lightly against the tip of my shoes. Her slight rubs become scrapes. The scrapes become foot nudges. Beanie's foot nudges become full-legged pushes against my feet. Her nanny doesn't come to my rescue. Since I receive no reaction from the nannies nearby, I am not even certain who Beanie's nanny is, or if the nanny is even in the activity circle. Ignoring Beanie's kicks is no longer possible. Finally, I peer down at Beanie and whisper, "Excuse me." She stops. I am powerless. If I speak to the nanny, she could possibly lodge a complaint about both the store and me. I cannot overstep my boundaries by asking the child to leave. I cannot reprimand

in any shape or form. Some of the nannies seemingly release their charges to my care, yet I possess neither the authority nor the desire to manage the children's behavior.

Finally, Ms. Long concludes that the gap between the early childhood classroom and the for-profit commercial world is too wide to be comfortably bridged. The organizational frame of the commercial setting dominates—the curricular, familial, and cultural frames were invited in for instrumental purposes of building customer satisfaction and increasing profits. At the end of the year, she returned to the classroom.

Discussion: Framing Teacher Education

Colleges and schools of education are the working studios in which the frames that shape education—and through which children, families, and teachers are viewed—are crafted. New frames may be constructed or found, familiar ones tinkered with, mended, and altered to serve the new realities these will contain. Schools of education bear a responsibility to children and families for making visible those frames that are hidden, by design or default. They can help prepare teachers for the realities of their children's lives and of the classrooms in which they will teach—not solely by presentation of teaching strategies, but also by preparing teachers to negotiate the finely stitched seams that will demarcate the boundaries of home, culture, and classroom. Narrow emphasis on the curricular frame can be, as Ms. Hernandez discovered in her work with graphic organizers, misleading. Her expectation that the curricular would upend the other frames, rendering these irrelevant to her, if only she were to intently focus on her goal, was soon dashed, paving the way for paralyzing teacher disappointment. Paradoxically, as Ms. Hernandez acknowledged the familial and affective frames and considered their impact on her students and on her role as teacher, she became better able to keep the curricular frame up front, working with her first-graders and sidestepping the cynicism that afflicted her colleagues.

The role of teacher as decision maker extends beyond the curricular decisions teachers make in the classroom. Teachers are no longer gatekeepers of the world of early childhood; the early childhood classroom is increasingly open to the outside world and, as Ms. Gregory reminds us in her discussion of her class in a homeless shelter, to situations and influences beyond the careful direction of the teacher. Teaching young children calls for careful classroom design, for spaces that will permit action and quiet reflection, solitude and group interaction, and especially for spaces in which multiple frames can coexist, in different configurations and at different times. The frames that predominate in the classroom inform and shape the many roles of early childhood teachers. When the curricular frame is centered, the early childhood teacher is performer: alternately storyteller, muse, mathematician, scientist, juggler (Sarason, 1999).

When the affective, familial, and cultural frames are centered, the teacher's role becomes lower keyed, less imbued with the verblike activity that *teaching* and *teacher* imply and that strategy-oriented workshops appeal to. Ms. Long's inability to respond authoritatively to the children who attended her bookstore readings was profoundly unsettling. Deprived of the context of school, her teacher identity was slowly eroded; what she referred to as "the teacher within" was gradually replaced by entertainer, whose institutional purpose was profit making. In her role as entertainer, Ms. Long permitted the curricular frame to drift toward the rear of the store. She no longer thought of what the children needed to hear, but found herself increasingly considering what might be pleasing to their ears.

Ms. Long's yearlong experience as a storyteller in a large retail bookstore may be read as a cautionary tale of the impact of the organizational setting on teaching and of what happens when educational experience serves the aim of corporate or personal profit. The recent proposal by New York City Schools Chancellor Joel Klein (Goodnough, 2002) to grant school superintendents a bonus of $40,000 if test scores significantly improve might be reconsidered in light of Ms. Long's experience.

Teaching, by nature, implies doing, whether setting out paints, teaching a lesson, leading an activity, or setting classroom limits. Teacher-as-listener and teacher-as-reflective-practitioner are less intuitively familiar to teachers who are accustomed to a tradition of doing and to the busyness that often permeates schools. Colleges and schools of education are in a unique position to educate teachers to be more thoughtful practitioners, who take the time to step back from the dominant classroom frame to consider other, invisible frames. Teacher education can help to prepare educators who are capable of interrupting the busyness that leaves no space or time for the real work of teaching or of leading the profession.

In the role of classroom director, early childhood teachers need to remain centered on a creative vision of their classrooms (Dewey, 1956). As they expand their practice to make room for familial and cultural frames, inevitable tensions arise between the frames of family and culture and that of curriculum (Johnson, 2002). Making room for cultural and linguistic variations within the framework of developmentally appropriate practice is a sensitive and complicated endeavor, as Ms. Santiago found in her work with preschool children and their families at a local Head Start center. In the case vignette reviewed, Ms. Santiago conceptualized her role as one of reflective practitioner and teacher researcher. She researched different perspectives and considered how she might make room for diverse cultural frames in her classroom. Ms. Santiago maintained a focus on the curricular frame, despite parental—specifically paternal—displeasure, especially regarding her nonsexist approach to educating young children.

Though the curricular frame is by far the most accessible to teachers, and the frame with which teachers appear most comfortable, this frame is easily threatened by the cynicism that can arise from disappointment in the work itself. Work with families is a large part of early childhood education practice; inability to establish solid working relationships with parents is commonly experienced by teachers as a personal failure and a deep professional disappointment. The danger to teachers is that, like Ms. Hernandez's colleagues, they may ultimately mirror the distancing moves of uninvolved parents, finally diminishing their personal and professional investment in the project of teaching. While schools of education can help teachers gain understanding of varied perspectives of parents, including those who maintain a cautious distance from school, schools of education need to also work with teacher education candidates to develop a strong sense of teacher identity that can sustain them through a career of challenging work assignments.

References

Bredekamp, S., and Copple, C., eds. (1997). *Developmentally Appropriate Practice in Early Childhood Programs*. Rev. ed. Washington, D.C.: NAEYC.

Bursztyn, A. (2002). "Conclusion: Reflections on Collective Identities." In C. Korn and A. Bursztyn, eds., *Rethinking Multicultural Education: Case Studies in Cultural Transition*. Westport, CT: Bergin & Garvey.

Clandinin, D. J., and Connelly, F. M. (1991). "Narrative and Story in Practice and Research." In D. A. Schön, ed., *The Reflective Turn: Case Studies in and on Educational Practice* (pp. 258–281). New York: Teachers College Press.

Connelly, F. M., and Clandinin, D. J. (1988). *Teachers as Curriculum Planners: Narratives of Experience*. New York: Teachers College Press.

Dewey, J. (1956). *The Child and the Curriculum/The School and Society*. Chicago: University of Chicago Press.

Elkind, D. (1981). *The Hurried Child: Growing up Too Fast Too Soon*. Reading, MA: Addison-Wesley Publishing.

Goodnough, A. (2002). "If Test Scores of Students Swell, So May Superintendents' Wallets." *New York Times*, September, 25, 2002, pp. A.1, B.4.

Goodson, I. (1992). *Studying Teachers' Lives*. New York: Teachers College Press.

Gopnik, A. (2002). "Bumping into Mr. Ravioli: A Theory of Busyness and Its Hero." *The New Yorker*, September 30, 2002, pp. 80–84.

Gregory, E., ed. (1997). *One Child, Many Worlds: Early Learning in Multicultural Communities*. New York: Teachers College Press.

Jalongo, M. R., and Isenberg, J. (1995). *Teachers' Stories: From Personal Narrative to Professional Insight*. San Francisco: Jossey-Bass.

Johnson, H. (2002). "An Ecological Perspective on Preparing Teachers for Multicultural Classrooms." In C. Korn and A. Bursztyn, eds., *Rethinking Multicultural Education: Case Studies in Cultural Transition*. Westport, CT.: Bergin & Garvey.

Keats, D. (1997). *Culture and the Child: A Guide for Professionals in Child Care and Development*. Chichester, UK: John Wiley.

Kincheloe, J. (1991). *Teachers as Researchers: Qualitative Inquiry as a Path to Empowerment*. London: Falmer Press.

Lincoln, Y., and Guba, E. (1985). *Naturalistic Inquiry*. Beverly Hills, CA: Sage Publications.

Lynch, E. W., and Hanson, M. J. (1992). *Developing Cross-cultural Competence: A Guide for Working with Young Children and Their Families*. Baltimore: Paul H. Brookes Publishing.

Postman, N. (1982). *The Disappearance of Childhood*. New York: Delacorte Press.

Sarason, S. (1999). *Teaching as a Performing Art*. New York: Teachers College Press.

Schön, D. (1983). *The Reflective Practitioner: How Professionals Think in Action*. New York: Basic Books.

Schön, D. (1987). *Educating the Reflective Practitioner: Toward a New Design for Teaching and Learning in the Professions*. San Francisco: Jossey-Bass.

Zigler, E., and Muenchow, S. (1992). *Head Start: The Inside Story of America's Most Successful Educational Experiment*. New York: Basic Books.

Chapter Nine

The Graduate Program in School Psychology: Imparting Responsive Practice

Florence Rubinson

As colleges and universities across the nation labor to create better programs to prepare teachers for the challenges of the twenty-first century, school psychologists continue to debate the role of school psychology in our nation's schools (Fagan and Wise, 2000). As the changing needs of schools and students spark educational reform throughout the United States, school psychologists must think about maintaining their relevance (Ross, Powell, and Elias, 2002). In response to the ever-changing educational climate, the Graduate Program in School Psychology at Brooklyn College recently embarked on efforts to revise its curriculum. Events certain to affect educational practice and the structure of schools in this century motivated this effort.

The first event was the effort by the New York State Education Department to increase standards for teacher certification. Although state credentialing in school psychology has not changed for the moment, standards are certain to increase for all related service professions. Movement on the state level to raise professional standards as well as changes proposed in the National Association of School Psychologists's standards for training and field placement programs (2000) sparked faculty conversations concerning our current curriculum and efforts to meet national and state standards as well as faculty's notions of best practice. Faculty contemplated whether these high standards of practice were possible in schools, considering the current educational climate.

The second event that spurred conversations around curriculum reform was the tragic shootings at Columbine High School in Colorado. Episodes of school violence sparked discussions among faculty and students and resulted in curricular changes and colloquia. A few years later the tragic events of September 11, 2001, occurred. In the midst of an event that overwhelmed many of our city's children and adults, school psychology students and faculty spent time in schools utilizing their crisis intervention skills to attend to the needs of schools and communities. Cumulative effects of this act of violence, combined with the stark horror of several school-violence incidents, led faculty to question the impact of mental health professionals in the schools.

Our students graduate as certified school psychologists trained to become valuable resources for children with learning and mental health needs. For example, our students possess the expertise to assist schools and families to deal successfully with many of the causes of violence. However, are school psychologists positioned in schools to use the skills they possess? If we assume the answer in most districts is no, we must first understand the factors that limit the utilization of a valuable resource in our schools. With this understanding, school psychologists can then position themselves in schools to do what really matters.

The Historical Dilemma

Throughout recent history, the dominant focus of school psychology has been the classifying of students with disabilities using standardized tests (Hutton, Dubes, and Muir, 1992; Lacayo, Sherwood, and Morris, 1981; Reschly and Wilson, 1995; Smith, 1984). Most school psychologists report that they spend over 50% of their time engaged in assessment activities (Curtis, et al. 1999). Since the early 1980s, an extensive literature in school psychology has advocated for broadening the school psychologist's role to include a wider range of services (Cheramie and Sutter, 1993; Gutkin and Conoley, 1990; Knoff and Curtis, 1996; Reschly, 1988; Reynolds, et al. 1984). School psychologists continue to express a desire to increase the depth and breadth of their role in schools, while teachers and administrators agree that school psychologists should increase both the variety and the quantity of functions they perform in schools (Kratochwill, Elliott, and Rotto, 1995; Reschly and Wilson, 1995). However, on this last point the literature is inconsistent, since other teachers and administrators appear satisfied with the school psychologists' involvement in assessment (Cheramie and Sutter, 1993; Hagemeier, et al. 1998). Since the advent of P.L. 94-142 in 1975 and later the Individuals with Disabilities Education Act of 1990 (IDEA), with its reauthorization in 1997, school psychology practice continues to emphasize psychoeducational evaluation, and school psychologists remain the gatekeepers of access to special education (Wilson and Reschly, 1996).

Growing controversy and dissatisfaction with psychoeducational assessment began soon after the passage of Public Law 94-142. Concerns focused on the significant numbers of children classified (or misclassified) as mildly learning disabled and the quality of special education services (Ysseldyke et al., 1983). Criticism was abundant (Galagan, 1985). The special education movement, which began with the best intentions, soon became subject to growing suspicions. On the positive side, youngsters previously placed in extremely restrictive educational environments or denied access to public education were provided with a free and appropriate public education and services in the least restrictive environment possible. Special education services, of which psychologists had become the gatekeepers as experts in normative assessment, soon became a maligned institution. Over the years, children were referred and tested with psychoeducational instruments and, based on these tests, overwhelmingly placed in special education (Esters, Ittenbach, and Han, 1997). In many districts the refer/test/place model was the only service delivery model available to school psychologists, and, more regrettably, it was the only way children in need of mental health and/or academic services could receive assistance. It is no wonder that as diminished outcomes for youngsters in special education became evident and criticism of special education abounded, school psychology received its share of criticism as well. The efficacy and morality of the special education segregation process and school psychology's role in promulgating the segregation cannot be defended. However, the utilization of school psychologists as simply psychometricians represented an underutilization of a potentially valuable resource, since school psychologists are typically trained to respond to a broad array of children's needs.

Early, as well as current, critiques of special education concerned overrepresentation of minority children. Although this issue was recognized soon after the passage of Public Law 94-142, it has never been resolved. In addition, a scarcity of minority psychologists has confronted the field from its beginning (Fagan, 1988). Fagan and Wise (2000) point to the persistent problem of a continued inability of the profession to recruit minority school psychologists in relation to the large numbers of minority children served. For example, a current survey revealed that school psychologists from ethnic minority groups represent only 5.5% of the entire profession (Curtis et al., 1999), while there is a significantly growing number of children of color and of those whose first language is not English.

The Current Dilemma

The reauthorization of IDEA in 1997 began a new era in school psychology practice. Instead of narrowly defined assessment functions, truly relevant processes could be designed by school psychologists, using both standardized instruments and nonstandardized tools. The role of the school psychologist has the potential to become even more multifaceted, with greater emphasis on prevention and intervention. The legislation provides a mandate for increased collaboration among professionals within the special and general education communities as well as with families. This frightens some school psychologists, since a very circumscribed method of evaluation has traditionally been our mandated reason for employment. The basis for this fear is to some extent realistic. Rather than reacting to these fears, school psychologists must reestablish their relevance by assuming major, varied, and expanded roles in the schools (Adelman and Taylor, 1998).

University trainers in school psychology must create programs that will be responsive to issues brought about by changes in societal and educational structures as well as advances in technology and research. By 2010 it is predicted that 38% of schoolchildren will be from minority backgrounds. People of color are already the majority in many urban areas (Lipman, 1998). School structure is undergoing unprecedented reform and must contend with major changes brought about by school-based management, the proliferation of integrated settings, and ever more demanding and prescriptive standards coupled with inadequate funding. While general education is overwhelmed with reform efforts seeking to increase standards, children with special learning needs are more than ever in general education classrooms, often with teachers unprepared to address their needs (Pugach and Johnson, 1995). Thus, educators, including school psychologists, are experiencing the confusion, resistance, and anxiety related to this period of unprecedented change in our nation. These negative emotions are heightened when one recalls the past educational reforms that did not produce much lasting effect.

Many of these issues are complex and somewhat conflictual, making them even more difficult to resolve. For example, standardized tests become more sophisticated each year as test developers tap increasingly sophisticated research and technology, yet normative testing continues to be severely criticized by some within school psychology and many outside the profession. Changing demographics in our nation's schools demand emphasis on cultural diversity and bilingualism, while, ironically, some districts eliminate bilingual education. One in four youngsters in this nation live in poverty, the single factor most strongly associated with academic failure, and these children experience higher rates of psychopathology (Tarnowski and Blechman, 1991). To cope with this situation, schools are often called upon to supply services not directly related to the acquisition of knowledge, yet the last decade has seen stricter adherence to academic focus and less support for ancillary services (Cobb, 1995).

Many conditions that school psychologists cannot control influence their practice. Yet we do need to be aware of these ever-changing contexts and must prepare for change as best we can. Assisting teachers in integrated classrooms, accurately and fairly addressing the needs of children from minority cultures, and preventing learning and emotional problems require a place in school psychology practice. It is abundantly clear that, in our current educational environment, we school psychologists must adapt to the changing needs of children, schools, and society if we are to remain valued professionals. Training for responsive practice is essential if school psychologists are to remain relevant in the changing context of American education.

What Matters in Schools?

Problem-Solving Paradigm and Its Relationship to Assessment

A broader role for school psychologists is linked fundamentally to the changing nature of assessment. Standardized testing administered by school psychologists should not be the first response to students' academic or behavioral difficulties. A test score, no matter how valid and reliable, provides little understanding of human behavior. Yet it is important to keep in mind that less reliance on standardized testing does not mean movement away from assessment but movement toward broader investigation (Canter, 1997). As school psychology practice evolves to include prevention, early intervention, teacher and parent consultation, and direct support for children, the character of assessment naturally changes to include a broader perspective. Assessment must expand beyond the scope of standardized tests to encompass alternative approaches for assessing learning and mental health problems within a broad ecological context. School psychologists must not simply become problem solvers and consultants to teachers, parents, and administrators, contributing an educational and psychological perspective to students' problems, but must also bring to their work an awareness of the economic, social, historical, and political contexts in which children reside.

The problem-solving paradigm is not new in school psychology; however, its recent representation is somewhat novel. As far back as the beginning of this century, Lightner Witmer's "psychological clinics" and G. Stanley Hall's "child study movement" were dedicated to ideographic problem solving designed to ascertain the causes of children's learning deficiencies. However, for Witmer and Hall the causes of behavior were presumed to reside solely within the child and required identification before appropriate educational treatment could be recommended (French, 1990). Although assessment utilized archival materials, interviews, observations, and tests, as it should today, diagnosis and intervention were solely child centered. A bit later, standardized tests were thought to bring objectivity to the problem-solving process by quantifying the extent of the problem (Fagan, 1995). Practitioners could apply so-called objective psychological knowledge in a disinterested way to benefit the client (Skrtic, 1995). Over the past few decades, there has been a shift to an ecological viewpoint, examining the impact of variables both internal and external to the student. As described by Henning-Stout (1994), responsive practice is designed to provide a much broader and a naturalistic perspective, which can lead to more relevant and direct intervention as well as effective prevention. Embedded in responsive practice is the notion that the learner and the environment compose a dynamic system, which develops within several specific contexts. As Henning-Stout asserts, if our inclination is to discover only deficient skill areas, we will focus on a narrow range of behaviors and be in danger of never developing a full understanding of the student. Although this evolution to an ecological approach is admirable, it does not go far enough when assisting children from diverse ethnic and language groups, those living in poverty, and gay and lesbian youth, as well as others. It is time to recognize the notion that human behavior, in this case the ability to learn, often does not neatly fit into a model adapted from the physical sciences, where human behavior is measured as if discrete and separate from the individual. Standardized testing will have its place within a much broader contextual framework. When standardized testing becomes only one aspect of a broad assessment, its impact on children will surely change.

As the professional organizations in school psychology encourage greater objectivity in practice, many trainers and practitioners adhere to a more subjective view of professional knowledge and practice, with less emphasis on prediction and control (Skrtic, 1995). Adequate assessment must assume the constructivist belief that human behavior cannot be separated from the social, cultural, and political venues in which it occurs

(Kincheloe, 1993). Responsive practice recognizes a myriad of contexts that impact the learner, some of which include child characteristics, home, family, school, classroom, community, race, and ethnicity, as well as the social and political climates. Each student brings to the classroom an idiosyncratic self, which is shaped by his or her unique experience. In order to effectively instruct the student, educators must attend to this experience. This more constructivist type of practice considers the multi-dimensional experience of both client and systems as essential in understanding assessment data. Henning-Stout (1994) tells the story of Jennifer, a third-grader responsible for the care of two younger siblings and how the youngster stayed up until midnight for her mother to return from work so she too could receive the maternal attention she required. As Jennifer's grades fell, the school's response was to evaluate for special education, without acknowledging that the life of this child was much broader and multidimensional. As advocates for children and as change agents, school psychologists must examine the political and social dimensions of their actions. Jennifer was born the eldest child in a poor family, most likely attended school with other poor and minority children taught by our least experienced teachers, and lived in a neighborhood with limited resources. Recognition of these facts might have come had evaluators permitted Jennifer and her mother to participate in the assessment in a meaningful way. Moreover, the eventual intervention might have been different.

The application of psychoeducational testing with ethnic and linguistic minority students, in particular, often evokes a vitriolic response from child advocates. The hostility directed toward intelligence tests is valid inasmuch as these instruments are used to sanction placement in settings in which educational opportunities are substandard. Standardized tests may or may not possess educational utility for some students; however, this issue is not nearly as important as improving the way in which we educate poor and ethnic minorities in this country. Whether we look at standardized tests or performance-based assessments, the fact remains that many poor, ethnic, and linguistic minority students are not achieving as well as majority students. The banning of intelligence tests in California, as a result of prolonged litigation, did little to improve the educational achievement of that state's minority population (Poggio, 1995). When standardized tests are utilized with caution and in conjunction with true ecological assessment, they become not instruments of evil but tools that can enhance understanding of a student. Ingraham (1999) supported this notion and argued that an ecological perspective is a more efficient and effective approach in working with diverse populations. Global scores for ethnic and linguistic minority students are generally not useful in understanding how a child learns and should never be used with children for whom the test has not been intended. The utilization of standardized instruments is advocated only when the test contributes to the educational success of the student (Lopez, 1997). Efforts need to go into establishment of quality education for all children, adjusted when necessary to fit the needs of individuals. Focus needs to be on equity of education for minorities and the poor, not on the utility of standardized tests (Hyman, 1993).

Training in school psychology must impart that the school psychologist's role is broader than administration of standardized instruments to place youngsters in special education categories. No longer is school psychology a field that seeks to create a successful learner by repairing some characteristic believed to lie solely within the child. Data from many naturalistic learning situations constitute authentic assessment (Skrtic, 1995). The field needs to move toward becoming more responsive to an ecological perspective, including the historical, social, cultural, and economic realities of children's lives, which involves assessment of students within a broad contextual framework in order to become more directly linked to intervention as well as to a greater emphasis on prevention.

Mental Health Interventions

Elimination of social and emotional learning is essential for effective learning and good mental health (Adelman and Taylor, 1998; Dryfoos, 1998; Flaherty, Weist, and Warner, 1996; Tyack, 1992). This requires attention when one considers the extent to which social-emotional concerns prevail among children. In a typical school of 1,000 students, there could be 180 to 200 youngsters requiring some type of psychological intervention (Doll, 1996). Data suggest that 15–22% of children and adolescents experience serious mental health problems that warrant treatment (Zill and Schoenborn, 1990). Other estimates of mental health problems found in children range from 11 to 26% (Brandenburg, Friedman, and Silver, 1990). Certainly, the increased environmental stressors experienced by many schoolchildren put them at risk more so than ever (Carlson, Paavola, and Talley, 1995; Power, et al. 1995).

The literature supports positive outcomes for mental health interventions in schools. This literature must not be ignored, since benefits are positive for students as well as schools in terms of better attendance and higher achievement and for society in terms of better employment opportunities and reduced costs for social services (Adelman and Taylor, 1998). Schools with psychologists on staff are certainly excellent places to house mental health services for children, particularly because many children with mental health problems do not typically access mental health clinics (Offord et al., 1987). Considering the increase in school violence and the prevalence of mental health problems in schools, school psychologists are in a position to assume a significant role as mental health providers to this country's youth. In this period of school reform combined with a public call to do something about increasing antisocial behavior in our schools, school psychologists can play a critical role in mental health service delivery. In order to deliver effective mental health services, school psychologists must be skilled at counseling, group work, consultation/collaboration, and communication. These traditional skills will be useful in service delivery to individuals and groups, but in order to assume a broader role, the school psychologist must be skilled in developing and maintaining effective mental health programming on the systemic level (Nastasi, 1998). A continuum of services including primary, secondary, and tertiary for moderate to severe mental health problems can be offered (Sandoval and Brock, 1996). Comprehensive program evaluation is necessary to address issues of acceptability, integrity, and effectiveness. This discussion suggests the need for preservice training to include counseling skills as well as a conceptual understanding and practical guidelines for effective mental health programming (Nastasi, 1998).

Effective mental health programming within a school, district, or municipality must go beyond planning and implementation issues to encompass understanding of the political and social aspects of school culture as well as the ability to counteract effects of many practices that undermine the education of some children. Socially mindful school psychologists can assist educators to examine their attitudes and practices that run counter to the mental health of children. As classrooms become more culturally and socially diverse, methods of instruction, assessment, and management must change to support a diverse student body. Without pedagogical flexibility, children who cannot conform to expectations of the dominant culture are often considered pathological. Overrepresentation of minority groups in special education has historically troubled most in the system, and a recent study confirmed that children's socioeconomic and ethnic status affects placement in special education classes (Frey, 2002). Academic segregation through tracking and special education placement often diminishes the self-worth of students. Curriculum constructed around the western European or American experience may seem irrelevant to students from varied cultures (Sleeter, et al. 1996). It is these toxic school environments that require intervention because they limit opportunities for some of our students. This discussion does not suggest that diverse students should not or cannot become competent and well-educated citizens. Rather, it insists that they must be educated in ways that respect their differences:

> It is time to look closely at the elements of our educational system, particularly those elements we consider progressive; time to see whether there is minority involvement and support, and if not, to ask why; time to reassess what we are doing in public schools and universities to include other voices, other experiences; time to seek the diversity of our educational movements that we talk about seeking in our classrooms. (Delpit, 1995, p. 20)

How Can School Psychologists Position Themselves in Schools to Do What Really Matters?

School psychologists can participate in the current reform movement only if their knowledge and skills significantly contribute to the educational success of all children. Training graduate students in relevant practice is a vital first step. If we continue to use standardized instruments, they must respect individual differences and be interpreted in ways that have educational relevance and direct linkage to instruction. In an attempt to provide assessments that inform and have greater utility for design and delivery of interventions, many tools are now available to the school psychologist and must be implemented along with standardized tests. Rigorous assessment must include the following elements: *curriculum-based assessments* that provide assessment within a curriculum, eliminating the need to translate assessment data into intervention techniques; *functional assessments* that furnish valuable information related to the motivations of behaviors; and *dynamic and flexible assessments* that allow ease of creating evaluations to match the nature of the students' problems. Collaboration with educators and families provides valuable contextual data necessary for relevant assessments of diverse learners. Qualitative interpretation of a variety of assessments is often more valuable than relying on quantitative data. Understanding the meaning as well as the function of behavior requires a contextual understanding of the child and his or her environment. The recommendations produced from assessment are in a sense the final and most important product of an assessment and what our consumers require in order to resolve problems. Thus, recommendations must be comprehensive, inform classroom instruction, and provide pragmatic interventions. It is important that school psychologists formulate recommendations in collaboration with teachers and family to ensure greater relevance. To do so, psychologists must have an understanding of instruction, the culture of the classroom, and the context of the family and community. Relevance to children, their families, and school staff is basic to the future of school psychology.

As the profession shifts away from the refer/test/place paradigm to more prevention-oriented and outcome-based paradigms, intervention becomes a more prominent activity of the school psychologist. School psychologists must convince school communities of the importance of mental health. The twenty-first century will require the practitioners in schools to become interventionists with regard to mental health problems. In a recent survey, a sample of school psychologists in California rated interventions for at-risk students and instructional interventions as the two most highly desirable topics for in-service training (Ingraham, 1999). Knowledge of effective intervention strategies is valuable but by no means all that is required to generate successful interventions. Understanding of behavior and a change in attitude in collaborative consultation is required to impart effective interventions. Knowing how to intervene effectively is certainly important. However, knowing how to involve educators and families in the intervention is essential for success.

Graduate programs must teach political astuteness and provide an awareness of organizational change and political influence. It is time for school psychologists to become politically well informed in order to successfully cope with issues of organization change and to create alliances with important individuals who wield both formal and informal power. These individuals make up the power structure in schools and range from teachers, who by virtue of their large numbers possess a good deal of power, to the formal power structure of district superintendents and state-level administrators.

Promote the profession to these individuals through our organizations. Inform them of accomplishments of school psychologists while maintaining high visibility for successful or nontraditional service delivery models (Franklin, 1995). Form alliances with legislators and office-holders to promote our cause. Do all that needs be done to ensure that power brokers understand the value of school psychology and what we are attempting to accomplish. Gravois (1998), in a symposium at the National Association of School Psychologists annual meeting, presented a model to influence policymakers through program evaluation. He suggested that to make policymakers more amendable to your agenda, come prepared with solid data and do what you can to make enhancements to them. For example, a written report on a project may help policymakers when it is time to procure funds for the next fiscal year.

What are school practitioners to do when schools are unwilling to restructure the role of the school psychologist? Professional associations can be a source of support and encouragement. State and national associations can provide nourishment for the struggle (Dawson, 1994). The field is not likely to change quickly; it is much more likely that change will occur in slow, plodding steps. Each responsively trained school psychologist, in small increments, will create an aggregate change from the bottom up. This may not be an encouraging vision, but it is nonetheless how change occurs within large institutions. Sarason's (1971) statement that school personnel often overestimate the degree to which a system restricts one's role, although referring to principals, may have relevance to all professionals wishing to change their role in schools. There is a potential for creating new roles and structures in schools (Rosenfield and Gravois, 1996). Not only should attempts be made at the building level to engage in relevant service delivery, but school psychologists who successfully engage in relevant practice must also inform and demonstrate what is possible (Nastasi, et al. 1998).

In order to promote much of what has been discussed in this chapter, the Graduate Program in School Psychology at Brooklyn College is not only undertaking preservice curriculum reform, but also conceptualizing an in-service program for practicing professionals. In our rapidly changing society, skills we acquire as graduate students become quickly obsolete. As the knowledge base in school psychology expands and societal needs become more acute, those trained in more decontextualized, traditional practice are at a disadvantage. It is our hope that continuing professional development will increase the knowledge base and skill level of practicing school psychologists.

Conclusion

Quality training that emphasizes responsive practice can provide school psychologists with an identity that will withstand challenges from others as well as allow the profession to guide best practice. The most innovative trainers and practitioners are currently moving from a primarily interventionist role to a more preventionist role, often involving systemic solutions. The notion of a proactive response at the very early stages of a problem or establishing systemic programs to inhibit potential problems is certainly superior to a reactive response (Hightower, Johnson, and Haffey, 1990; Will, 1988). Although the literature has endorsed such practice for the past 20 years, it is not commonplace in most school districts.

Given the changing demographics in our nation's schools, it seems likely that education can move forward only when the efficacy of a contextual emphasis becomes common practice. Contextual practice requires the school psychologist to reflect continually on school culture, community, and family and considers class structure and the marginalization of many groups. This type of practice will not be achieved through a national evaluation system or through the standards movement, as difficult as it is to be against higher standards. Recognizing and addressing the diversity that students bring to the learning experience and training all professionals at the preservice level to value this diversity may be the only way to achieve healthy reform. In the author's experience, the journey from training to responsive practice is difficult for many of our graduates, but not impossible. National and state organizations as well as a vast literature provide the blueprint for responsive practice. Utilization of these resources coupled with reflection on practice, as well as quality training, is critical to the professional reform process.

References

Adelman, H., and Taylor, L. (1998). "Mental Health in Schools: Moving Forward." *School Psychology Review*, 27, pp. 175–190.

Brandenburg, N. A., Friedman, R. M., and Silver, S. E. (1990). "The Epidemiology of Childhood Psychiatric Disorders: Prevalence Findings from Recent Studies." *Journal of the American Academy of Child and Adolescent Psychiatry*, 29, pp. 76–83.

Canter, A. S. (1997). "The Future of Intelligence Testing in the Schools." *School Psychology Review*, 26, pp. 255–261.

Carlson, C., Paavola, J., and Talley, R. (1995). "Historical, Current, and Future Models of Schools as Health Care Delivery Settings." *School Psychology Quarterly*, 10, pp. 184–202.

Cheramie, G. M., and Sutter, E. G. (1993). "Role Expansion in School Psychology: The Need for Primary and Secondary Prevention Services." *Psychology in the Schools*, 30, pp. 53–59.

Cobb, C. T. (1995). "Defining, Implementing, and Evaluating Education Outcomes." In A. Thomas and J. Grimes, eds., *Best Practices in School Psychology III* (pp. 325–336). Washington, D.C.: National Association of School Psychologists.

Curtis, M. J., Hunley, S. A., Walker, K. J., and Baker, A. C. (1999). "Demographic Characteristics and Professional Practices in School Psychology." *School Psychology Review*, 28, pp. 104–116.

Dawson, M. M. (1994). "Will the Real School Psychologist Please Stand Up: Is the Past a Prologue for the Future of School Psychology–School Reform Issues?" *School Psychology Review*, 23, pp. 601–603.

Delpit, L. (1995). *Other People's Children: Cultural Conflict in the Classroom*. New York: The New Press.

Doll, B. (1996). "Prevalence of Psychiatric Disorders in Children and Youth: An Agenda for Advocacy by School Psychology." *School Psychology Quarterly*, 11, pp. 20–47.

Dryfoos, J. G. (1998). *Safe Passage: Making It Through Adolescence in a Risky Society*. New York: Oxford University Press.

Esters, I. G., Ittenbach, R. F., and Han, K. (1997). "Today's IQ Tests: Are They Really Better than Their Historical Predecessors?" *School Psychology Review*, 26, pp. 211–223.

Fagan, T. K. (1988). "The Historical Improvement of the School Psychology Service Ratio: Implications for Future Employment." *School Psychology Review*, 17, pp. 447–457.

Fagan, T. K. (1995). "Trends in the History of School Psychology in the United States." In A. Thomas and J. Grimes, eds., *Best Practices in School Psychology III* (pp. 59–68). Washington, D.C.: National Association of School Psychologists.

Fagan, T. K., and Wise, P. S. (2000). *School Psychology: Past, Present, and Future*. Washington, D.C.: National Association of School Psychologists.

Flaherty, L. T., Weist, M. D., and Warner, B. S. (1996). "School-Based Mental Health Services in the United States: History, Current Models, and Needs." *Community Mental Health Journal*, 32, pp. 341–352.

Franklin, M. (1995). "Best Practice in Planning School Psychology Delivery Programs." In A. Thomas and J. Grimes, eds., *Best Practices in School Psychology III* (pp. 69–79). Washington, D.C.: National Association of School Psychologists.

French, J. L. (1990). "History of School Psychology." In T. B. Gutkin and C. R. Reynolds, eds., *The Handbook of School Psychology* (pp. 3–20). New York: John Wiley.

Frey, A. (2002). "Predictors of Placement Recommendations for Children with Behavioral or Emotional Disorders." *Behavioral Disorders*, 27, pp. 126–136.

Galagan, J. E. (1985). "Psychoeducational Testing: Turn Out the Lights, the Party's Over." *Exceptional Children*, 52, pp. 288–298.

Gravois, T. A. (1998). *Designing Evaluation to Improve Instructional Consultation in Schools*. Paper presented at the annual meeting of the National Association of School Psychologists, Orlando, FL.

Gutkin, T. B., and Conoley, J. C. (1990). "Reconceptualizing School Psychology from a Service Delivery Perspective: Implications for Practice, Training, and Research." *Journal of School Psycholgy*, 28, pp. 203–223.

Hagemeier, C., Bischoff, L., Jacobs, J., and Osmon, W. (1998). *Role Perceptions of the School Psychologist by School Personnel*. Paper presented at the annual meeting of the National Association of School Psychologists, Orlando, FL.

Henning-Stout, M. (1994). *Responsive Assessment: A New Way of Thinking about Learning*. San Francisco: Jossey-Bass.

Hightower, A. D., Johnson, D., and Haffey, W. G. (1990). "Best Practices in Adopting a Prevention Program." In A. Thomas and J. Grimes, eds., *Best Practices in School*

Psychology II (pp. 425–439). Washington, D.C.: National Association of School Psychologists.

Hutton, H. B., Dubes, R., and Muir, S. (1992). "Assessment Practices of School Psycholosists: Ten Years Later." *School Psychology Review*, 21, pp. 271–284.

Hyman, I. A. (1993). "A Response to a Letter from a Special Education Parent." *Education Week*, 56.

Ingraham, C. L. (1999). "Towards Systems Interventions in Multicultural Schools: Practitioners' Training Needs." *The School Psychologist*, 53, pp. 72–76.

Kratochwill, T. R., Elliott, S. N., and Rotto, P. C. (1995). "School-Based Behavioral Consultation." In A. Thomas and J. Grimes, eds., *Best Practices in School Psychology II* (pp. 519–538). Washington, D.C.: National Association of School Psychologists.

Kincheloe, J. L. (1993). *Toward a Critical Politics of Teacher Thinking*. Westport, CT: Bergin & Garvey.

Knoff, H. M., and Curtis, M. J. (1996). "Introduction to Mini-series: Organizational Change and School Reform: School Psychology at the Professional Crossroad." *School Psychology Review*, 25, pp. 406–408.

Lacayo, N., Sherwood, G., and Morris, J. (1981). "Daily Activities of School Psychologists: A National Survey." *Psychology in the Schools*, 18, pp. 184–190.

Lipman, P. (1998). *Race, Class, and Power in School Restructuring*. Albany: State University of New York Press.

Lopez, R. (1997). "The Practical Impact of Current Research and Issues in Intelligence Test Interpretation and Use for Multicultural Populations." *School Psychology Review*, 26, pp. 249–254.

Nastasi, B. K. (1998). "A Model for Mental Health Programming in Schools and Communities: Introduction to Mini-series." *School Psychology Review*, 27, pp. 165–174.

Natasi, B. K., Varjas, K., Bernstein, R., Pluymert, K. (1998). "Mental Health Programming and the Role of School Psychologists." *School Psychology Review*, 27, pp. 217–232.

National Association of School Psychologists. (2000). *Standards for School Psychology Training Programs and Field Placement Programs*. Washington, D.C.: National Association of School Psychologists.

Offord, D. R., Boyle, M. H., Szatmari, P., Rae-Grant, N. I., Links, P. S., Cadman, D. T., Byles, J. A., Crawford, J. W., Blum, H. M., Byrne, C., Thomas, H., and Woodward, C. A. (1987). "Ontario Child Health Study. II. Six-Month Prevalence of Disorder and Rates of Service Utilization." *Archives of General Psychiatry*, 44, pp. 832–836.

Poggio, J. (1995). *Expert Report of Dr. John Poggio*. Sacramento, CA: Public Advocates.

Power, T. J., DuPaul, G. J., Shapiro, E. S., and Parrish, J. M. (1995). "Pediatric School Psychology: The Emergence of a Subspecialty." *School Psychology Review*, 24, pp. 244–257.

Pugach, M. C., and Johnson, L. J. (1995). *Collaborative Practitioners, Collaborative Schools*. Denver, CO: Love Publishing.

Reschly, D. J. (1988). "Special Education Reform: School Psychology Revolution." *School Psychology Review*, 17, pp. 459–475.

Reschly, D. J., and Wilson, M. S. (1995). "School Psychology Practitioners and Faculty: 1986 to 1991–1992 Trends in Demographics, Roles, Satisfaction, and System Reform." *School Psychology Review*, 24, pp. 62–80.

Reynolds, C. R., Gutkin, T. B., Elliott, S. N., and Witt, J. C. (1984). *School Psychology: Essentials of Theory and Practice*. New York: John Wiley.

Rosenfield, S. A., and Gravois, T. A. (1996). *Instructional Consultation Teams: Collaborating for Change*. New York: Guilford Press.

Ross, M. R., Powell, S. R., and Elias, M. J. (2002). "New Roles for School Psychologists: Addressing the Social and Emotional Learning Needs of Students." *School Psychology Review*, 31, pp. 43–52.

Sarason, S. B. (1971). *The Culture of the School and the Problem of Change*. Boston: Allyn & Bacon.

Sandoval, J., and Brock, S. E. (1996). "The School Psychologist's Role in Suicide Prevention." *School Psychology Quarterly*, 11, pp. 169–185.

Skrtic, T. M., ed. (1995). *Disability and Democracy: Reconstructing (Special) Education for Postmodernity*. New York: Teachers College Press.

Sleeter, C. E., Gutierrez, W., New, C. A., and Takata, S. R. (1995). "Race and Education: In What Ways Does Race Affect the Educational Process?" In J. L. Kincheloe and S. R. Steinberg, eds., *Thirteen Questions: Reframing Education's Conversation* (pp. 181–190). New York: Peter Lang.

Smith, D. K. (1984). "Practicing School Psychologists: Their Characteristics, Activities, and Populations Served." *Professional Psychology, Research and Practice*, 15, pp. 798–810.

Tarnowski, K. J., and Blechman, E. A. (1991). "Disadvantaged Children and Families." *American Psychologist*, 20:4, pp. 338–339.

Tyack, D. B. (1992). "Health and Social Services in Public Schools: Historical Perspectives." *The Future of Children*, 2, pp. 19–31.

Will, M. (1988). "Educating Students with Learning Problems and the Changing Role of the School Psychologist." *School Psychology Review*, 17, pp. 476–478.

Wilson, M. S., and Reschly, D. J. (1996). "Assessment in School Psychology Training and Practice." *School Psychology Review*, 25, pp. 9–23.

Ysseldyke, J., Thurlow, M., Graden, J., Wesson, C., Algozzine, B., and Deno D. (1983). "Generalizations from Five Years of Research on Assessment and Decision Making." *Exceptional Educational Quarterly*, 4:1, pp. 75–93.

Zill, N., and Schoenborn, C. A. (1990). *Developmental, Learning and Emotional Problems: Health of Our Nation's Children, United States, 1988*. Advanced Data, no. 190, November 16, 1990. Washington, D.C.: National Center for Health Statistics.

Chapter Ten

The Changing Faces of Literacy

Carolina Mancuso

Literacy is sorcery.
—James Moffett

In the Sputnik era of my elementary school days, my passion for reading and writing stories nearly drowned in the ocean of space. The race to the moon, which precipitated a wave of curricular change weighted heavily toward math and science, was probably my first experience (recognized decades later) of the vagaries of educational policy and its potential to sweep students from the paths that give their schooldays a dose of *joie de vivre*. Science did intrigue me, but language gripped my heart and soul.

Literacy back then sprouted in the garden of Dick and Jane. Desperately in love with words and stories and the characters who used them to beckon me, I didn't really notice that Dick and Jane were part of the status quo of the 1950s and I was not. Despite the sting from teasing about the clothing my immigrant mother sewed for me or about my darker skin ("near-white," in the immigration categories), success in reading and writing kept me from feeling a total misfit in a community where my ethnicity and class hovered near the bottom rung of the social ladder.

Neither of my parents had extensive educations. It would be their children who escorted them into the foyers of institutions of higher learning. They were, however, self-educators and avid readers, and our house had its share of dark hardcover volumes on glassed-in shelves; multiple dialects and languages (burgeoning as my four siblings, far older, also brought their school languages home); many and varied musics on piano, trumpet, clarinet, and drums as well as radio and record player; and even a television when I was still a young child. All of these connected us to the outside world even as we held onto the cultural tenet that dictated "not calling attention to ourselves" in a less than welcoming society.

This heritage of literacy—even beyond my father's call to "learn the standard language"—propelled me to succeed in school. Though I suffered dutifully with math and yearned to be better at science, I always rejoiced in reading and writing, in whatever form. Unfortunately, that form was largely worksheets and basal readers. In the Catholic school I attended, we were neither encouraged nor allowed to write our own stories; book reports and essays were the *pieces du touts jours*. Those who read and wrote well basked as others envied them, seated as we were according to our averages. Those who read with mediocrity, often the big boys in the back of the room, daydreamed out the half-shaded windows and got away with little else under Sister's watchful eye and ready ruler. Those who struggled to read would disappear from our class each September, only to turn up in assemblies and in church sitting with other classes, earlier grades we had just survived. There was often a student or two among us kept back from the grade ahead.

It would be decades before I questioned what stood in the way of those students' reading and writing lives. At the time, pity forced up an occasional Hail Mary, but we were taught not to question, only to accept things as they were. In later years, that thinking, theory, and practice, which resulted in or contributed to student failure, would evoke for me the failure of teacher education in a period when "part to whole" teaching was the norm; language skills were isolated from each other and from students from the real world, enacting and foreshadowing a critical failure in democracy. What had become of Dewey's early twentieth century admonitions that students' interests and choices should lead the way (Dewey, 1909)?

The Revolution in English

Ironically, though reading and writing have occupied center stage from the little red schoolhouse on, notions about teaching them differently have been long in coming and often short in sticking. There is a history of revision in conceptions of literacy, with the historical context and use of the term itself steeped in irony. Willinsky (1990) notes that the word "literacy" dates back to the late nineteenth century, when the *Oxford English Dictionary* credited it to the *New England Journal of Education* in 1883 (p. 14). Interestingly, however, it is predated by the term "illiteracy," referring in the seventeenth century to a lack of awareness of letters and reading. In the fifteenth century, "literate" described someone who could read and write; earlier it was mostly linked with elite and religious orders

(p. 14). According to a traditional definition in use in the 1980s in Australia,

> literacy must include both spoken and written language, the latter involving both reading and writing. Literacy therefore is to be defined . . . as the mastery of spoken language and reading and writing. This is a much broader definition of literacy than is usually accepted. A more common definition would include only the written language—reading and writing. We wish to emphasize the more general nature of literacy and underline the continuities between spoken language and written forms of language. Literacy is directly involved with written language: common knowledge would have us believe so. However, we also expect literate people to speak fluently, to show mastery of the spoken language. Consequently, a definition of literacy should recognize this, particularly when studying the development of language skills. It is thus in this broad sense that we use the term "literacy." (Garton and Pratt, 1998, p. 1)

However, that "broad sense" at the time was on the verge of yet more change, following two decades of development in the teaching of English, precipitated in 1966 by the three-week-long landmark English Coalition Conference at Dartmouth in New Hampshire. With "Democracy through Language" and "What Is English?" as chosen themes, representatives from English-speaking countries all over the world shared educational policies, structures, pedagogy, and curricula. The proceedings led to the founding of the International Federation for the Teaching of English (IFTE), formally constituted in 1983 and still going strong. A seminal event, the Dartmouth Conference deeply transformed the study of English through all levels of instruction.

In the next twenty years, a pattern of various interlocking experiments emerged in literacy theory and practice, such as whole language; the Growth through English model and related developments in Language for Learning and Writing across the Curriculum; sociopsycholinguistic variations with schema theory; reader-response theory; and transformational reading, including innovations of the Writing Process Movements and the Bay Area Project, subsequently the highly successful National Writing Project (Willinsky, 1990 p. 5).

The momentum was propelled by decades of research and application in cognitive function in learning and in social and cultural theory (Vygotsky, 1978; Bakhtin, 1981; Bruner, 1986; among others). Reading as mere decoding gave way to the vital understanding of reading as a meaning-making activity. Language took its rightful place in education, as its four facets—listening, speaking, reading, and writing—were acknowledged as essential to learning in all disciplines. Writing, specifically, with a history of neglect outside of English classes, was highlighted in terms of "process" rather than "product" and encouraged across the curriculum. Process writing, with its freewrites and repeated drafting, began to displace the five-paragraph formula; writing to learn, or writing as discovery, dislodged the discouraging notion that "real" writers know what they want to say before they pick up a pen. Further, the invisible "I" burst through the myth of objectivism, gradually even in the academy; reader-response theory upset the New Criticism in schools and settled in for the long haul; and writing and/or reading workshops took classroom procedures by storm, offering previously unheard of opportunities to teach cooperation, encourage peer tutoring, and foster collaborative writing.

Notwithstanding the evolution of English teaching begun in 1966, alarming statistics about the lack of literacy proficiency in the United States were released in the mid-1980s by NAEP (the National Assessment of Educational Progress), triggering a widespread and long-term response in research and development of literacy programs. In his landmark book, Kozol (1985) described the crisis in shocking terms, citing statistics for illiteracy in various cultures in the United States and pointing out that 60 million adults, or one-third of the adult population, were functionally illiterate, with 25 million unable to read poison warnings, letters from their children's teachers, or the newspaper and 35 million others reading at levels precluding complete survival needs in the society (p. 4).

A new phase of transformation had begun. The seeds of postmodernism had sprouted on Dick and Jane's old turf, promising to redecorate every nook and cranny of the language and literacy classrooms. Nooks and crannies, in fact, surged as coveted decor for classrooms, where "learning centers" still retain their cachet.

At the same time, an additional thrust occurred through efforts to professionalize the field of teaching. Teachers' quests for agency in classrooms, schools, districts, and even larger domains of education, along with the proliferation of teacher research in the real world of K–12 classrooms, solidified a deep concern for democratic principles amid recognition of blatant inequities in American schools.

A third momentum, a hybrid in the garden of postmodernism, pushed literacy further into the limelight, where it currently finds itself. That impetus blossomed in the continuing recognition of not just one (literal reading and writing) but multiple literacies in the onslaught of technology and massive amounts of accessible information. Thus, researchers and practitioners have become concerned with ever-expanding categories of literacy necessary for survival and growth in an increasingly complex world: among them, visual, numeric, computer, cultural, emotional, and critical, as well as medical, economic, media, environmental, consumer, and global literacies. In a 1988 call for manuscripts, *Language Arts*, the journal of the Elementary section of the National Council of Teachers of English, questioned the direction of literacy teaching in a plea to consider the implications of plurality in school and beyond:

> "Literacy" is one of our most commonly used educational terms, implying, in its singular form, a uniformity in goals, expectations, and assumptions for all reading/writing and for all readers/writers. However, recent research shows us clearly that literacy is different in different social and cultural settings. In addition, we have learned that different types of discourse (e.g., literary, informative, persuasive) and even texts within a type of discourse (e.g., stories shaped differently) require different kinds of reading and writing. Finally, more and more we are viewing the reading and writing of print as part of an analogously larger "reading" and "writing" of visual media, technology, other people, society— ultimately one's world. (p. 537)

Literacy had thickened into a vine of massive complexity. But what had it actually come to mean? Whose literacy, and how to teach it? By the next decade, the explosion of language and literacy practices, as well as those yet to take seed, inspired the umbrella term "New Literacy" (Willinsky, 1990, p. 4). In providing a name for strategies developed since 1966, Willinsky notes that the most interesting aspect they share is the reconceptualization of literacy as altering classroom life and traditional roles of teacher and student. More than with just instructional techniques, the New Literacy is concerned with reinvigorated thinking about literacy (pp. 3–4), a trend building over many years. Understanding literacy as meaning making rather than simply decoding underscored each of these modalities, as did the implementation of students' choice of materials. This was accompanied by a strong effort to "*shift the control of literacy from the teacher to the student*" (author's italics) and to promote a "*social process with language that can from the very beginning extend the students' range of meaning and connection*" (author's italics) (p. 8).

This conception stands in opposition to definitions of literacy as performance at the levels required on standardized tests and use of classroom practice to prepare for such tasks. It defies a formulation of literacy as competence that students do or do not achieve at certain arbitrary levels. Like Dewey's (1909) example of drilling students for swimming without allowing them into the water, Willinsky uses the analogy of bike-riding as transportation rather than display of skill. All learning, including literacy, involves engaged intention and purpose to improve skill. With this concern foremost, the New Literacy displaces traditional methods of teaching reading and writing and "moves the locus of intention and purpose to the student as much as possible, rather than letting it reside in the teacher and the curriculum" (p. 8). Willinsky further elucidates the necessity of authentic and contextualized literacy events by noting that

> "literacy" is nothing in itself. Literacy is understood as the working of language in its written form, in reading a novel of a favorite author or writing a resignation letter, and that work takes place in a setting which contributed to its meaning, whether in a classroom or an office; the nature of that experience of literacy in the classroom is what constitutes an education. This . . . [reflects] the educational philosophy of John Dewey, who held that the classroom is poorly conceived as a preparation for life; it should be treated as the thing itself. (p. 9)

Change continues in the twenty-first century, as certification in master's level literacy programs (formerly known as reading programs) is under revision to address current needs. Previously, a single certificate served K–12 classroom reading teachers as well as schoolwide reading specialists. However, some states, such as New York, have instead initiated two certificates, one in birth–6 and the other in 5–12, encouraging greater specialization in each area.

On the early literacy level, many contrasting models of reading have surfaced, perhaps the best known being the "commonsense" (or transmission) model and the "sociolinguistic" (or transactional) model. As Weaver (1994) explains, the first is based on the assumption that reading and comprehension are achieved through moving from smaller to larger parts, using a bottom-up approach, from deep structure to surface, outside to inside, text to reader (p. 41).

The sociolinguistic/transactional model, while acknowledging that some part-to-whole methodology is involved in learning to read, arises from an assumption that for the most part, the reverse is enabled—whole to part, top down, surface to deep, inside to outside—by an essential transaction between reader, text, and social and situational context. That is, *making* meaning of a text requires *bringing* meaning to the text, i.e., activating schema theory (p. 42).

Weaver (1994) cautions against an erroneous dichotomy between these approaches as "phonics" and "whole language" (p. 50). She asserts that whole language has evolved more comprehensively, as a "philosophy of education, drawing upon many more lines of research and encompassing far more than just the development of reading, or even literacy" (p. 59). In this framework, educators aim less at the direct teaching of reading and more at "*guiding and supporting students in developing as independent readers, writers, and learners*" (author's italics) (p. 59).

Particularly at the early literacy level, many teachers have embraced a procedure of "balancing" the best of both models, helping children learn through individualized instruction, perhaps even participating in making the choices they need.

There are numerous other controversies regarding the teaching of literacy. Another highly debated topic falls in the realm of discourse theory and the implications of literacy's power and status in a society where the dominant culture often maintains exclusionary attitudes toward other discourses. Delpit (1995) and Gee (1996), who have deliberated in this area for some time, have found fertile ground in the context of New Literacy for reaffirming the valuing of discursive varieties among diverse students and making a linguistic spectrum part of the curriculum, while introducing students to multiple forms of representation, with no form honored over another. Understanding language variations can be very helpful to students whose mother tongue is a dialect of a standard language. To learn that there is a linguistic term, *code-switching*, for learning the speech of different discourses is a liberating concept. Being able to change codes as one changes social settings can empower students at any age. It is also useful to know that, according to Weinreich, a standard language is a dialect with an army and a navy behind it (Pinker, 1994).

Another group of students, English Language Learners (ELL), or "linguistically different youth," need access to develop both in their native languages and in English, requiring bilingual and biliteracy classes (Faltis and Wolfe, 1999). Similarly, learning disabled students may labor for years to learn the most basic aspects of literacy and to have their special needs addressed over various stages of their development. One such student, who referred to himself as a "creative learner" after years of being labeled learning disabled, describes the boost in his confidence in working with a tutor consistently for several years. In a book cowritten by the two, he gives an in-depth description of his struggle to use strategies that would enable him to read and write (Lee and Jackson, 1992).

Though much of literacy research and development has been focused primarily on young children, the new certificate in secondary-level teaching underscores the growing need for concentrated work with middle school and high school students. In urban schools, remedial students abound, with English classes often overtaken by literacy block classes for students reading far below grade level. And while literacy skills grow better in the soil of fascinating context, the need for student choice of materials, while necessary for young learners, is paramount for older ones.

It is here that the philosophical kernel of the New Literacy, best described in terms of a critical dimension of literacy, offers the promise of a pedagogy centered on preparing students with higher-order thinking skills for an active role in democracy. Critical literacy, with its multiple definitions, stems from critical pedagogy and is grounded primarily in Dewey's focus on creating a democratic society with a moral, humane, and activist citizenry, as well as in Freire's efforts to awaken the subordinate classes to realities of exploitation within the social structure, and Vygotsky's theories on meaning making in social contexts (Shor and Pari, 1999).

The theory and practice of critical literacy allows students to read (and write) more of the world (and the word) while focusing on the realities of their own and others' life circumstances as well as links to various aspects of popular youth culture. It extends their learning by encouraging them to analyze texts in terms of embedded relationships of power and domination. They learn to critique social constructions of knowledge; political and socioeconomic contexts; origins of worldviews; and possibilities for liberating and transforming society. Gradually, complex levels of thinking—including analysis, synthesis, application, and evaluation—take root.

Many teachers have found that applying critical literacy to popular youth culture taps a great potential for student engagement in secondary classrooms. Popular culture, viewed by critical theorists as a site of ideological struggle between subordinate and dominant groups, stresses its significance in awakening students to the role of literacy in their lives, beyond traditional academic forms (McLaren, 2003; Morrell, 2002).

Using popular media as critical literacy texts extends the power of schema theory by allowing students to access prior experience not only to link with school knowledge but also to validate interests not usually allowed in an educational setting. Making connections such as these increases comprehension and impels the creation of new knowledge. As students bring in literacy practices they use outside of school and explain facets of popular culture to teachers and peers, they may feel empowered to take ownership of and contribute to the curriculum, viewing themselves as participants and even coteachers. Thus, popular culture in the literacy classroom offers a powerful way to push through the "fourth wall" traditionally separating school from life.

One extended exploration of this approach, which focused on hip-hop music, culture, and mass media, was conducted over an eight-year period with urban adolescents (Morrell, 2002). The study found that many students, previously disengaged in school, were motivated through projects conducted in their communities, acting as authorities on subject matter from their own lives, connecting experiences with cultural texts, and becoming critical researchers and change agents as they constructed their own texts within the project (Morrell, 2002).

The many recastings of literacy theory and practice over the years has not precluded a major share of bickering and trampling in Dick and Jane's hallowed garden. There are occasional respites in the so-called "reading wars," but they are short-lived while various political factions jump on the bandwagon of one or another (often recycled) controversy, aided and abetted in no small part by the widespread venture of corporate publishing into educational media. The literacy "political football" has become as subject to manipulation by the media and the vagaries of power as any discipline (perhaps more so). In those policy-level debates, it unfortunately often appears that students remain the last to be considered. Years passed before a truce of sorts inspired the no-brainer that the needs of individual children should determine when, if, and how particular curricular components should be used.

Repackaged literacy programs are marketed continually. Government intervention has, most recently, framed the Bush administration's No Child Left Behind initiative. Most of the programs, whether commercially or educationally produced, offer variations on conflicting themes, both new and old. In the meantime, any conference of professional education organizations can reveal the "businessification" of teaching as the newest "Curricula R Us." A walk through the aisles of book displays at such a conference reveals one after another salvaged literacy program, some innovative enough to stay around and others as quickly dispensed with as the holiday season's newest toy.

The Changing Faces of Teachers and Teacher Education

Teachers who reflect criteria of race, ethnicity, class, gender, and age have settled into the education classroom in part to address the need for large numbers of new teachers in the face of waves of retirement. Whatever their ages, they will need to look back at their own language-learning experiences to grasp the succession of events in the second half of the twentieth century and situate themselves in the context of its literacy curricula.

In these tumultuous times of both criticism and praise for teacher education, many prospective and developing teachers in large numbers still choose the rigor of university programs over short-term technical programs. In this society, teaching, especially in urban settings, is commonly denigrated and considered a second-hand career ("do," don't "teach"); teachers receive sympathy over their low salaries and their having to work with difficult students in poor conditions. However, attitudes toward teaching may have improved slightly, perhaps because of the need for a new crop of teachers—a kind of supply-and-demand respectability. Teacher candidates frequently reveal similar responses from families, friends, and previous coworkers.

From years of working with pre- and in-service teachers, I have found their courage and commitment highly inspiring in light of such disregard. Entering one of the most critical—and criticized—professions, some bring with them attitudes steeped in the culture. In addition, just about anyone schooled here can declare himself or herself an expert in advising educators. Students of teaching, themselves, may view specific solutions with certainty without having any in-depth knowledge about the problems. Such solutions sometimes arrive in the trappings of technical rationality, which keeps teacher students searching for help with formulae, lesson plans, and the minutiae of classroom life. On the other hand, many also envision teaching in terms of relationship, community, creativity, and improvisation as well as rigorous knowledge, information, and insight.

Studies in foundations of literacy can guide candidates toward examining the roots of literacy as well as the implications of particular perspectives and how they have helped or hindered what is really at stake: the best preparation for youth in the most equitable way in unwieldy and contentious school systems. Reviewing historical, political, sociological, psychological, and philosophical underpinnings of language learning exposes many inequities in North American schooling.

Both preservice and in-service teachers need to review or acquaint themselves with the varieties and components of literacy programs past and present. Many aspects of content, instruction, and assessment must be addressed both in the university classroom and in students' placements in the schools. Students of teaching must seek creative ways to use content knowledge in curriculum. They must learn about the growth and development of children who hail from diverse backgrounds. They must examine their own practices, reflecting on how children react to lessons and to classroom procedures. It is essential that teacher students become familiar and stay current with research in the field. In addition, they must make a firm commitment to engage regularly in research in order to advance awareness of teacher knowledge.

To combat the lingering effect of technical rationality on the teaching profession, teacher educators must maintain focus on praxis, linking theory with practice. Exploring a broad and deep view of educational practices over time can yield critical insights into how learning takes place, how teaching styles and choices affect learning, and how we can best serve students who have diverse needs. Further, as professionalization of the field increases, there is a greater call for teachers to be agents of change. Agency, beginning in classrooms, can extend its impact into other classrooms, schools, broader educational domains, and the community. It also opens the door to policymaking, a potential that teacher candidates must explore. Not relegated only to adults and professionals, the understanding and practice of agency in the world is what schoolchildren need to learn as well, observing their teachers as models.

Teachers model for students in other ways as well, e.g., by demonstrating meaning making, engaging in inquiry with them, enacting holistic teaching and learning—linking mind, body, and spirit—and constructing learning communities where all are respected, multiple viewpoints are valued, and everyone actively teaches and learns. At the same time, teacher educators must also engage in these practices, maintain an attitude of openness toward teacher students and their needs, and create an atmosphere in which students feel free to ask about the decisions of our practices.

Education students need to experience as much as possible the basic practices they are and will be using with their own students. To understand the role of listening, speaking, reading, and writing in all learning, they must experience those roles as well as discuss and reflect on how learning is enhanced by them. Reading and writing workshops, process writing, reflective practice, meta-cognitive exercises, and other such activities must be part of classroom procedures in the university.

One last aspect of teacher preparation is perhaps among the most important: the quest for self-awareness and understanding, an ongoing search for self-actualization. Outside the pedagogically rooted concerns of teaching, perhaps the single most momentous endeavor a teacher should take on is knowing—and remodeling—the self in preparation for enduring development. To understand the self, teachers must reflect on and examine the assumptions and beliefs that guide their perceptions and actions. Only by becoming conscious of attitudes that inform them can they determine which attitudes they should cultivate and which they should change. They must examine the roles of teachers and learners in the context of current beliefs and controversies regarding the place of literacy in all instruction, particularly in urban schools among children with diverse abilities and varied cultural, educational, and economic backgrounds. A vital part of teaching is the endeavor to help students toward self-knowledge as well, encouraging them to create and maintain community in the classroom and to situate themselves in the society.

The Changing Faces of Students

The faces of students in urban classrooms today have not so much changed as finally been recognized. They reflect the changing demographics under way for many years in the United States but often ignored until trouble comes our way. Many students live in neighborhoods and attend schools where inequity is rampant. Both schools and homes reflect the great poverty that ravages our cities. Yet, day after day, devoted teachers enter those decaying school buildings and give voice to their heart's desire, the growth of children entrusted to their care. They bring the hope and joy that Freire (1998) speaks of in creating a "pedagogical space," a space shared between teacher and student (p. 69). Teacher educators, he says, must address the indispensable qualities for a teaching practice, qualities actually created by the practice itself:

> a generous loving heart, respect for others, tolerance, humility, a joyful disposition, love of life, openness to what is new, a disposition to welcome change, perseverance in the struggle, a refusal of determinism, a spirit of hope, and openness to justice. (p. 108)

To see the face of literacy blossom on each student must be the source of joy and hope.

References

Bakhtin, M. M. (1981). *The Dialogic Imagination: Four Essays*. Trans. C. Emerson and M. Holquist (eds.). Austin: University of Texas Press.

Bruner, J. (1986). *Actual Minds, Possible Worlds*. Cambridge, MA: Harvard University Press.

Delpit, L. (1995). *Other People's Children: Cultural Conflict in the Classroom*. New York: The New Press.

Dewey, J. (1909). *Moral Principles in Education*. 1975. Carbondale: Southern Illinois University Press.

Faltis, C. J., and Wolfe, P. M., eds. (1999). *So Much to Say: Adolescents, Bilingualism, and ESL in the Secondary School*. New York: Teachers College.

Freire, P. (1998). *Pedagogy of Freedom: Ethics, Democracy, and Civic Courage*. Trans. P. Clarke. Lanham, MD: Rowman & Littlefield.

Garton, A., and Pratt, C. (1998). *Learning to Be Literate: The Development of Spoken and Written Language.* 2nd ed. Oxford: Blackwell.

Gee, J. P. (1996). *Social Linguistics and Literacies: Ideology in Discourses.* 2nd ed. London: Taylor & Francis.

Kozol, J. (1985). *Illiterate America.* New York: Doubleday.

Lee, C., and Jackson, R. (1992). *Faking It: A Look into the Mind of a Creative Learner.* Portsmouth, NH: Boynton/Cook.

McLaren, Peter. (2003). *Life in Schools: An Introduction to Critical Pedagogy in the Foundations of Education.* 4th ed. Boston: Allyn & Bacon.

Morrell, E. (2002). "Toward a critical pedagogy of popular culture: Literacy development among urban youth." *Journal of Adolescent & Adult Literacy,* 46(1), pp. 72-7.

Pinker, S. (1994). *The Language Instinct: How the Mind Creates Language.* New York: William Morrow.

Shor, I., and Pari, C., eds. (1999). *Critical Literacy in Action: Writing Words, Changing Worlds.* Portsmouth, NH: Boynton/Cook.

Vygotsky, L. S. (1978). *Mind in Society: The Development of Higher Psychological Processes.* Cambridge, MA: Harvard University Press.

Weaver, C. (1994). *Reading Process and Practice: From Socio-psycholinguistics to Whole Language.* Portsmouth, NH: Heinemann.

Willinsky, J. (1990). *The New Literacy: Redefining Reading and Writing in the Schools.* New York: Routledge.

Chapter Eleven

Toward a Counterhegemonic Multicultural Grammar

Lee Elliott Fleischer

Introduction: Writing into Power

Recently, I acquired a book on grammar entitled *The Grammar Book: An ESL/EFL Teacher's Guid*e (Celce-Murcia and Larsen-Freeman, 1999). As I combed through the pages, I took notice of the subtitles: "A Pedagogical Grammar, Not a Linguistic Grammar," "Which Grammar," "The Form of Words," "Discourse Communities," and so on. My interest was more and more piqued as I began reading the content of these pages. Imagine, I thought (reflecting on my lifelong struggle to write well), me, intrigued by a book on grammar—a subject I hated!

It's not that I don't want to "write well," be understood, and communicate my thoughts effectively. Throughout my childhood school years and later in my academic career, first as a teacher and finally as a professor of education, I have been plagued and stigmatized by the fear of writing. But, then, upon reading portions of *The Grammar Book*, it hit me: There are no absolute rules of grammar! Everything is relative to the discursive communities one inhabits in the cross fire of cultures, ideologies, and power relations we experience consciously or not so consciously as we write, speak, and hear words.

In his *Pedagogy of the Oppressed*, Paulo Freire (1970) speaks of becoming humanized as an act of cognition, knowing the word, naming (reading and writing) the word, and identifying and overthrowing the word of the oppressor as people collaborate as coinvestigators to explore and name new words based on love, trust, respect, humility, and mutual care. In approaching those who are oppressed, those not having a voice or words that speak to their histories, identities, and cultures, Freire examines illiterate people and the effects of their illiteracy, and how they identify with words that maintain their status as objects of others' words, silenced and submerged in a culture of oppression, immobilized from speaking or emerging from their silence with words that could name, rewrite, and rebuild their worlds. As a consequence, Freire advises liberating educators to record "apparently unimportant items," including expressions, vocabulary, and syntax of the oppressed. He reminds us to suspend our need to "correct" their "incorrect pronunciation but, rather, appreciate the way they construct their thought" (p. 111). Citing Joao Guimaraes Rosa, a Brazilian novelist, the idea is to "capture authentically not the pronunciation or the grammatical corruptions of the people, but their syntax, the very structure of their thought" (p. 111).

In today's schools of education, as well as in public schools across the United States and elsewhere, the emphasis is clearly not on capturing students' "structure of thought." Rather, fueled by the immense push for standardization in the last century, and more recently in the last twenty years, the dogma has been to emphasize standardized or "correct" writing and reading skills (Delpit, 1986), predetermined by "correct" rules of grammar, aligned to predetermined standardized curricula packages, standardized examinations, and state and national programs and goals. There have been many others, including chapter contributors in this book, who have argued that this agenda of standardization is linked, both directly and indirectly, to a multiglobal corporate capitalism, to racism, to sexism, and to other macro forces of power (Apple, 1999; Chomsky, 2000; Kincheloe, 2002).[1]

What critics of the new world corporate order of schooling have not completely realized, with their emphasis on scientific positivism and technical deskilling of teachers, is the additional need to expose, more theoretically and practically, the subtle links and connections among people in public schools (the micro context) and in the intervening terrain (the meso context), or mixed spaces, who are in constant or potential emergence and battle with the "powers that be" (the macro context). The first two contexts lie squarely in the arena of discursive communities that can and do exist among students and teachers in the classrooms.

A plethora of ethnographic studies in the last twenty-five years (Apple, 1983; Everhart, 1983; Giroux, 1981; King, 1983; MacLeod, 1987; Willis, 1977) have already validated the existence of resistant discursive cultures—partially submerged, partially emerging—as potential bases of power for a supportive popular base of resistance knowledge and action in schools. A discussion in this chapter will further advance how this base of power may be an adequate point of reference to ignite effective and informed resistance against being engulfed by the present-day hegemony of corporate schooling, teacher practices, and teacher education programs. Attention must be paid to how the webs and alignments of corporate- and state-

mandated curricula and testing get caught up within the discursive formations of doubt, deconstruction, and holding patterns of fear and immobi-
lization. For example, few people writing about schools and professional
practices have identified those "in-between" layers or levels of schooling;
they have not linked people and the state/corporate/media representations
that penetrate both layers or levels of battle, the macro and micro. Within
these discourses, the power of the macro context gets enmeshed and filtered through the powerless. By investigating how the powerless resist the
powerful, we may glimpse metonymies and, on a more microscopic level,
signifiers outlining the anatomies of these invasions. Resistance, including
the experience of struggle one feels when attempting to write "correctly,"
provides a venue of discourse for students and teachers to react and eventually reshape the subtle and not so subtle forms of standardization. Is not
one of the most oppressive experiences of schooling the inability to write
what one feels, and the feeling of humiliation and eventual stigma one
acquires when repeatedly corrected?

Through my experiences teaching graduate and undergraduate education courses with the assistance of an interactive software program, I
am able to observe the written discussions of my students. In these online
discussions, I have noticed that my students respond to each other concerning complex subject matter with a (previously unexhibited) clarity
and quick-flowing ease, albeit with run-on and grammatically flawed
sentences.

For example, one student,[2] in an open letter to her classmates, reveals
her world of struggle, indecision, rivalry, and oppression:

> Many of you feel as if you don't know what you are doing. And I'm sure you have
> watched enough [of the TV show] *Felicity* to know that you are not the only one
> living in the scenario of that twenty-something finishing college and not know-
> ing what to do. You ask yourself every day what you should be smarter/thin-
> ner/more successful than the person next to you by now. What we forget is, that
> the person next to us is likely more miserable than you are. You think that every
> one else is excelling faster than you, they have all the luck, that they are confident
> and headed in the right direction. You worry that you made the wrong choices,
> that you will end up broke or enslaved by an unrewarding job, but mostly you
> worry about what the world will think of you.

In another written dialogue, this same student, who left the corporate
world to become a teacher, cites her views on "oppression." She writes:

> Not to be cynical, but I think this problem (oppression) will never end. People are
> complex, and we can never hope to change the face of human nature entirely.
> Oppression is mainly learned, but not entirely, some people just get satisfaction

out of making others feel inferior, some people are insecure and need to push down others to make themselves feel better. We see this in people's nature as young as toddlers in preschool, we wish to assert our power, we wish to feel important, we must feed our ego, even if it is at others' expense. As we get older we take this to a new level, we get satisfaction out of holding people beneath us, at believing that people of a lower socioeconomic are worth less, because as long as there is someone beneath us, we aren't doing so bad after all.

She continues to relate her story as a middle manager:

> Can you honestly say that every time you were in a position of power (I was a corporate manager for quite a while) you encouraged and helped those beneath you to exceed you, or be your equal, I can't. I was one of the most leanient [*sic*] and trouble-making managers my company has ever seen, always fighting for the rights of my workers, teaching them to be self-sufficient, and how to get ahead, but in my heart I know I couldn't let some get too far, or else where would I be? In a perfect world my company would encourage people to work in teams and get involved, but in most (like mine) managers have to be scared that if they are out-performed, then that employee may take their job. So how do you change a culture as a whole?

In these examples, and countless others, I was struck by my student's ability to create vivid and moving images of the oppression and pain of ordinary people. Through online written dialogue, unhampered by the pressures of conventional rules of grammar and standardized English, my students overcame their writing inhibitions and revealed an eloquence and "power" not seen in their other written assignments.

While I have written about the terrain of culture wars and student resistance relative to how kids form their identities within dominant identity formations experienced in freshman core courses at a city university (Fleischer, 2000), I was, and still am, a product of schooling in a larger urban public school system and society. Living in such a world, similar images to that of the student cited above are experienced as I talk, think, and write. As I observe the online discourses of my preservice and fledgling teachers, these written images have left their fingerprints of power on me.

Reflecting on my early days of public schooling, the fears associated with my inability to write obeying grammatical or "correct" rules constantly return to me. I am left with an uncanny sense of aloneness. I recall my high school and undergraduate days, when I wrote paper after paper and never felt that my ideas counted. I remember all too painfully the way my teachers and professors would flood my words with their red ink, making grammatical corrections, deletions, and lines and loops carrying one clause over and under another. In time, I became ashamed and afraid to write; I was unable to overcome the debilitating influence of teachers who would not see beyond the grammar to appreciate my creative thoughts and ideas.

Today, as an educator, I see how the same destructive experiences have gripped my students, and even my professorial colleagues. In my most recent post at a suburban technical college, my colleagues continually express apprehension about writing. These professors are at ease with charts, tables, and bulleted lists, but chronically procrastinate when they are faced with the challenge to write about their scholarly interests. Pressure from the college administration to upgrade the school image with more scholarship and research authored by faculty has left many of them demoralized. In depressed whispers, these professors confess their inability to write and publish.

As Freire (1970) maintains, "the word is more than just an instrument which makes dialogue possible; accordingly, we must seek out its constitutive elements" (p. 87). Once we begin to map out or theorize the "constitutive elements" that make up the word, the syntax of sentences, as Freire explains, we may begin to understand how people think in words and use grammatical structures and, conversely, how words and grammatical structures do thinking for them. By doing this, links between the dominant standardized system of writing and the writing of the people may be explored in terms of the variegated discursive formations that interpose and filter words. Through the constitutive elements making up words, syntax, and grammar, we may further explore how speaking, listening, and writing acts are linked to power relations that subjugate, stigmatize, and sway us from imagining how words and their structures may project images that portray a more equal, just, and democratic society and world. To accomplish this, we would have to confront how words dash our hopes, raise our fears, and stop us from expressing and writing in such power arrangements. To begin a discourse or discursive community that begins to filter words that speak to us and carry our stories of justice, freedom, and democracy will require the construction of a counterhegemonic and multicultural grammar discourse that will make our own voices correspond to emerging discursive formations within and against the existent and dominant hegemonic discursive formations of grammar.

Hegemonic Discursive Formations of Grammar

This chapter offers a critical perspective on the literacy of grammar, with a poststructural orientation toward reconceptualizing writing as more than the "good" or "correct" form of English. Rather, grammar is conceptualized as occurring on a field of battle, whereby the form becomes the locus of struggle for expression and communication between dominant and dominated groups of classes. This means that problems of verb agreements, or correct word uses, do not have a once-and-for-all correct application. Grammar and the way we write, think, and form syntax must respond to the contexts of politics, ideological controls of language, and power. When ideology and language are understood to form a discourse, the possibilities of breaking out or reconstructing an alternate discursive formation in replacement of or adjacent to the existing discursive formation will become real, as opposed to imaginary.

In schools, lessons are taught and reinforced in a way that erases the notion that class exists in American society and thus in turn reinforces the idea that the individual is essentially free. This, however, hides the battle of grammar from groups that are marginalized, unequal, or struggling to obtain the American dream. The ideology offered to all is that success equals going to school and working hard; we learn not to question dominant practices, including the "proper" form of writing. In recent years, the ideology of working hard, going to school, and writing the "good" or "correct" form of English has been further complicated by the fact that minority groups themselves advocate the acquisition and learning of standard English (Delpit, 1986) and believe that speaking and writing "correctly" are the way to go to gain acceptance. Minority group members have already bought the message of the American dream without examining the filter of their words.

These filters—or, as critical and poststructuralist theorists speak of them, subject-positions, signifiers, and chains—illustrate how words and their meanings are formed within constitutive structures. Just recall how we sometimes talk to think rather than think before talking; or how we think as we are talking when in close proximity to an attentive listener to our words; or how we think better on our feet, literally walking (Cranny-Francis, 1995), as our bodies begin to talk and think without the constraints of sitting in a chair positioned in a classroom. Recall how we often forget something upon leaving a room, yet know the feeling that communicates images that we have forgotten something but don't know its content; or, as we speak, we forget what we were about to say, but then, after a lapse of time, hearing another's voice or words, suddenly the forgotten thought and its content shoot through us in our speech. How often have we experienced these slips, slides, and stoppages of speech? Do they not reveal how tentative, slippery, and rather arbitrary the archaeology of grammatical knowledge can be? Are they the constitutive structures of grammar that Freire points to?

It may be argued then that it is in the subject-position of being an individual, filtered by dominant discursive forms, that the American school ideology and politics, through which minority-group individuals seek to read, speak, and write, are grounded. And, as is the central argument of this chapter, it is in and through such subject-positions and their accompanying discursive forms that a particular filter operates to install or anchor us into a construct linking the many to the macro entities of power, which gives them the illusion that they are independent and free citizens. Recall how the student described earlier, who left her manager position to become a teacher, thinks of herself in relation to others; how she is constantly aligning her self-image to what others will think; how the culture in the workplace creates fear. Her thoughts reveal a defeated person, an "I" on display, in fierce competition with others and always fearful of those with the power to render her inferior or take away what is hers.

The "I"—or, the ideological expression of the self-sufficient, essentialized subject-position we all occupy at the moment of writing or speaking—is a subject-position that subtly communicates a dichotomous message experienced when we write the next word, the next sentence, the next clause, and the next paragraph. The images cross into us constantly: Is this word use "correct"? Will my audience comprehend my words because they share with me a similar or the same discursive community that either aligns or breaks with the hegemonic and dominant discourse community of writing? As Kincheloe and Steinberg (1997, p. 38) ask, why do words when strung together always have to be constructed in a linear way between subjects and predicates? One may further ask: How is the insistence of the linear stringing of words according to their classifications as noun, verb, or object related to the dominant syntax of standardized schooling that students and teachers must undergo in the act of writing? And still further, what happens when cross-group or subgroup resistances to the standardized or dominant language supplant the rules of grammar or transform them by "code-switching"? And how are these changes of language, with new rules set by an emerging and resistant discursive group, maintained as rigorous yet in communicatively complex ways?

Often ignored in texts of grammar and pedagogy is that the "correct" form of grammar and syntax derives its norms and parts of speech from several groups, and that it fights for its legitimacy across many spaces. As poststructuralist and literacy critics have known for many decades and have offered analytical concepts for critiquing such formations through "heteroglossia" or "hybrid" subject-positions (Belsey, 1980; Brooks, 1984; Eagleton, 1991; Hawkes, 1977; Pecheux, 1982; Trudgill, 1974; Williams, 1977), signifiers and their associated chains interlocking dominant discursive formations form cultural blocs that emerge as competing discursive formations within and across dialects and discourses (Bove, 1990; Brooks, 1984; Bredin, 1984a; Coward and Ellis, 1977; Davis and Schleifer, 1989; Grossberg, 1994; Hall, 1997; Heath, 1977; hooks, 1997; Pecheux, 1982; Willeman, 1979), or implant new accents and words that produce "in-between" or "third spaces" that are both productive and legitimate ways to establish new and "real" definitions of what is correct or legitimate syntax and grammar in the fight for hegemony (Bhabha, 1989; Rutherford, 1989; Volosinov, 1973). By hegemony, and taking an insight from Gramsci (1971), we mean that these subject-positions and discourses are themselves constantly in movement, in negotiation, and shifting indecisively between the established group norms determining what constitutes the "proper" or "correct" grammar and the disestablished group norms resistant to the dominant group's variations and subnorms on the same theme.

It is on the battlefield of discourse that some norms emerge as the "correct" forms of English and grammar while others become marginalized as "slang," "street talk," and "incorrect." Others remain "out there," circulating, waiting to be named. It is on this same battlefield, however, within the established norms already defining "correct" or "proper," that accommodations and negotiations become possible as new norms and new grammatical constructions emerge. Thus, the Ebonics debate and other controversies currently relevant to bilingual education in America have emerged and continue to be an unsettled and politically sensitive terrain in school curricula and teacher education preparation programs in schools of education. For example, while many have supported the notion of English Only or English First programs, there is, at the same time, the obsessive need to overcome and eliminate the "bi" part of the program, thereby eliminating the indigenous language of the two-language program.[3]

This chapter will show how the "standard" or "correct" form of writing occurs within not one but several discursive formations, in which a battle for dominance is fought about who defines which norms are "correct" or what is legitimate syntax and grammar. In revealing these struggles, we can describe a new experience that offers students and teachers other subject-positions and signifiers that break open the hegemony of the individual or unified subject-position of the "I" and the "correct" form of grammar. By breaking out of these subject-positions, perhaps constructing new subject-positions and signifiers, this chapter hopes to liberate individuals' fears of writing by showing prospective writers (and those who will teach writing and related subjects in which "correct" writing is so powerful as sanctioned by standardized curricula) how, as they write about the fear of writing, they may simultaneously release and take notice of new and alternate subject-positions that exist, metonymically, within or alongside the dominant subject-positions of the "correct" or "proper" forms of grammar.

The Metonymies of Words and Grammar

In the beginning of her book *In My Mother's House: A Daughter's Story*, Kim Chernin describes her frustration in conveying her story with words. The experience of feeling multiple subject-positions, existing side by side in words, in a metonymic relationship to each other, is constructed. Chernin illustrates this construction in the following passage:

> When I first began to work on *In My Mother's House* I recorded my mother telling her stories, then transcribed the tapes. The words (transcribed) missed her, they suffered from her absence. It was hard to believe that they were the same words. That made me aware how many things, when spoken (and written) are *words beside words*. The silence that strings them together, the excited rush that carries them out, the brightness of their delivery, the slower measure by which they pause, falter, hesitate, almost stop, suddenly veer off and get going again, with a sharp exhalation of breath, a small dark hand waving the specter away. Spoken words carry, and make use of the incidental. . . . To get my mother to sound like my mother on a (written) page, I had to find a voice that was as richly textured as her presence, a voice that could, being a paper voice, rely entirely on itself. . . . It had to sound like my mother literally sounded; it had to have something of her in it but something of me as well, of the way I had listened to her voice throughout our life together. (1994, p. x)

Chernin's desire to find a link between her words and the words of her mother sets up a problem of metonymy: locating the parts—words—in the whole and how the parts together make up meanings of the whole and beyond. If she had read poststructural literary criticisms, she would be looking for chains of words or signifiers making up meanings that exceed the whole, such as desire. Like Chernin's desire, we begin to create new spaces for norm construction and locate new chains of word meanings leading to submerged groups who have been silenced, within and alongside their words and the dominant forms of grammar, words alongside words, clauses alongside clauses, sentences alongside sentences.

Moreover, we may discover how words are strung together alongside other sentence constructions and their strings of words, some intersecting each other as slurs of words become articulate and as other words bring to light new meanings overlaying old meanings and silences.

Approaching words and grammar this way, educators and educators of teachers may come together within a chorus of grammatical constructions, instead of producing alienating rules superimposed on those who are different or from diverse communities and cultures, histories, identities, and life struggles. Such an approach would provide many with the confidence necessary to enable them to guess or imagine how writing can occur without taking on the "proper" and linear grammatical subjects, objects, nouns, or verbs or, further, on a deeper level, locating the unified subject-positions of the individualized "I"'s or self-mages of a person, grounded in the ideology, language, and politics of American education and its teacher education programs.

The dominant or established grammar, or the literature on the so-called universal structures constituting oneself as a solitary "I," whether "innate" or "deep," has been long espoused by the early Chomsky (Mehta, 1971) since the 1960s.[4] Freire, however, goes further than Chomsky in humanizing the world through dialogue, through the power of the word that we speak and write. Freire argues that dialogue is instrumental in raising a critical consciousness in getting to know the world as an object of cognition, and further, to know its constitutive elements, so we may all become knowledge makers in the process.

Getting beyond the essentialized, acontextualized, or noncontradictory structures of grammar, Freire suggests a constructive program of teaching and curriculum making that probes deeper into the ideological layers that make up grammar and syntax. He urges us to do the same as long as we reflect and act: two components making up the dialogical relationship between teacher and taught and between human and world. It is unclear, however, what Freire means by reflection occurring within action. He has not located the degrees of consciousness from unconscious reflection that occurs within talk and writing. Recall the everyday examples provided earlier of the unconscious thought process we all experience when we suddenly remember what we momentarily forgot, or the feeling we get once we leave a room that something (albeit what?) is missing. I argue that the same feelings may be revealed or be a part of the images of reflection that flash through us as we are writing grammatically correct or different (not incorrect) sentences. If Freire had employed Lacanian linguistics (Lacan, 1977) or sociolinguistics (Bryson, 1990; Hodge and Kress, 1988; Trudgill, 1974) or postcolonial translation theory (Auer, 1999; Bassnett and Trivedi, 1999) or historical (Smith, 1998) and political linguistic theory (Laclau and Mouffe, 1985; Dentith, 1994) or feminist Marxist theory (Ebert, 1992; Hennessey, 1993; McRobbie, 1994), he might have noted that the unconscious is constituted like a language or that one signifier slides over and refers to another signifier; as some signifiers become sutured in the place we receive or make meaning or accept as correct grammatical rules or constructions, while other places—signifiers sliding over signifiers—reveal meanings and images as being in constant movement, revealing places to construct alternate rules or positions where a clause may be offset or how words (subjects, verbs, objects of sentences) may be located nonsequentially. Thus, in some groups, verbs are deleted or overstressed, as in "Her doing this" or "He be doing this," the former omitting the verb, the latter taking an additional verb for emphasis, as recorded by Gee (1990) and by Perry and Delpit (1997) in the Ebonics debate.

The implication of this poststructural grammatical perspective is realized when "correct" grammar is transformed into various and different grammars, thereby creating new maps, diagrams, and rules in our teacher education courses and programs. With these new constructions, we may create as well as detect at what points the intrusion of one grammar or language is imposed on another. In this detective work, we may also inadvertently create moments of correction or of violation and violence as defined democratically by those from a variety of cultures, identities, histories, classes, genders, sexual preferences, and powers. As I have learned in my years as a professor at a large urban city university, it should be sufficient to say that a multiplicity of grammars coexist alongside one another, just as there are as many groups constituting a social whole of a university or a school of education. That grammars overinscribe one another (at times one grammar becoming dominant) places writers and the writing act into the subject-position of politics and hegemony making up the battle lines between "correct" writers and marginalized and "incorrect" writers, the latter stigmatized by writing as taught in monological, not dialogical, practices composing the corpus of grammatical knowledge taught in schools of education and in public schools.

While we have already mentioned several examples illustrating how grammar becomes essentialized, emptied of sub- and countergroup resistance and resonance, this chapter also argues that a third terrain exists in writing that permits other subject-positions to enter and exist in the discourse of writing. These subject-positions (and the signifiers they are constituted from) act as relays or links between the surface and deep structures proposed by Chomsky, which may become occupied and experienced by the writer as passing glimpses or metonymic images representing links between the deep or macro institutions (of the economy, state, and media), the intermediate or in-between institutions (of cultural, political, and discursive groups as experienced in school communities), and the micro level of self as a signifier (see my "Conclusion" section below) that is obscured by the formal and "correct" surface levels and structures of grammar. As one writes subjects/nouns/objects/verbs in "correct" grammar, then, one may also experience other discursive formations creeping in, allowing for different sequences of subjects/nouns/objects/verbs, positing the writer as a circulating subject-position and signifier of words. That is to say, he or she writes with sliding signifiers, resisting becoming anchored in dominant representations of correctness.

"When I Come Back to Reality"

An example of writing from two subject-positions at the same time comes from a journal of one of my undergraduate education students. As a recent Russian immigrant, she wrote about the New York City mayoral race and the lack of discussion on the subject of education. She expressed her displeasure about the candidates' failure to debate about the drastic school budget cuts. She commented:

> The vow of candidates to rehabilitate the New York City public schools remains no hope when I come back to reality. I am extremely disappointed by receiving a letter in this school year that informs parents about severe cuts in funding for education.

At first, I began to correct her paragraph. I inserted the plural noun in the first line to read, "The vows by candidates," prompting the change of the singular "remains" to "remain," and then transformed the last clause by inserting "hopeless" in lieu of "no hope when I come back to reality." Thus, the original first sentence was changed to: "The vows by candidates to rehabilitate New York City public schools remain hopeless."

Having one of the metonymic experiences previously described, I later began to question my corrections: Was I being intrusive and censoring what the student was trying to communicate? What about the student's assertion "when I come back to reality"? Was she thinking/writing her thoughts as structures of grammatical authority of the dominant discursive community that did not make it possible to communicate her desires or represent them adequately? Who was I to "correct" her words? Why shouldn't her authentic words, and through them, her feelings, and the "reality" of her immigrant or outsider status, be heard and counted in a dominant discursive community?

Her placement of the words "when I come back to reality" does indeed suggest a reality in relation to the dominated discursive community: that of the immigrant and outsider. We hear in her words a mingling of several communities of discourse. In accepting her words "as is," and suspending our knee-jerk reaction to correct them, we can assist her, and so many others like her, by forming a basis for a multicultural, counterhegemonic grammar.

Toward a Multicultural Counterhegemonic Grammar

In resisting or avoiding the self-conscious or embarrassed subject-positions inherent in the fear of writing, correction, and ridicule, we can write authentically and begin simultaneously to see a metonym complex—edges and links to other subject-positions. This metonym complex decenters the unified subject, permitting the many selves of the writer to represent and be represented by their multicultural group affiliations and relations (class, ethnic, gender, sexual preference, etc.) as well as to begin to form their own counterhegemonic group norms of writing, without fearing the immediate trigger responses of others' corrections; or, proactively, to prepare themselves for a counterattack by the dominant discourse and its reactions in support of "correct" grammar.

Once writing is conceptualized as a multicultural and counterhegemonic enterprise, words may be written within various subject-positions and circulate in various discursive formations. Those who write about power and the fear of writing may simultaneously begin to release other positions of the hegemonic subject/object/noun/verb sequences, and begin to carve out or create spaces that, in effect, create relays that transform subject-positions of school authority or the "correct" grammar. Thus, the act of writing may become decentered from its original position of ownership by the individual, re-creating new structures,[5] signifiers, and subject-positions linked to complexes of chains interlocking the construction of group norms and their speaking and writing communities into a counterhegemonic multicultural grammar of writing.

A Framework for a Counterhegemonic Multicultural Grammar of Writing

The notion of discursive formations (Pecheux, 1982) provides a basis for reconceptualizing or rediagramming various subdiscursive structures, shifting dominated group norms within and against the dominant norms to be included in the "correct" forms of grammar and writing. This shift may be diagrammed through the concept of discursive formations and their chains of circulating signifiers and subject-positions, thus allowing one to see the extent to which one group represents itself as having the "correct" grammar or writing form within its discourse without falling necessarily into the grips of a deficit or deviant model. Instead, the "proper" English and grammar, with its "proper" nouns, verbs, subjects, and objects, operate on a playing field of difference. That is to say, the dominant group's hegemony operates no longer from the norm(s) or subject-positions that marginalize competing groups. Rather, communication is grounded on a multiple set of norms, breaking with the dualism of correct versus incorrect. In this way, links to the subnorms of each speaking group can be traced as relays that may or may not contribute to the whole or to the solidarity or communication of people in terms of their differences of discourses as opposed to their own distinctive dialects. So, for example, when one says, "I understand," relying on the syntax of the dominant discursive community of "correct" English, one may simultaneously be a member of a sub- or countercommunity group of discourse and rephrase "I understand" as "I got your bag."

Probing deeper, however, what those in the dominant group fail to examine is how language as a discourse is framed within chains of Western thinking and associated meanings, grounded in a unified or individualized subject-position that separates thinking from writing and placing the latter in a superior hierarchical position. Thus, in both instances—"I understand" and "I got your bag"—the "I" is similarly positioned to respond to other speakers hierarchically rather than with mutual respect and trust, as a coconstructor of the rules of grammar. In a subsequent paper, I will argue that the notion of discursive formations breaks with and penetrates these Western chains of unified subject-positions that dichotomize I and We, communication and chaos, thinking and writing, seeing and saying, knowledge and ignorance, truth and falsity, power and impotence, standard writing and slang. I will also describe how discursive formations, as an analytic, peel open many layers acting as intervening terrain, permitting one to further examine how hegemonic and ideological struggles are fought out in language on the level of circulating signifiers, producing resistant forms of grammar and its norms or reproducing established grammar and its respective norms.

Such an approach offers a more penetrating view of power as a field, comprising various discursive structures, such as subject-forms and subject-positions within which group norms are constructed and, in this process, how such constructions provide glimpses or traces revealing metonymic chains of signifiers already circulating in discourse as images and flashes shooting through our writing consciousnesses of discourse.[6] These metonymic chains point to the fixing, unfixing, and transfixing of subject-positions or images, positing correct grammatical places for nouns, verbs, subjects, and objects and providing the basis for a counter-hegemonic and multicultural grammar. Within this field of grammatical construction, we can see the shifting and sliding of power as it constructs, deconstructs, coconstructs, and reconstructs writing and simultaneously positions writers to question, guess, and ultimately (by cooperating with each other) imagine a change in the structures of writing so that they express their desires, diverse cultures, histories, politics, group norms, and identities over and against the established norms and groups and their chains of signifiers. Hence, the norms determining the "correct" stringing together of words may now be reconsidered and changed.

Conclusion:
The Subject/Writer as a Traveling Signifier of Power

Thus, the subject/writer may be reconceptualized as more than writing into power but as simultaneously traveling as a signifier of power, thereby linking both subjects of writing: the subject of the dominant and standard English and the subject of the sub-, counter-, or dominated discursive group community. In between these two memberships, language is constituted as a chained as well as a circulating discursive form. By using the notion of norms, a determination can be made in tracing which groups affect the movement of signifiers—nouns, subjects, verbs, and objects—within a field of power, as speaking/writing group members penetrate the individualistic subject-positions of individual speaker/writer. This understanding of language may provide a new basis for redefining grammar and reopen language as a composite of many interests, each seeking to retake the field of language in a counterhegemonic power struggle.

Additional arguments may then be mounted to show how the teaching of writing, speaking, and reading can be a counterhegemonic enterprise. We can thus reshape education and its written forms so that they are no longer an extension of the wealthy and privileged, linked to corporate and capitalist systems, and can thereby provide spaces for critical and creative citizenship (Apple, 1999; Giroux, 2000; Kincheloe, 2002).

The main objectives of this paper have been to show that when we open spaces for a counterhegemonic multicultural grammar, three things happen: (1) we see the extent to which our fears are individualized and identified into subject-positions of complicity in a given dominant discursive formation, (2) in another discursive formation, we see the extent to which our writing creates spaces or new subject-positions and group norms for critical reflection, counterdiscourse, and dis-identification, and (3) we see the extent to which our writing is occurring within a series or chains of subject-positions and signifiers, constituting the writer as the intersection of groups and institutions of school and society in the construction of group norms, as opposed to individualized identities or subject-positions.[7]

In this poststructural context of understanding the signifier as a subject or, on other levels, the signifier as a subject circulating within a web of discursive formations constituting grammar, a call is made for further theorizing and research and an understanding that further extends Freire and Macedo's (1987) argument, namely: To read the word is to read the world and, therefore, to rewrite and change the world. This bold formulation of literacy needs to be accompanied by a critical theory of discourse that allows one to read the world and read the word through a complex of discursive structures, revealing the extent to which the world and the word are linked and crossed by the chains and circulating signifiers and subject-positions and their norms of the dominant and the dominated groups, and how these structures affect one to make, to write into, and finally, to take power.

We need to address the contradiction in schools of education that claim to practice multiculturalism and critical literacy, yet only reproduce existing hierarchical power relations. Many of these schools of education do not provide a critical theory of discourse or the critical complex education called for by Joe Kincheloe in the first chapter of this book. They do not provide a basis for preparing emerging or practicing teachers to help students overcome their writing inhibitions and fears; nor do they help teachers construct more just, democratic, equitable, and multicultural forms of teacher education programs and schools of education.

Notes

1. Some of Giroux's works (1991, 1992, 1994) seemed, for a period of time in the early 1990s, to point to research "between borders" on this subject. His research since that period goes no further to explain in a rigorous way the constitutive structures of language and power.

2. I have received permission and wish to acknowledge Tara Dennis, a student in my graduate foundation class, for the use of her words to illustrate the condition of struggle that students, like herself, are experiencing today.

3. I am indebted to my former colleague at Brooklyn College, Dr. Luis Reyes, presently a visiting professor at Hunter College, for daily emails, newspaper articles, and Web site downloads on this subject. For example, "The Power of Words: What Parents Mean by 'Bilingual Education,'" http://www.publicagenda.org/specials/thankful/thankful7.htm (accessed November 8, 2002), reveals how one-sided the campaign for English Only campaigns are under the banner of bilingual education when sponsored by ultraconservative, Washington, D.C.– and New York City–based pressure groups.

4. Chomsky was one of the first language theorists to discuss "universal," "generative," and "deep" structures of grammar that underlie the surface structures—subjects, verbs, nouns, and objects—that constitute syntactical constructions. For example, Chomsky's "John is easy to please," as opposed to "John is eager to please," locates a shifting or sliding of the proper noun (John) from the passive object to the active subject. While Chomsky locates two levels coexisting between surface and deep structures of grammar and their corresponding movement, he ignores, on other deeper and wider levels, the impact of and relations between culture, politics, and proactive groups resisting and redefining grammar in speaking communities, revising definitions of the "correct" positioning of subjects, nouns, verbs, and objects. For example, young people use the Afrocentric contractions and deletions of the absent *be*, as in "You be doing this?" or, omitting the verb altogether, "You doing this?"

5. As Deleuze (1988) said, locating the signifiers or words as "rhizomes" means to identify new forms of syntax and grammar (new "statements," "diagrams," or "maps," linking the micro to the macro, parts of the whole) and, metonymically, how the parts of the whole exceed the whole, revealing how nonhierarchicalized relations of power may "assemble" between hierarchical relations of power. Or, as Pecheux (1982) identified, modifying Althusser's (1971) analytic, on those planes between ideological apparatus institutions (i.e., schools, media, marketplace, civic associations) and the repressive institutions of society (the state, courts, military, and police) lie discursive formations and their respective signifying/signifier activities, acting on the plane of grammar and syntax, substituting, deleting, and re-creating new syntax and grammar within a given era and society.

6. Giddens (1977) has referred to this type of consciousness as "dis-consciousness."

7. I am struck by how Gilles Deleuze understands the subject not as a unitary or hierarchicalized discursive structure but, rather, as an assemblage, a complex criss-crossing of flows or points—in Deleuze's words, a subject without organs, a "groupuscule" or "rhizome." This is very different from understanding nouns, subjects, verbs, etc., in one linear sequence. As Deleuze and Guatarri (1983) explain, the rhizome is an image of interlocking and circulating webs of discourses in which a "rupture" occurs "each time . . . segmentary lines [hierarchical paths of power] explode into a line of flight, but the line of flight is part of the rhizome." Hence, to both authors, "[t]hese lines never cease to refer to one another, which is why dualism or dichotomy can never be assumed, even in the rudimentary form of good and bad. A rupture is made, a line of flight is traced, yet there is always the risk of finding along it organizations that restratify everything, formations that restore power to a [hierarchical] signifier, attributions that reconstitute an [individualized] subject"(p. 18).

References

Althusser, L. (1971). *Lenin and Philosophy and Other Essays*. New York: Monthly Review Press.

Apple, M. (1999). *Power, Meaning, and Identity: Essays in Critical Educational Studies*. New York: Peter Lang.

Apple, M. and Weiss, L. (1983). *Ideology and the Politics of Schooling*. Philadelphia, PA: Temple University Press.

Auer, P. (1999). *Code-Switching in Conversation: Language, Interaction, and Identity*. New York: Routledge.

Bassnett, S., and Trivedi, H., eds. (1999). *Post-Colonial Translation*. New York: Routledge.

Belsey, C. (1980). *Critical Practice*. London: Methuen Books.

Bhabha, H. (1989). "The Third Space." In J. Rutherford, ed., *Identity: Community, Culture, and Difference* (pp. 207–221). London: Lawrence and Wishart.

Bove, P. (1990). "Discourse." In F. Lentricchia and T. McLaughlin, eds., *Critical Terms for Literary Study* (pp. 55–65). Chicago: University of Chicago Press.

Bredin, H. (1984a). "Metonymy." *Poetics Today*, 5, pp. 45–58.

Bredin, H. (1984b). "Roman Jakobson on Metaphor and Metonymy." *Philosophy and Literature*, 8:1, pp. 89–103.

Brooks, P. (1984). "Narrative Desire." *Style*, 18:3, pp. 313–327.

Bryson, B. (1990). *The Mother Tongue: English and How It Got That Way*. New York: William Morrow.

Celce-Murcia, M., and Larsen-Freeman, D. (1999). *The Grammar Book: An ESL/EFL Teacher's Course*. 2nd ed. Boston: Heinle & Heinle.

Chernin, K. (1994). *In My Mother's House: A Daughter's Story*. New York: HarperPerennial.

Chomsky, N. (2000). *Chomsky on Miseducation*. Lanham, MD: Rowman & Littlefield.

Coward, R., and Ellis, J. (1977). *Language and Materialism: Developments in Semiology and the Theory of the Subject*. Boston and London: Routledge and Paul.

Cranny-Francis, A. (1995). *The Body in the Text*. Victoria, Australia: Melbourne University Press.

Davis, R. C., and Schleifer, R., eds. (1989). *Contemporary Literary Criticism: Literary and Cultural Studies*. New York: Longman Press.

Deleuze, G., and Guattari, F. (1983). "Rhizome." In *On the Line* (pp. 1–63). New York: Semiotext(e).

Delpit, L. (1986). "Skills and Other Dilemmas of a Progressive Black Educator." *Harvard Educational Review*, 56:4, pp. 379–385.

Dentith, S. (1994). *Bakhtinian Thought*. New York: Routledge.

Eagleton, T. (1991). *Ideology: An Introduction*. New York and London: Verso.

Ebert, T. (1992). "Ludic Feminism, the Body, Performance and Labor: Bringing Materialism into feminist Cultural Studies." *Cultural Critique*, winter, pp. 1–35.

Everhart, R. (1983). "Classroom Management, Student Opposition, and the Labor Process." In M. Apple and L. Weiss, eds., *Ideology and Practice in Schooling*. Philadelphia: Temple University Press.

Fleischer, L. (2002). "Writing about the Fear of Power, Writing into Power." *Educational Change: A Journal of Role Analysis and Institutional Change*.

Freire, P. (1970). *Pedagogy of the Oppressed*. Trans. Myra Bergman Ramos. New York: Continuum Press, 2000.

Freire, P., and Macedo, D. (1987). *Literacy: Reading the Word and the World*. South Hadley, MA: Bergin & Garvey.

Gee, J. P. (1990). *Social Linguistics and Literacies: Ideology in Discourses*. London: Taylor & Francis.

Giddens, A. (1977). *Studies in Social and Political Theory*. New York: Basic Books.

Giles D. (1988), *Foucault*. Trans. D. Hand. Minneapolis: University of Minnesota Press.

Giroux, H. (1981). "Hegemony, Resistance, and the Paradox of Educational Reform." *Interchange*, 12:2–3, pp. 3–26.

Giroux, H. (1991), "Modernism, Postmodernism, and Feminism" in Henry Giroux, ed., *Post-Modernism, Feminism, and Cultural Politics*. Albany, New York: State University of New York Press.

Giroux, H. (1992), *Border Crossings: Cultural Workers and the Politics of Education*. New York: Routledge.

Giroux, H. (2000). *Impure Acts: The Practical Politics of Cultural Studies*. New York: Routledge.

Giroux, H. and McLaren, P. (1994), *Between Borders: Pedagogy and the Politics of Cultural Studies*. New York: Routledge.

Gramsci, A. (1971). *Selections from the Prison Notebooks*. New York: International Publishers.

Grossberg, L. (1992). *We Gotta Get Out of This Place: Popular Conservatism and Postmodern Culture*. New York: Routledge.

Hall, S. (1997). "The Goldsmith Lectures." In *Race: The Floating Signifier*. Northampton, MA: Media Education Foundation.

Hawkes, T. (1977). *Structuralism and Semiotics*. Berkeley and Los Angeles: University of California Press.

Heath, S. (1977). "Notes on Suture." *Screen*, 18:4, pp. 47–76.

Hennessy, R. (1993). *Materialist Feminism and the Politics of Discourse*. New York: Routledge.

Hodge, R., and Kress, G. (1988). *Social Semiotics*. Ithaca, NY: Cornell University Press.

hooks, b. (1997). *Cultural Criticism and Transformation*. VHS tape. Northampton, MA: Media Educational Foundation.

Kincheloe, J. L. (2002). *The Sign of the Burger: McDonald's and the Culture of Power*. Philadelphia: Temple University Press.

Kincheloe, J. L., and Steinberg, S. R. (1997). *Changing Multiculturalism*. Bristol, PA: Open University Press.

King, N. R. (1983). "Play in the Workplace." In M. Apple and L. Weis, eds., *Ideology and Practice in Schooling* (pp. 262–280). Philadelphia: Temple University Press.

Lacan, J. (1977). *The Four Fundamental Concepts of Psycho-Analysis*. Trans. Alain Sheridan. London: Hogarth Press.

Laclau, E. and Mouffe, C. (1985). *Hegemony and Socialist Strategy: Towards a Radical Democratic Politics*. New York: Verso.

MacLeod, J. (1987). *Ain't No Makin' It: Leveled Aspirations in a Low Income Neighborhood*. Boulder, CO: Westview Press.

McRobbie, A. (1994). *Post-Modernism and Popular Culture*. New York: Routledge.

Mehta, V. (1971). *John Is Easy to Please: Encounters with the Written and Spoken Word*. New York: Farrar, Straus, and Giroux.

Pecheux, M. (1982). *Language, Semantics, and Ideology*. Trans. Harbans Nagpal. New York: St. Martin's Press.

Perry, T., and Delpit, L., eds. (1998). *The Real Ebonics Debate: Power, Language, and the Education of African-American Children*. Boston: Beacon Press.

Smith, A. M. (1998). *Laclau and Mouffe: The Radical Democratic Imaginary*. New York: Routledge.

Rutherford, J. (1990). "A Place Called Home: Identity and Cultural Politics of Difference." In J. Rutherford (ed.), *Politics of Identity, Community, Culture, and Difference*. London, England: Lawrence and Wishart.

Trudgill, P. (1974). *Sociolinguistics: An Introduction*. Harmondsworth, UK: Penguin.

Willeman, P. (1978). "Notes on Subjectivity." *Screen*, 19:1, pp. 41–69.

Williams, R. (1977). *Marxism and Literature*. Oxford, UK: Oxford University Press.

Willis, P. (1977). *Learning to Labor: How Working Class Kids Get Working Class Jobs*. New York: Columbia University Press.

Volosinov, V. N. (1973). *Marxism and the Philosophy of Language*. Trans. L. Matejka and I. R. Titunik. Cambridge, MA: Harvard University Press.

Chapter Twelve

Students' Perceptions of Schools of Education

Koshi Dhingra

A school of education positions itself squarely in the midst of a variety of relations and collaborations that are part of the fabric of school, society, and the university. Some of these relations and collaborations involve the liberal arts and science departments, the Board of Education, school settings, informal learning centers such as museums and zoos, to say nothing of the city at large, with all the ongoing social issues being reported on the news and experienced by teachers and their students. How does the school of education define itself, positioned as it is amid these complex relationships? What roles are played by the school of education in the university, in schools, and in the community?

Students Views on the Roles of the School of Education

My first instinct, when considering these questions, was to wonder what my students' views were. After all, they are very familiar with such important aspects of the school of education as the courses offered and patterns of communication with administration, advisors, and faculty. I teach elementary and secondary science education courses in a public, urban university. In a graduate class on teaching science in the elementary classroom, where the range of teaching experience was 0 to 30 years, I asked my students to complete a brief questionnaire on their views on the role of a school of education. All of my students live and work in New York City; most of them are currently teaching in public schools. I had placed six items on the questionnaire that respondents could check off, as well as an open-ended question asking them for additional roles they felt a school of education should play. Below is the list of roles for the school of education that most of my students agreed were important. Eleven of the twenty-five students checked off all six items listed below, and six students checked off five of the six items.

- Provide coursework needed to better understand ideas about effective teaching and learning

- Provide opportunities to discuss teachers' personal questions and problems about teaching and to hear other teachers' issues

- Provide networking opportunities with other teachers and administrators from other schools and districts

- Help teachers learn about local resources that will improve their teaching

- Get teachers certified to teach in New York City

- Teach content in science and other areas

In the eyes of most of my students in my elementary science methods class, the school of education needed to be engaged in a range of activities that would provide coursework in content and pedagogy, provide ongoing professional support and guidance, introduce new teachers to the teaching profession by helping them with the steps of the certification process, facilitate peer support and discussion, and instruct teachers on valuable local resources they can use to enrich their classroom curricula.

In another graduate class I teach—a seminar on educational research that represents the final course in the masters program—I facilitated a conversation among ten secondary science teachers. Initially, when the question I put before them was "What is the role of a school of education?" the conversation was focused on critiques of their own experiences. Issues such as lack of available courses, degree of advisement on which courses to take, and so forth received the greatest talk time. It was clear that these students had not had the opportunity to voice these and other critiques to faculty or administration. From this, one important emergent theme was the need for a school of education to get feedback from its students on an ongoing basis. More often than not, the only feedback we ask our students for is the course evaluations they complete toward the end of the semester. However, how does my course fit in with others they have taken, with what they themselves teach (if they are currently teaching), with the contexts in which they work, and with what they feel they need most help with in their professional development? These are questions that the average course evaluation does not address. Not only do faculty and administration need to hear student perspectives on these questions, but also students need to articulate their thoughts in order to feel that the school of education is more than a requisite transition place that they pass through in order to meet state and city whims about teaching certification. For a school of education to be a place for serious professional development, students need to be treated like professionals. The first step to this end is to listen. I agree with Weiner (2000), who suggests that each successful program of teacher preparation should draw on the strengths of its teacher candidates and operate in a distinctive context. Thus, each program will probably be different. What they should all have in common is an appreciation of the significance of context and who the teacher candidates are.

Since I was interested in hearing my students' larger perspectives on the role of a school of education, I shifted the conversation to a hypothetical new school of education, somewhere in a different state, that they were to create. Most of my students referred to the major role that schools of education played in the area of apprenticeship, which they saw as needing to be sustained on three levels: field placements in different school settings, student teaching (a semesterlong internship), and mentoring by school of education faculty for new teachers once they begin teaching. It seems that a key need, at least as perceived by these urban teachers, is for a set of well-planned, guided experiences in the school culture. Such experiences could ground discussions pertaining to educational theory so that the close relationship between theory and practice becomes transparent to all.

Other roles of the school of education mentioned by students included the need to educate teachers about the importance of relationships with the parent community, informal learning centers, and the workplace. These were areas they felt that they were figuring out for themselves over the years and thought that it would have been very helpful if they had learned about the significance of these relationships sooner.

The Theory/Practice Dichotomy

The issue of apprenticeship is tightly linked to perceptions about the school of education's critical role of providing practical experiences and guidance, as opposed to focusing on theory. The notion that faculty tend to lead professional lives cloistered from the reality of school and all that teaching entails in the real world is a popular one among the student populations with whom I have worked at three different universities. Hopkins (1981) writes that the problems of integrating theory and practice cannot be understood without reference to the ecology and environment in which teacher education occurs. Given that most schools of education sit at the fringe of the university campus—both geographically and figuratively—the questions become: In what ways does the university perceive the roles of the school of education? In what ways does the school of education carve out a unique role for itself as it attempts to be a part of the university? How do education faculty see their roles vis-à-vis the traditional faculty role at liberal arts and science departments? Hopkins posits that the theory/practice integration issue became problematic when teachers' colleges moved onto the university campus and became subject to the university's norms and to the tenure and promotions criteria that traditionally emphasize research and publication, as opposed to professional involvement in schools and educational policy. If we agree that an important role of the school of education is to participate in and support local educational innovation, how does the school, as part of the university institution, regard faculty who focus on this rather than on the traditional research and publication valued in the liberal arts and sciences?

Lortie (1977) comments on the apparent intellectual segregation of educational theory and pedagogical practice that he observed in his well-known sociological study, *Schoolteacher*. He wonders if this segregation is caused by compartmentalized instruction—perhaps education students are not expected to apply theory to practical matters. He proposes that teacher apprenticeships be developed such that prospective teachers have many opportunities to observe and discuss a range of teachers and classrooms.

What is educational theory and where does it come from? How is it relevant to classroom practice? What is the teacher practitioner's role in advancing new theory? These basic questions need to be addressed in order for theory and practice to be integrated. Although it is common for education students, in my experience, to think about theory as being almost analogous to an instructional manual for teaching, I always point out that I use "theory" to refer to a range of conceptual lenses, helpful in making sense of pedagogy and the context in which it takes place. In a profession that is as context dependent as teaching, it is impossible to use theory prescriptively, as one can in the natural sciences. However, theoretical perspectives allow teachers to make sense of experiences and phenomena in deeper dimensions and allow for greater insights than would otherwise be possible.

My own strategy in teaching is to speak about the theory/practice link explicitly in the courses I teach, to talk about the relationship between developing one's own personal philosophy of teaching and one's classroom practice. I do this by making my own teaching methods transparent. For example, in the elementary science teaching course in which I surveyed students as described earlier, I asked students to tell me what they thought some aspects of my philosophy of teaching were after having been involved in a three-week water exploration that culminated in group presentations of their unique questions, their methods of exploration, their findings, and their new and remaining questions. Similarly, after an activity in which pairs of students each received a different issue of the Science section of the *New York Times* and were asked to select any piece in their issue and talk about some ways they might use the article in their teaching, I asked them again to tell me what they thought constituted my philosophy of teaching, learning, and science. The value of purposeful social interaction in learning, learning is best done by doing; science comprises tentative knowledge claims, science is often about playing or exploring—these and other comments demonstrated their understanding not only of the rationale for some of the things I asked them to do in my course, but also of the ways in which theory informs personal philosophy and, hence, practice. In order for teacher candidates to internalize and make meaning of the discourse of educational theory, education faculty need to find ways to help students articulate the relationship between theory and what they see happening in a classroom. When it comes to theory, the role of the school of education is much more than informing education students of the ideas of Piaget, Vygotsky, Dewey, and others—it is having them critically assess these ideas in the light of their own experiences and use them to shape their personal and evolving sets of philosophies of teaching and learning in their discipline. It is coaching them—in every course they take—on being a reflective practitioner and providing them with the intellectual tools, represented by educational theory, to craft their approach to their profession most constructively.

Teaching is a field in which it is of the utmost importance that practitioners be reflective. They need to continually see how the political, social, and economic circumstances in the school, community, and world affect their students and, consequently, their own professional lives. Teachers' responses to a student's behavior or an environmental issue such as street noise affecting the classroom need to incorporate a consideration of the social context. However, such reflection does not necessarily produce satisfying solutions; Weiner (1999) discusses various reasons why urban teachers face challenging situations for which they often have no solutions. I think, nonetheless, that being cognizant that one's personal philosophy of education has everything to do with the myriad decisions one makes as a teacher every day is critical in the professional development of a teacher. This is what distinguishes a teacher as a professional from a teacher as an automaton. A reflective teacher will learn from her experiences—both in the school of education and in her own classroom—and will make connections between them. She will try, as far as the system allows her, to treat her students as individuals and to teach in intriguing and innovative ways. She will be aware of the host of sociocultural factors in which her school, her classroom, her students, and her self are embedded.

School/College Collaborations

Professional development schools (PDSs), another concept students in my graduate research class referred to as an important aspect of their ideal school of education, is an effort to invent a coalition that brings together universities, schools of education, and public schools. Darling-Hammond (1994) characterizes PDSs as "a special case of school restructuring: as they simultaneously restructure schools and teacher education programs, they redefine teaching and learning for all members of the profession and the school community" (p. 1). The PDS is meant to allow for a synergistic relationship between the school and the school of education; teacher candidates gain practical experience in school settings in which they can see exemplary teaching modeled, and schools are provided with assistance from university faculty in curriculum development and so forth. It is, in short, an effort to address the theory/practice dichotomy as well as to address the role of the school of education in the community. However, research does not indicate that PDSs actually meet these goals. In a study describing collaboration between an urban school district and a large teacher preparation program at a university with an emphasis on the teacher as social justice educator, the researchers found that actual commitment was modest. Only a few education faculty, mostly nonsenior, were involved (Su in Weiner, 2000). Such token involvement sends the message that the venture is not critically important and tends to produce little positive results. Again, it seems that in the absence of a reorganization of the ways in which the university culture perceives the worth of faculty contributions to the practical endeavors that often constitute running a school well, the pressures of producing publications that measure well in one's academic career outweigh faculty's interest in being involved in PDSs.

At a meeting on the possibility of forming a PDS that I attended recently, teachers from a high school and faculty from a school of education were both in attendance. The high school and the school of education had a historical connection, owing to the fact that part of the high school was located on the university campus. However, numerous teachers and professors pointed out a lack of a common space, time constraints, and the absence of a structure that would facilitate informal or formal contact between high school teachers and college faculty. Teachers presented a number of reasons why they were present at the meeting and supported the idea of the development of a PDS. A first-year teacher suggested the possibility of added support by instituting a forum in which professors, student teachers, cooperating teachers, and interested teachers could participate. Another teacher talked about how she felt that her autistic kids felt empowered by the connection to a college, even though it was merely geographical at this stage. Similarly, college faculty spoke positively about the gains they and their students could experience by participating in a PDS. Several individuals brought up the need for tangible recognition, financial or otherwise, in order for a structure to be set in place. All the best intentions would not be sufficient to institute organized, ongoing interactions in the absence of a clear validation of the efforts of high school and college faculty. This was the note that this meeting ended on, with apparent agreement from all attendees. The next steps clearly are for the school of education and high school administrations to articulate the ways in which faculty participation will be valued.

Intra-university Collaborations

As a secondary science educator, I have students who take many science courses in the natural science departments. I hear from them about a sense of a lack of connection between these courses and their education courses. The majority of the science courses they take consist of graduate students en route to a degree in that science, which contributes to the education students' sense of not fitting in. Further, the faculty who teach these courses, as members of the science departments, generally make little reference to the field of education or to classroom practice. I wonder how my students would feel if education faculty like myself were more visible in the natural science departments, and vice versa? Collaborations between the school of education and other departments have the potential of enriching curriculum in all departments involved. Prakash (1986) presents four models for teacher preparation programs. The most radical of these models calls for spreading teacher education throughout all departments and doing away with a separate school of education. The school of education would, by its very absence as a distinct entity, "move from being a minor professional school of uncertain purpose . . . to the broker for an entire campus" (Judge, in Prakash, 1986). In this scheme, faculty from the school of education would work cooperatively with faculty members from the humanities, sciences, and social sciences to revise the undergraduate curriculum so that future teachers would learn both content and pedagogy from instructors who modeled innovative teaching methods. This model raises the commitment to teaching across the entire campus. However, it does not address the differences between teaching in school and in college, and politically it is not viable since it does away with the school of education as a distinct entity on campus. To what extent can we move toward the educational value of the interdisciplinarity proposed by this model while maintaining the current structure of the school of education? Heads of departments and faculty members in the liberal arts and sciences need to have conversations with faculty from the school of education who see the value of interdisciplinary projects. With appropriate encouragement from college administration, interested faculty can work cooperatively on curricular and pedagogical issues together or they can partner up and try team-teaching a course. The school of education, together with the other departments, can model innovative teaching methodology to all students as a result of collaborations within the university. Thus, the school of education can take on an educational role within the university for faculty interested in thinking about new approaches to teaching. Why not have a science educator like myself talk to a biologist about different approaches in teaching biology? Conceivably, as a result of conversation, both of us would benefit.

The Teacher-Researcher

Many researchers have written about the value of action research. Duckworth (1986) presents her view that there are two objectives of teaching—first, to put students in contact with the phenomena directly related to what they are studying and, second, to have students try to explain the meaning they make out of the experience (and to be able to account for their understandings). Teaching, for Duckworth, is largely an attempt to understand a number of things: how best to construct curriculum that is meaningful and engaging, how one's students think about the subject matter being discussed, how to involve those students who seem relatively uninvolved, how to manage the classroom so that things move smoothly, and so on. Research, similarly, is done in an attempt to understand. A teacher-researcher is therefore in the best position to generate research questions of interest to her; to gather data in the form of observations, interview transcripts, student work, or whatever makes most sense to her; and to interpret her data in light of her knowledge of the nature of the school, her understanding of who her students are and her personal reflections of her own goals and motivations as a teacher. Her research will generate new questions and teaching approaches that will nurture her professional life in many ways, while at the same time contributing to "theoretical and pedagogical discussions on the nature and development of human learning" (Duckworth, 1986, p. 494). The task before the school of education, thus, is not merely to prepare teachers, but to prepare teacher-researchers.

Informal Learning Environments

Recent national commissions on teacher education recommend to "reinvent teacher preparation and professional development for teachers to have continuous access to the latest knowledge about teaching and learning" (National Commission on Teaching and America's Future, 1996). The American Association for the Advancement of Science (1990) urges science teachers to exploit the resources of the larger community beyond the school, since children learn from a wide range of sources: museums, television, movies, and so forth. Further, Brown and Campione (1994) posit that Vygotsky's "zone of proximal development" can include effects of cultural artifacts such as museum exhibits, books, film, and so forth, since the zone defines the distance between current levels of comprehension and levels that can be accomplished in collaboration with other people or powerful artifacts. Such artifacts function as mediational means, just as talk does, resulting in the appropriation of words and concepts.

If we want to make clear the connections between the theories on social learning (put forth by Vygotsky and others) and our practice, we need to adopt deliberate strategies to that end, both at the school of education and in K–12 schools. If we see our students' educations as works in progress, curriculum needs to ensure greater continuity in students' experiences as they move from classroom to beyond (Lemke, 2001). If we want students to bring themselves into the classroom, as opposed to practicing the "cognitive apartheid" referred to by Cobern (1996), then we need to find ways for their worldviews to have access to classroom agendas. Inclusion of meaningful, informal science experiences in classroom conversation is one strategy that makes explicit the link between social learning theories and teaching practices. It encourages more students to participate in the conversation (Dhingra, 1999). Science is viewed as being inclusive and relevant (as opposed to exclusive and unrelated to students' lives) when the curriculum extends beyond the classroom in meaningful ways.

In order for teachers to accept and integrate new approaches and practices, they should be involved substantially with the reform effort, which involves partnerships among teachers, researchers, administrators, and educators (van Driel, Beijaard, and Verloop, 2001). Museum/school partnerships constitute effective agents for reforming science education. However, in the absence of effective teacher education with a focus on the power of informal science-learning experiences and learning experiences in the museum context, museum/school partnerships frequently end up being no more than field trips that are not entirely connected to the classroom curriculum. Science teachers in urban schools frequently feel the pinch of insufficient resources, and yet science museums in the same urban settings are rich in recent research and primary source materials placed in their real-world context. These methods, ideas, and artifacts have the potential to help students understand scientific ideas and phenomena. It therefore seems natural to hope for a connection between museums, teacher preparation, and classrooms. However, it also seems to be the case that simply introducing science classes to museums is not an effective teaching strategy to reach this goal. Prior research (Dhingra et. al., 2001) points to the value of involving museum experiences in science teacher education. Partnership between a school of education and a major institution was seen to facilitate powerful learning experiences affecting classroom practice in positive ways. However, the study also pointed to the need for the limitations (represented by school structures that prevented teachers from using museum resources in the classroom curriculum) to be addressed in a variety of ways. The collaboration between museum and school of education has the potential of being a powerful one. School administrators can be included in informal learning experiences at the museum in the hope that they will recognize the value to their schools of being involved with the museum. Coordinated interaction of the informal and the formal gives teachers new knowledge of how they learn and how to use those insights and resources for teaching. This study represents a model worth exploring as we try to address science content knowledge and pedagogical content knowledge in impoverished urban schools by identifying and using rich resources, such as museums, parks, zoos, and botanical gardens.

In a study on the construction of science on television (Dhingra, 1999), the distance between the worlds of formal school science and informal television science was perceived as being fairly wide by many student participants in this study. If, as Cobern (1996) suggests, the goal for science education is the fostering of scientifically compatible world-views, then popular television programming, which in the minds of student viewers contains scientifically relevant content, is a significant contributor toward such worldviews. Guided participation in discussion and activities grounded in the context of television programs that students are familiar with would increase student perceptions of the relevance of school science in their everyday interests and lives. However, if teachers are not open to the use of such material, students will continue to feel that school science has little to do with their everyday world. Television represents the everyday world; there are characters and situations on television that many students are familiar with or relate to. The medium is a tremendous resource as motivation, point of reference, or basis for critique in the classroom.

A school of education, it seems, needs to help teachers think about education broadly and to see clearly the tight relationship between theory and practice. What does it mean to learn? In what ways can connections between formal and informal learning be made explicit? How can all students participate in classroom conversations, and what do such conversations have to do with their everyday lives? Where are the resources we can all use to learn? This is a challenging set of tasks, given that it is sandwiched between layers of certification-related paper pushing, a variety of course requirements, state standards and standardized tests, and institutional constraints and politics.

References

American Association for the Advancement of Science (1990). *Science for All Americans*. New York: Oxford University Press.

Brown, A. L., and Campione, J. C. (1994). "Guided Discovery in a Community of Learners." In K. McGilly, ed., *Classroom Lessons: Integrating Cognitive Theory and Classroom Practice* (pp. 229–270). Cambridge, MA: MIT Press/Bradford Books.

Cobern, W. W. (1996). "Worldview Theory and Conceptual Change in Science Education." *Science Education*, 80:5, pp. 579–610.

Darling-Hammond, L. (1994). "Who Will Speak for the Children? How 'Teach for America' Hurts Urban Schools and Students." *Phi Delta Kappan*, 76:1, pp. 21–34.

Dhingra, K. (1999). *An Ethnographic Study of the Construction of Science on Television*. Doctoral dissertation, Columbia University.

Dhingra, K., et al. (2001). *Museum-College-School: A Collaborative Model for Teacher Preparation*. Paper presented at the annual meeting of the American Educational Research Association, Seattle, WA.

Duckworth, E. (1986). "Teaching as Research." *Harvard Educational Review*, 56:4, pp. 481–494.

Hopkins, D. (1981). *It Is True What They Say about Theory and Practice?* Paper presented at the Conference of the Western Canadian Association for Student Teaching, Vancouver, British Columbia, Canada (ED256708).

Lemke, J. (2001). "Articulating Communities: Sociocultural Perspectives on Science Education." *Journal of Research in Science Teaching*, 38, pp. 296–316.

Lortie, D. C. (1977). *Schoolteacher: A Sociological Study*. Chicago: University of Chicago Press.

National Commission on Teaching and America's Future (1996). *What Matters Most: Teaching for America's Future*. New York: Author.

Prakash, M. S. (1986). "Reforming the Teaching of Teachers: Trends, Contradictions, and Challenges." *Teachers College Record*, 88:2, pp. 217–240.

van Driel, J. H., Beijaard, D., and Verloop, N. (2001). "Professional Development and Reform in Science Education: The Role of Teachers' Practical Knowledge." *Journal of Research in Science Teaching*, 38:2, pp. 137–158.

Weiner, L. (1999). *Urban Teacher*. New York: Teachers College Press.

Weiner, L. (2000). "Research in the 90s: Implications for Urban Teacher Preparation." *Review of Educational Research*, 70:3, pp. 369–406.

Chapter Thirteen

The Experience of Experience: Haphazard Stories about Student Teaching

Philip M. Anderson

> *Critical pedagogies . . . necessarily embrace experience, confessions and testimony as relevant ways of knowing.*
> —bell hooks

I plan to write about experience from experience. In what follows, among other things, I will recall my experiences as a student teacher and a supervisor of student teachers. I plan to make several points:

- Student teaching is a central feature of teacher preparation because of the power of experiential learning, even though colleges and schools do not structure that experience in any consistent or meaningful way.

- As professionals we have few scholarly ways in which we can talk about classroom experience and, though experience is part of our vocabulary of practice, it is not a central feature of our research.

- Experience in teaching, unlike experience in learning, is not problematized in ways that allow for reflective professional development and practice.

- Colleges do not respect experiential learning as part of the mission of higher education, and, as a result, student teaching supervision is not properly supported by college budgets.

Tinkering with the current model of college-sponsored student teaching can solve none of the problems above.

These problems haunt every teacher education professional in the colleges. We know that "classroom experience" only *begins* with student teaching. We "educationists" are frequently accused of not having enough classroom experience anyway. But experience is not our mise-en-scène: Our status in the culture of higher education does not rest on our experience but on our knowledge.

Interestingly, much of our professional knowledge is about experiential learning. In the end, the content versus process argument is about formal knowledge versus experiential learning. But because colleges do not define college classroom experience in ways that reflect our understanding of experiential learning, the student teaching experience, for one, remains haphazard and unpredictable. And until colleges take responsibility for the experiential learning of their teacher preparation students, student teaching will remain an "add-on," an almost extracurricular feature of teacher education.

The answer to the first problem above, problematizing and eventually defining teaching "experience," might solve the second problem, getting college administrations to take experiential learning, student teaching in particular, seriously. The first problem requires research, and it requires research of a different color. I remember either Michael Apple or Herbert Kliebard making a telling observation in a course I took once upon a time: Though we have a history of educational curriculum and policy in the United States, we have no history of actual practice.

While I recognize that this situation has changed somewhat since twenty years ago, it seems to me that a history of "practice" would need to be gathered from stories of practitioners. There has been some important research on teacher narratives in recent years. But, as teacher education professionals and serious academics, I believe we do not trust narratives of experience. I will not speculate here but instead argue that ignoring "experience" in favor of "research" creates some conflicts for us as teacher educators.

Calling my own bluff, I will present a few stories from *my* experience. My experience has a completeness from which I will claim a particular type of authority. I completed an undergraduate teacher education program with student teaching. I have served the profession as a teacher, student teacher supervisor, teacher education faculty member in public and private universities, education department chair, education dean, and director of a Ph.D. program in educational studies. I have some stories to tell.

My student teaching took place in Wisconsin in 1972, my senior year of college. I had completed a preparatory course sequence in teaching English, with the "methods" course taught by someone who had begun teaching in 1927. Yes, 1927. I have never met a more dedicated teacher educator or *more experienced* teacher in my life. When it came to supervising me in the classroom, there were too many student teachers for her to supervise each individually. So, some of us were assigned someone else as our university supervisor. I do not remember whether I felt rejected or not by being assigned to the "other" supervisor. My late wife's father, a professor at the same university, later told me that my English methods instructor thought I was arrogant. It seems to me that he told me this with some point in mind, though I am not sure what it was.

The significance of being assigned to the "other" supervisor is that there was only one person in college who was a teacher educator who specialized in English, my professor who had begun teaching in 1927. So, a wonderful English professor who specialized in eighteenth century literature, and had *no experience* in teacher education, was assigned to cover us leftovers. He was a big fan of Samuel Johnson, and like many eighteenth century specialists, took some pride in displaying the reported personal habits of mind of the object of his scholarly affection. I felt a confused affection for the man myself: He later reported to my former father-in-law that he thought I had something to offer the world.

Not to put too fine a point on the matter: The two choices for supervisors at my state university in 1972 were either the most experienced English teacher in the world or someone who had no experience at all. I got the one with no experience at all. Since I didn't listen to anyone in those days, this was probably the better choice. "Dr. Johnson" visited me twice during the spring semester at the local high school and thought I did just fine. My cooperating teacher, one of the more experienced and, simultaneously, progressive teachers I have ever met, thought I did just fine too. I got an "A" in student teaching with the caveat that I shouldn't be so arrogant and I should listen more. I spent the next year getting a master's degree in English before looking for my first teaching job, and everyone knows that that experience will not make you less arrogant.

I also remember one other thing about my student teaching experience from the point of view of the student teacher: Student teaching is a huge disruption in the life of future teachers who at that moment happen to be seniors in college. We aspiring middle-class kids put up with the inconvenience, cost, and unfairness of it because we had no choice: We needed our teacher certification to get a job. One of the most interesting lessons I learned during my years as an Ivy League education professor was that upper-middle-class and rich kids didn't have to put up with this limitation on their undergraduate experience.

I remember several instances where Ivy League undergraduates with whom I was working decided not to pursue student teaching. It wasn't because they would be teaching in private schools and would not need student teaching for certification or that they would enter some "Teach for America"–style alternative. Instead, since most students completed all of this college's requirements by the end of the seventh semester, the last semester (the spring semester, when we did student teaching) was reserved for "having fun." No sensible Ivy League student could forsake the prospect, after the stress of three and a half years of studying, of having some fun during the final semester.

But, back to the disruption of lives of ordinary students during student teaching. Since I attended a rusticated university as an undergraduate, as most of the colleges west of the Hudson are, there were never enough student teaching placements available in the small college town. I at least was assigned to the local high school. Some of my friends and intended future colleagues needed to pack up and move to a town in the next county. In my case, having managed nicely for three and a half years without a car, I was forced to find a car to travel to the cornfield on the other side of town where the new consolidated high school perched. For those of you from warmer places and those who might think I was lazy as well as arrogant, no one walks two miles anywhere in Wisconsin during February or March.

I managed both the disruption of my senior year and the responsibilities of student teaching somehow. Remember that I got an "A" in student teaching. To this day, I am not sure why I got it. There did not seem to be any clear sense of what I was supposed to learn nor any goals I was supposed to attain except to be a "good" teacher. I guess I was a good teacher.

As a former colleague used to say to me, possibly with a twinkle in his eye, "The thing our new graduates need the most is something we can't give them: five years experience." Of course, this statement is true, but it also illustrates the problem with our professional thinking about "experience." Starting with Dewey, it has been clear that educational experience in formal settings is not "naturalistic." Experience, in a formal educational sense, needs to be structured. And yet, the only real structure we appear to have for student teaching is administrative rather than pedagogical. Experience, as an educational aim, is more than time spent doing something. Lots of teachers with lots of experience are really bad teachers.

This observation brings us back to the next chapter in the narrative. After teaching in a public high school (thoroughly unsupervised) for a few years, I became a full-time graduate student in curriculum and instruction at the University of Wisconsin–Madison. In exchange for the university paying me a maintenance wage and tuition to attend, they expected me to work for the university. In my program, we supervised student teachers.

I was a graduate student during the low point of teacher preparation and teacher hiring in the second half of the 1970s (disco flourished during this time period, so you can see what desperate shape the culture was in). Counting my major professor, the only English education professor senior enough to survive the faculty purges of 1973–75, there was need for only two of us graduate students to cover all of the student teachers in English at a major university.

In addition to bonafide English teacher candidates, this number included a few Big Ten athletes who would become full-time coaches when they got their first school jobs and several theatre arts majors who could pretend to be English teachers while pursuing their thespian careers. Not surprisingly, cooperating teachers and students alike universally praised this group of beautiful and animated future soap stars. They could have been teaching anything. In a couple of cases, if memory serves, they *were* teaching anything.

The other graduate student assigned student teaching supervision along with me had never taught in a school. She had *no* experience. The following year, after she left, I believe I had to supervise fifteen student teachers while completing my graduate studies. You get the idea. Any way you look at it, these students were not getting the best supervision possible. But the university was getting it done cheaply. And remember, Wisconsin was the epitome of a progressive university in those days—most places would have done less with less.

Working with those future English teachers, I learned a lot about teaching, even if they learned less from me. I also learned what all experienced supervisors know, that cooperating teachers are all different. Each cooperating teacher, good or bad, managed the mentoring of the novice in her (sometimes his) own particular way. There were common characteristics of good teaching they demonstrated generally, though not all of them could articulate those characteristics to a novice.

Many of these cooperating teachers had clear ideas about preservice teacher deficiencies, in particular their English subject-matter preparation for teaching high school. They harbored little hope that repeated suggestions would be heard by an English department they never saw.

Instead they visited their frustration on us, English education types who actually ventured into the schools. I learned early on to remind cooperating teachers that the department of curriculum and instruction was allowed no say over the curriculum in the English department. By the by, I completed significant coursework in the English department during that time, and no one ever mentioned the essential questions of English teaching at the high school at which I worked except to wonder why a smart (and appropriately arrogant?) graduate student such as myself was "over there" in the education program.

However, the real issues surrounding student teaching and its supervision by the university came to me after I graduated and was admitted to the professorate. I quickly found that as a pedagogy specialist, my workload was different from that of other professors. It was even different from that of the educational foundations and educational psychology professors. The difference was student teaching supervision. I calculated that I was spending four times as many hours teaching or observing students than other professors were.

I also discovered that student teachers were paying significant amounts of money for "extra" tuition that never came back to the education programs. Since my first full-time job was at an Ivy League university, you might imagine how much money those extra credits translated into. The money was captured in the general fund and probably used to support the classics department and the laboratory technicians for the chemistry department. It certainly was not used to provide additional supervisors, more training, or more compensation for the cooperating teachers. It was free money. And the cooperating teachers never got a free lunch from it.

The fact that I was spending four times as much time on student contact did not impress the senior faculty who were in educational foundations or educational psychology. The research and publication standards for tenure and promotion were the same for everyone. Any deviation would be unfair to hardworking faculty researchers everywhere. The other pedagogical specialists and I would commiserate, but we were powerless in the face of sham notions of collegial equity.

All pedagogical specialists out there will of course want me to mention that the seminar that accompanies student teaching in most colleges is done for "free" by the pedagogy professor, and program advising frequently does not carry any released time. For years I have believed that providing an equitable workload for pedagogy specialists has been resisted by college administrations because doing so would require hiring more of us. We already had the money from the extra tuition collected for student teaching to hire more. But that is another story.

Six years later I was not invited to pursue tenure at my Ivy League college, probably because I was not arrogant enough. I moved to an urban college where teacher education was a staple of the college's advertised mission. Here, I thought, would be a place that appreciated the complications in the life of a professor who also supervised student teachers. Of course, whether a college is public or private, elitist or egalitarian, the goals of higher education do not allow for proper consideration of the needs of student teachers or professors of pedagogy.

Luckily for me, the students at this urban college were some of the best, hardest-working, and most appreciative students on the planet. Becoming a teacher was a big deal. They were aspiring to the middle class, these students from, literally, all over the world. We did the best we could with the resources we had. I found cooperating teachers who were genuinely interested in the mentoring of novice teachers (they couldn't be doing it for the minuscule remuneration). I found assistant principals of English who acted as colleagues with no remuneration whatsoever. I found that we made a difference in the experience of these student teachers. For me, the hours spent trying to find a parking spot near a high school in Queens was always worth it.

This utopian vision was marred only by the fact that there was no common understanding of what the student teaching experience was supposed to be or what it was supposed to do. Each disciplinary program at my college operated under different assumptions, depending on the college faculty member directing the program. Cooperating teachers in the field, whom we had no contact with other than when we "visited" the school, operated under differing assumptions based on discipline, school, neighborhood, country of origin, and possibly religious and/or ethnic background.

Since the pedagogy specialists couldn't visit every student in these large programs ourselves, we were very fortunate to find an abundance of retired staff developers and assistant principals who were available to help with the supervision of large numbers of student teachers. And they of course had many different ways of approaching the task and carried many different assumptions of the purpose of the student teaching experience.

After ten years of building a program and educating future English teachers, I became a department chair and then eventually dean of education. Given my experience, I figured that I knew how to fix— even transform—student teaching. Of course, I had no experience of being a chair or a dean and had no idea how the constraints of the college-funding scheme operate. I soon found that there was never enough money or other resources to maintain existing programs. And, as an education dean, one constantly hears how *expensive* student teaching is: Can't we have the supervisors cover more students than they currently do?

I made a dent here or there. I actually think I helped the scientists who normally serve as provosts these days to understand some of the issues. I may have actually increased the budget in a few small areas. We hired some good faculty, primarily pedagogy specialists, to manage the education of our future teachers. But, in the end, nothing was really different. In the end, nothing can be different. Colleges do not support experiential learning for professional preparation. And in this new era of limited funding for academic programs, colleges will not choose to invest more resources in experiential learning situated off-campus.

In what universe would this vision of apprenticeship supervision be acceptable? In one sense it is the same story as thirty years ago, even in the face of major recommendations, and requirements, for change promoted by state departments of education. Colleges are still allowed to collect money for student teaching and not support education programs with the money. Colleges, as a matter of course, or even as a matter of ideology, do not support experiential learning as central to their mission. Requiring educational faculty to do more with experiential learning puts us at odds with our own institutions.

On the other hand, colleges appear to be supporting more "internships" these days, primarily as partnerships with businesses. The financial piece is shared with the companies, who have something to say about the experience. In fact, the apprenticeship is seen as a partnership between the college and the business, not something the college is visiting upon the business for the academic benefit of the college. Colleges understand that relationship—and share costs and goals.

Teacher education has a problem with that structure, since the public schools are our "business" partner. The public schools are directed and funded by the same people who direct and fund the public universities (and supplement private universities). You would think that, under those circumstances and that synchronous structure, all of these continuing problems could be solved.

But, instead, new state regulations for teacher certification require more experience during the teacher preparation coursework (in New York it is roughly twenty hours per course prior to student teaching) and more student teaching hours. At the same time, those authorities are reducing funding for university programs. Given the lack of funding and resources for the current situation, anything could happen. And anyone could be managing the supervision of future teachers.

Here's my modest proposal: Nothing short of changing the way state education funding is distributed is needed. I would suggest that funding be directed to school sites that are the equivalent of "teaching hospitals" for medical internships. These professional development schools would be "co-owned" by the public schools and the universities, which would take responsibility for the professional education of teachers. I know this is not a new idea, but it is an idea that still has not been seriously attempted except by privately financed pilot projects.

Current attempts to reduce funding for experiential learning in colleges while maintaining, or even increasing, preservice teacher experience requirements are doomed to failure. The state governments and regulating bodies that claim to take experiential learning seriously must in turn finance professional development sites. (I say this knowing that many states have reduced funding for teaching hospitals.) Without an attempt to fundamentally change the current system of college-supervised student teaching, financed almost solely by goodwill, it will collapse.

Barring any actual change in the funding of teacher preparation in the colleges, here is my radical proposal: Require the schools to take the responsibility for experiential learning through the induction process. Fund and work with the schools to accomplish what many teachers have said they have wanted to do, take over the responsibility for experiential learning by replacing student teaching with a school-based, first-year apprenticeship. At least you know someone with teaching experience will do the supervision.

I realize that the neoconservatives have been pushing this same idea. And I realize that neo-cons see the apprenticeship model as the first step in eradicating the influence of liberal "educationists" permanently. I think the apprenticeship model is a risk we need to take, if for no other reason than that the schools will then take responsibility for induction into teaching in ways that they are allowed to avoid now. Both experiential learning theory and current research on situated cognition tell us that we need better induction models. A strong induction model could make student teaching obsolete.

And, to return to my business partnership model above, the schools would have a full share in the collaboration. Let's face it—under the current student teaching framework, we college types still act as if we don't trust the schools to manage their own new recruits. Let's go to the schools and make them full partners in teacher preparation by requiring them to manage the experiential learning of new teachers. I think college professors and schoolteachers could find some common stories to tell and pass on to the initiates.

Out of those common stories should also emerge a discourse of experience that probably could be the center of professional research. The focus would then be on the *experience* of the working professional rather than the limited topics we use to chide the teacher for not *knowing*. College professors would be expected to communicate with teachers as colleagues rather than view them as objects of study. Recentering our professional aims and educational study on the experience of teaching would make for a whole different story.

Afterword

Working on the Future: Concluding Thoughts

Alberto M. Bursztyn

I recognized Crystal's name on the roster of graduate students enrolled in Methods of Educational Research, a course I teach in the master's program in special education. I remembered her as an undergraduate student in another course, Urban Children and Adolescents: Development and Education, I had taught in the preservice teacher education program four years earlier. At the time, Crystal was a curious and idealistic young woman, a first-generation college student eager to "give back" to her struggling immigrant community. I wondered if she would still be a passionate young person committed to learning, to "bettering" herself, and to teaching as a way of making a worthy contribution to others. Or, I feared, was she returning to college with broken dreams; enrolling in classes only because she was required to do so by the school system that employed her? Was she another wounded romantic who had downscaled her dreams to permanent teacher certification and a steady job? I also questioned the roles that colleges and schools of education play in sustaining hope, not only for prospective and returning teachers, but also for society at large.

Teaching graduate courses at Brooklyn College's School of Education, I regularly encounter graduates of our preservice programs who, like Crystal, return to our institution for a master's degree in education. As a group, they report widely varying experiences working in our local schools. While they praise their preparation in our programs, they sometimes relate having lost their enthusiasm in the face of unexpected obstacles and challenges. Some seem defeated and cynical, even burned out, after a relatively brief stint in difficult assignments. Still others report feeling energized by their work and even more devoted to their chosen profession.

Faced with the challenges of their new teaching assignments, teacher thinking about education, school reform, and teachers' ability to make a difference is quickly transformed. New teachers complain that bureaucratic oversight and unsympathetic administrators regulate their work-lives, while the pressing organizational needs of their schools stifle their ideas and creativity. Some refer to their worklives in the language of survival, where hope has withered and the goal of reaching the end of each day is the propelling force. Alienation and isolation are the common denominators for these disillusioned teachers. In contrast, new teachers who report satisfying teaching assignments also report supportive interactions with colleagues and school administrators. A sense of school community clearly contributes to these teachers' engagement with their work.

Mindful of my role in shaping expectations, I often confront the tension that emerges from a false dichotomy: whether to prepare students to adapt to the "harsh realities" of urban public schools or, conversely, to encourage future teachers to be change agents in schools and society. It is the second option that I find most meaningful and that sustains my own teaching. It is also what powers the imagination of most teacher candidates and gives meaning to their work. When teachers work to build communities and to develop collaborative relationships, they form the support structures that allow them to thrive in difficult classrooms and under-funded schools. Preparing students to work in the real world need not imply that they should dismiss their commitment for social change in favor of "classroom management." When schoolchildren are subjected primarily to control, their education suffers. Clearly teachers need to learn how to organize and structure their classrooms, but those efforts should not come at the expense of promoting student learning and growth (Darling-Hammond, 1998).

Schools of Education as Sites of Hope

Returning graduate students with newly acquired cynicism should not be ignored or blamed for their soured dreams. If teachers are to find satisfaction in their work, they need to recover a sense of courage and hope. I argue here that urban colleges and schools of education can be sites where hope is restored and where purposeful work toward social justice can support the aspirations of students and faculty alike. Recognizing the challenge that educators face, Maxine Greene (1996), reflected on the hope tied up in teaching:

> Given what we see—the neglect, the cold carelessness, the rampant greed—it will take courage to succeed in education. It will take a new kind of hope, a new shaping of possibility, a new venture into the unpredictable. But, then, utopias are never predictable. We can choose ourselves for something caring and humane and daring. We can only begin. (p. 313)

Faculties of schools of education could begin by asking the question that Greene poses: whether our role in preparing educators embraces hope, whether we are choosing for ourselves to care and to dare. Although we may reflexively respond that our work fosters hope and courage among our students, we need to reflect on how, individually and collectively as institutions, we relate to the urban realities among which we work. The space between rhetoric and action is vast.

On writing about how middle-class Americans choose to live in their cities, Adrienne Rich (1979) identified three prototypical approaches that, I believe, have implications for teachers and teacher educators. The first option, the *paranoiac*, refers to individuals who perceive the city as a dangerous place; they are suspicious of others and prefer to live behind locked doors. This worldview is rooted in the need for protection from a hostile environment. Another type seeks to create an isolated, self-indulgent way of living: She called this approach *solipsistic*. These city dwellers claim to love their town but would not dare use public transportation or venture outside well-traveled physical and psychological boundaries. While they may enjoy the city's arts institutions and cultural life, they are apathetic to the needs of others around them. The third way, which remained unnamed, Rich considered the best choice; it is one whereby individuals see the city as a site of both hope and difficulty. Here city dwellers ask: What can *I* do? This stance implies that one is not merely an accidental visitor in one's life, a tourist who remains uninvolved. Rather, we respond to a city that demands our love because we cannot remain indifferent when others are struggling and, by addressing a shared humanity, we can contribute to the city's hope and our own (Rich, 1979).

In urban education, we encounter this typology in the ways that teachers and teacher educators approach their work. As with any human typology, Rich's framework does not describe a set of mutually exclusive options but rather functions to identify the primary orientation of individuals, an orientation that is subject to change with life experience and education. We can identify how our own orientations may have changed over time or even how competing tendencies can coexist, generating conflicting interests. We witness these tendencies in schools and in colleges and schools of education on a daily basis. Few teacher candidates rush to fill positions in the most troubled schools; similarly, professors of education often become disillusioned by the troublesome politics of dysfunctional, poor school districts and schools and typically retreat to safer and more predictable collaborations. While most educators uphold an ideal of commitment for all children, we work, for the most part, in circumscribed ways, occasionally retreating behind locked doors to assuage our anxieties and suspicions.

Yet the work of education has been, historically, that of preserving hope. The impulse to fix a broken society by working with its children still resonates with most educators, even when they disagree passionately about what needs fixing and how this should be done. Educators carry into their work implicit visions of social transformation that range from conservative dreams of returning to a glorious past (Hirsch, 1996) to emancipatory notions of achieving a just and progressive society (Greene, 1998). Adrienne Rich's typology is relevant here; the way we choose to live in the city reflects the values and visions we overtly or inadvertently transmit to our students. If our actions betray our words, we only breed cynicism among our students.

Education cannot be a neutral enterprise because it is laden with the competing expectations of social order and social transformation. To educate is to care. Hannah Arendt (cited in Gordon, 2001) wrote about education in terms of love and responsibility:

> Education is the point at which we decide whether we love the world enough to assume responsibility for it and by the same token save it from the ruin which, except for renewal, except for the coming of the new and young, would be inevitable. And education, too, is where we decide whether we love our children enough not to expel them from our world and leave them to their own devices, nor to strike from their hands their chance of undertaking something new, something unforeseen by us, but to prepare them in advance for the task of renewing a common world. (pp. 54–55)

Arendt was well known for her distrust of utopian visions because they could lead to totalitarianism; still she believed that education should prepare children for taking responsibility for the world. In her view, the work of education is to help children become familiar with the world and feel secure in it so that they may have a chance to be creative and develop the moral convictions to attempt to change it (Gordon, 2001). Taubman (2001) is similarly troubled by the notion that teachers' hope for their students may impose on them limitations and restrict their path toward self-identity. He proposes to teach "without hope," that is to care deeply for our students while refraining from prescribing a path for them and their aspirations.

From Schools to Utopia: An American Tradition

Although the task of renewing a common world is not often directly addressed in the preparation of educators, it is tacitly embedded in the educational project. In its origins, American public education was intended to strengthen children's character and morality by teaching them to read the scriptures and thus curtail satanic influences. But soon educators and policymakers developed a more expansive vision, one in which schools could become vehicles for social transformation and renewal (Bailyn, 1960). In fact, a century of educational change and reform initiatives have sought to impact not only on schools, but also on the way that schools prepare children for life in this culture. In essence, school reform initiatives have been the most tangible policy efforts to pursue utopian visions (Tyack and Cuban, 1995).

At the dawn of the twentieth century, public education assumed the task of shaping a homogeneous nation out of disparate streams of immigrants. In a land of perennial optimism, Americans have generally turned to education to achieve their personal ambitions and have trusted schools' promise to bring about an idealized society. For example, John Dewey (1899), echoing Thomas Jefferson's belief that education should prepare citizens to govern themselves, stressed the potential of schools to lay a firm foundation for modern democracy. He proposed a utopian vision in which the school would become

> an embryonic community life, active with the types of occupations that reflect the life of the larger society, and permeated throughout with the spirit of art, history and science. When school introduces and trains each child of society into membership within such little community, saturating him with the spirit of service, and providing him with the instruments of effective self-direction, we shall have the deepest and best guaranty of a larger society which is worthy, lovely, and harmonious. (pp. 43–44)

Dewey worked to translate his vision into pedagogic practice at the University of Chicago Lab School and laid the foundation for a democratic pedagogy that engaged learners in meaningful activities, but commercial and industrial paradigms quickly overshadowed and subverted his approach. His Lab School at the University of Chicago remained a beacon of progressive education long after he left for a teaching post at Columbia University, but schools elsewhere began to resemble factories. Ravitch (2000) described the emerging vision of the time as brutally pessimistic. Children encountered a differentiated curriculum based on performance on intelligence tests, and their progress was carefully monitored through standardized measures. Dewey remained an influential figure in education, but his philosophy was more likely to be adopted by elite and private schools than by those serving the poor and urban populations.

The factory model of school organization was premised on the efficient use of public resources; children were to be prepared for work in factories or the professions, according to their measured aptitude. This model of education is still with us and, despite countless reform efforts, is more entrenched than ever. Tracking is subtler now, but still commonplace, with special education and alternative programs channeling underperforming students to dead-end outcomes. Intelligence tests have been replaced with other high-stakes standardized measures, but these serve the same sorting function. It is noteworthy and ironic that learner-centered approaches and humanistic traditions in pedagogy, which have been enthusiastically adopted in the most exclusive private schools, are derided as ineffective and unscientific in the public education sector.

It is instructive to search the historic roots of ability sorting policies in U.S. schools. The idea of conducting systematic intelligence testing of all pupils was introduced by the leading psychologists of the day. Lewis Terman (1919), a leading proponent of IQ tests for social control and the American sponsor of the Stanford-Binet Test, championed the use of tests to emulate policies that had been effective in sorting conscripts for various roles in World War I. Terman believed that education had little influence on intelligence and proposed that American society organize itself to the benefit of the gifted while seeking ways of isolating and controlling the intellectually weak. The Social Darwinism and eugenic ideology he epitomized gained substantial strength throughout the 1920s and 1930s. The use of intelligence tests in schools was so pervasive that the trend became known as the Testing Movement. The group administration of IQ tests continued unabated until the 1960s. The ideology that had originally supported its use had fallen out of favor years earlier. After World War II, the racist agendas for social organization resonated too closely with Nazism and Fascism and were largely shunned in this country. The eugenics project exemplifies the dark utopian vision that Arendt so feared could return to the American imagination and find support among policymakers.

Social control on the basis of race and class, or their surrogate—measured mental ability—are not defunct ideas. In the past decade, the prominent psychologists Herrnstein and Murray wrote *The Bell Curve* (1994), a provocative text condensing years of research in multiple fields. In this widely read text, they took up and defended social stratification on the basis of measured intelligence. The book was well received in influential academic and political circles, despite the authors' biased interpretations and misuse of data (Kincheloe, Gresson, and Steinberg, 1997). Taking a social engineering perspective, they argued that racial minorities and the poor do not benefit enough from education to warrant the cost of extant programs in schools. They concluded that resources should be allocated for preparing an elite of intelligent students, controlling and isolating those considered least cognitively endowed and resistant to learning. Herrnstein and Murray's utopian vision for a well-ordered society where the powerful elite remains in control resonates with the racist ideology popular before World War II. The credibility assigned the authors of *The Bell Curve* in social science circles suggests that eugenics has not disappeared, but has simply gone underground in the face of a discursive environment that makes overt racism taboo. Clad in scientific language, the racist idea of social control based on measured intelligence can reemerge as a respectable proposition.

Public discourse on educational policy and priorities reflects philosophical assumptions about society and ways of shaping the future. As Tyack and Cuban (1995) have observed, efforts at educational reform are in fact attempts to reshape society. The intensity of the public debates reveals the passionately held beliefs and aspirations of individuals and groups. Yet reform efforts have been primarily "top down," emerging from the offices of policymakers and imposed on the lower levels of the educational hierarchy. Ideas from the trenches, that is, from teachers, parents, and grassroots organizations, generally lack the clout to force changes in the system (Fullan, 1993). Yet it is those who lack institutional power who have challenged the system with a moral voice to remain open and committed to democracy. For example, during the dark days of the McCarthy hearings, W. E. B. Du Bois (1970) stated:

> [W]e should fight to the last ditch to keep open the right to learn, the right to have examined in our schools not only what we believe, but what we do not believe; not only what our leaders say, but what the leaders of other groups and nations, and the leaders of other centuries have said. We must insist upon this to give our children the fairness of a start which will equip them with such an array of facts and such an attitude toward truth that they can have a real chance to judge what the world is and what its greater minds have thought it might be. (pp. 230–231)

Some of the more notable successful challenges to the education establishment centered on access, such as the movement to end racial segregation and the grassroots organizing that led to free public education for children with disabilities. Perhaps the disillusionment with desegregation policies, which have been largely circumvented, and the massive failures of special education have diminished expectations for what schools can do. Diane Ravitch (2000) suggested that utopianism has declined in

American society as a consequence of universal access to education. Access has not yielded equity, and consequently the expectations of social transformation have declined.

Following the lead of Hirsch (1987, 1996), it can be argued that conservative educators have found the answers to educating the next generation somewhere in the idealized past; they passionately advocate for a return to earlier approaches to teaching and loyalty to the Western canon. Their approach may be understood as an attempt to legitimize and perpetuate the current distribution of power (Aronowitz and Giroux, 1988). Liberals have also abandoned a grand vision for social change; they often join with neoconservatives to support privatization, school choice, vouchers, and charter schools. They seem to share the expectation that schools, even if improved, will not significantly reshape society. Educational goals for both conservatives and liberals have become more modest, focusing on academic rigor and measurable outcomes, without much thought given to the curriculum or pedagogy. The larger unresolved questions, such as funding inequities, racial segregation, and curriculum content have receded from the public discourse.

Ideas that flowed from utopian visions in education have left their mark and continue to speak to issues of practice, if not to social change. Dewey's progressive education ideas, for example, continue to be implemented through project-based learning and through an emphasis on democratic processes in the classroom (Tanner, 1997). Similarly, Terman's idea about sorting students by ability level is still common practice in the public schools, as is the use of standardized testing. Contemporary modern utopian projects include efforts to educate all children with special needs in regular classrooms (Skrtic, 1995) and the Reggio Emilia approach to an arts-suffused, child- and community-centered model of early education (Edwards, Gandini, and Forman, 1993). Multicultural education, which sought to create an inclusive and proactive approach to address individual and collective identities, gained substantial acceptance before it became marginalized in a high-stakes testing climate (Bursztyn, 2002).

Critical Pedagogy

Schools of education, particularly in urban settings, now face the challenge of defining themselves anew. In a political climate of control and accountability that seeks to reduce the role of educators to technicians who "deliver instruction" through "empirically validated methods," education faculty must choose between acquiescence and resistance.

Faculty must choose between collusion in the move to disempower teachers and diminish their role in curriculum development and implementation and insistence upon support for the autonomy and creativity of teachers and other professionals who work in schools.

Current public policy initiatives on education, driven by prevailing political ideologies, focus on learning standards, accreditation, and other efforts to regulate instruction. Many education theorists have distanced themselves from this discourse, dismissing the standards movement as a manifestation of elitist efforts to bring about centralized control of local schools. The poststructuralist vision of school reform includes major power realignments, together with the abandonment of positivistic and foundationalist constructions of teaching and learning. For example, Giroux (1988) advocates a radical emancipatory pedagogy that challenges dominant assumptions and opens up new possibilities by critically exploring the marginalized space of student cultural experience. He conceptualizes the tensions between students and the structures of legitimate power, language, history, and culture as a *field of struggle*. When incorporated into the curriculum, the field of struggle serves to challenge normative standards of mainstream schooling (Demetrion, 2001). Similarly, Kincheloe and Steinberg (1996) and McLaren (1994) suggest that critical pedagogues must confront the ways of seeing that dominate traditional liberal and conservative critiques of schooling. Moving beyond these analytical forms, critical pedagogy seeks to elucidate to students and teachers how schools work by exposing student sorting processes and the ways that power influences the curriculum.

The current postmodern focus on power in education, rooted in Bourdieu's (1976) concept of reproduction of culture schemes through social institutions, particularly schools, and in Freire's (1970) concept of critical pedagogy, has gained ascendancy in educational theorizing. Identifying power as an organizing force in education, these thinkers encourage a radical reexamination of methods and purposes of schooling, beyond those issues that dominate the public discourse on curriculum content and methodology. Aiming to redefine education, they dispense with the prevailing modern meta-narratives; these are described as masking the will to power that excludes and marginalizes others (Lyotard, 1984). Within postmodern, poststructuralist frames, ideas of social utopias flourish; endemic to these discourses, however, is a lack of agreement on how to resolve competing claims between the primacy of power structures and individual agency.

Though not given to promoting prescriptions for social change, Richard Rorty (1989) nevertheless puts forth his own conception of education as a vehicle to realize a utopian vision. His contribution is notable because it is less focused on issues of power. He begins with a notion of humans as consisting of "centerless networks of beliefs and desires whose vocabularies and opinions are determined by historical circumstance" (p. 200). Rorty redefines education as a process of self-formation and self-creation forged in the crucible of language. He suggests that the process of socialization dominates education for children, focusing on the world as it is. Beyond eighteen years, education should be dominated by what he terms individuation, or self-creation. In his utopia the conditions are such that individuals share in solidarity the selfish hope that the little things around which they have woven their final vocabularies will not be destroyed. Rorty believes that not all individuals are likely to arrive at a full capacity for self-formation and self-creation, thus leaving unresolved the possibility of an inherent stratification of people within his social utopia.

Unlike modern utopian visions, postmodern and poststructuralist writings are less focused on practice and may be better described as critiques of education and schooling. Their agendas address directions for change by exposing unexamined assumptions and exposing injustices. Kincheloe and Steinberg (1996) explain that their students often experience critical pedagogy as mysterious and frightening, since it challenges basic assumptions about schooling. The students are particularly disturbed by the idea that education can be deployed to undermine their own efforts to gain socioeconomic mobility and control over their lives. The two authors describe how students gradually come to understand the connection between mainstream social assumptions and their evolving view of themselves as future teachers and to realize that their transformative role as educators is not always rewarded in the world of education. Kincheloe and Steinberg are keenly aware that preparing teachers to be change agents means preparing them to enter into conflict with the organized power structures of schools. Maintaining commitment to change, though, requires conviction and an understanding of what needs to be changed and how this can be accomplished (Sarason, 1993). While postmodern and poststructural philosophies provide intellectual underpinnings, they offer little guidance regarding the pragmatics of school change.

Reconsidering Utopia

The school as an engine for social justice and social transformation is yielding to a technicist institution that both prepares and sorts children for different roles in an increasingly bifurcated society. Schools, particularly in the large cities, are told to live up to the standards of wealthy suburbs without the benefit of equitable funding and resources (Kozol, 1991). When they predictably fail, they are blamed for their circumstances and become subject to corporate takeovers. In this zeitgeist of commodification, schools are portrayed as a major drain of local tax revenues and as potential sources of corporate profit. Rather than the embryonic version of our society's future, schools now have the potential to become the sites where hope dies for the sake of profit.

Schools of education cannot be indifferent to the plight of teachers and public schools. To maintain their integrity, they must develop counternarratives and theoretical arguments to rekindle hope for education as a vehicle to a more democratic and just society. But this effort cannot be limited to rhetoric. Education faculty and colleagues and liberal arts that prepare future teachers must engage in collaborative and meaningful work that exemplifies our expectations for our students. Inevitably, the road to utopia begins at home.

References

Aronowitz, S., and Giroux, H. (1988). "Schooling, Culture, and Literacy in the Age of Broken Dreams: A Review of Bloom and Hirsch." *Harvard Educational Review*, 58:2, pp. 173–194.

Bailyn, B. (1960). *Education in the Forming of American Society*. New York: W. W. Norton.

Bourdieu, P. (1976). "Les conditions sociales de la production sociologue; sociologie coloniale et decolonisation de la sociologie." In H. Moniot, ed. *Le Mal de Voir*. Paris: Union General d'Edition.

Bourdieu, P., and Passeron, J.-C. (1977). *Reproduction in Education, Society and Culture*. Trans. Richard Nice. Beverly Hills, CA: Sage.

Bursztyn, A. (2002). "Conclusion: Reflection on Collective Identities." In C. Korn and A. Bursztyn, eds., *Rethinking Multicultural Education: Case Studies in Cultural Transition* (pp. 185–196). Westport, CT: Bergin & Garvey..

Darling-Hammond, L. (1998). "Education for Democracy." In W. C. Ayers and J. L. Miller, eds., *A Light in Dark Times: Maxine Greene and the Unfinished Conversation* (pp. 78–91). New York: Teachers College Press.

Dewey, J. (1899). "The School and Society." In M. S. Dworkin, ed., *Dewey on Education* (pp. 33–90). New York: Bureau of Publications, Teachers College, Columbia University, 1959.

Demetrion, G. (2000). "Reading Giroux through a Deweyan Lens: Pushing Utopia to the Outer Edge" *Educational Philosophy and Theory*, 33:1, pp. 57–76.

Demetrion, G. (2001). "Discerning the Contexts of Adult Literacy Education: Theoretical Reflections and Practical Applications." *Canadian Journal for the Study of Adult Education*, 15,(2), pp. 104-127.

Du Bois, W. E .B. (1970). "Education and Work." In P. S. Foner, ed., *W. E. B. Du Bois Speaks*. New York: Pathfinder.

Edwards, C., Gandini, L., and Forman, G. (1993). *The Hundred Languages of Children: The Reggio Emilia Approach to Early Childhood* Education. Norwood, NJ: Ablex.

Freire, P. (1970). *Pedagogy of the Oppressed*. Trans. Myra Bergman Ramos. New York: Herder & Herder.

Fullan, M. (1993). *Change Forces: Probing the Depths of Educational Reform*. Bristol, PA: Falmer Press.

Giroux, H. A. (1988). *Schooling and the Struggle for Public Life: Critical Pedagogy in the Modern Age*. Minneapolis: University of Minnesota Press.

Gordon, M. (2001). *Hannah Arendt and Education: Renewing Our Common World*. Boulder, CO: Westview Press.

Greene, M. (1996). "Plurality, Diversity, and the Public Space." In A. Oldenquisted ed., *Can Democracy be Taught?* Bloomington: Phi Delta Kappa Educational Foundation.

Greene, M. (1998). "Educational Visions: What Are Schools for and What Should We Be Doing in the Name of Education?" In J. L. Kincheloe and S. R. Steinberg, eds., *Thirteen Questions: Reframing Education's Conversations*. New York: Peter Lang.

Herrnstein, R. J., and Murray, C. (1994). *The Bell Curve: Intelligence and Class Structure in American Life*. New York: The Free Press.

Hirsch. E. D. Jr. (1987). *Cultural Literacy: What Every American Needs to Know*. Boston: Houghton Mifflin.

Hirsch. E. D. Jr. (1996). *The Schools We Need and Why We Don't Have Them*. New York: Doubleday.

Kincheloe, J. L., Gresson, A., and Steinberg, S. R., eds. (1997) *Measured Lies: The Bell Curve Examined*. New York: St. Martins Press.

Kincheloe, J. L., and Steinberg, S. R. (1996). *Thirteen Questions: Reframing Education's Conversations*. New York: Peter Lang.

Kincheloe, J., S. Steinberg, and P. Hinchey (1999). *The Postformal Reader: Cognition and Education*. New York: Falmer Press.

Kozol, J. (1991). *Savage Inequalities: Children in America's Schools*. New York: Crown.

Lyotard, J.-F. (1984). *The Postmodern Condition: A Report on Knowledge*. Trans. Geoff Bennington and Brian Massumi. Minneapolis: University of Minnesota Press.

McLaren, P. (1994). *Critical Pedagogy and Predatory Culture: Oppositional Politics in a Postmodern Era*. London: Routledge.

Rich, A. (1979). *On Lies, Secrets, and Silence: Selected Prose, 1966–1978*. New York: Norton.

Ravitch, D. (2000). *Left Back: A Century of Failed School Reforms*. New York: Simon & Schuster.

Rorty, R. (1989). "Education without Dogma: Truth, Freedom and Our Universities." *Dissent*, 36:2, pp. 198–204.

Sarason, S. B. (1993). *The Case for Change: Rethinking the Preparation of Educators*. San Francisco: Jossey-Bass.

Skrtic, T. M. (1995). *Disability and Democracy: Reconstructing (Special) Education for Postmodernity*. New York: Teachers College Press.

Tanner, L. N. (1997). *Dewey's Laboratory School: Lessons for Today*. New York: Teachers College Press.

Taubman, P. M. (2001). "Teaching Without Hope: What's Really at Stake in the Standards Movement, High Stakes Testing, and the Drive for 'Practical Reforms'" *Journal of Curriculum Theorizing*, 16:3, pp. 19–33.

Terman, L. M. (1919). *The Intelligence of School Children: How Children Differ in Ability, the Use of Mental Tests in School Grading and the Proper Education of Exceptional Children*. Boston: Houghton Mifflin.

Tyack, D., and Cuban, L. (1995). *Tinkering toward Utopia: A Century of Public School Reform*. Cambridge, MA: Harvard University Press.

Contributors

PHILIP M. ANDERSON is professor of secondary education at Queens College, and professor of urban education and executive officer of the Ph.D. Program in Urban Education at the City University of New York. His scholarly publications center on aesthetics, reader response, curriculum development, and cultural theory. His current research examines the inherent contradictions within cultural theory and curriculum practice in the United States.

ALBERTO M. BURSZTYN is an associate professor of school psychology and special education at Brooklyn College, CUNY. Born and raised in Argentina, he is a graduate of Brooklyn College, NYU, and Columbia. Prior to becoming an academic he worked for a decade in the New York City public schools as a teacher, psychologist, and administrator. His current scholarship focuses on the school paths created for children identified as needing special services, psychological assessment of culturally diverse students, and urban school reform. He has been looking at schools critically since prekindergaten. He is also a visual artist working in a variety of media.

KOSHI DHINGRA has taught science to first graders through twelfth grade as well as science and science education at schools of education in the New Jersey and in New York City. She currently resides in Dallas, Texas, with her husband, Arun, and their three children.

LEE ELLIOTT FLEISCHER, raised and educated in New York City, is currently a professor of education at Empire State College, State University of New York. Lee loves serious in-depth debate into the politics of knowledge as well as cracking open new doors of knowledge hitherto not discussed in the educational and exploratory social science circles. His current research mainly focuses on critical, poststructural, and qualitative perspectives of the narrative; counterhegemonic struggles of peoples all over the world; and the impact all of this stuff has in schools.

MORDECHAI GORDON is an assistant professor at Quinnepiac University. He was born in Israel and moved to Tennessee as an adolescent. His areas of research encompass the philosophy and sociology of education and Jewish studies in education. He is the author of an American Educational Studies Association Critic's Choice award for his book *Hannah Arendt and Education: Renewing Our Common World*.

NORA E. HYLAND is an assistant professor in the Graduate School of Education in the Department of Learning and Teaching at Rutgers, the state university of New Jersey. She was an elementary school teacher in Brooklyn for eight years. She is a scholar/activist whose research and scholarship include work on teaching for social justice, developing antiracist teaching by building relationships between communities and schools, and action research with teachers and community members to investigate and improve their practice for liberatory ends. Her work is primarily ethnographic and action oriented. She is currently working on developing models of teacher education and professional development for urban schools.

HAROON KHAREM is an assistant professor of education at Brooklyn College. He taught in the federal prison at Rockville, PA, before completing his doctoral studies at Penn State University. A scholar of African American history and studies, he is also a mentor and professor in the New York Teaching Fellows Program. His recent articles deal with images of African Americans, African Free Schools, and the Moors in Spain.

JOE L. KINCHELOE is a professor of education at the CUNY Graduate Center in the urban education Ph.D. program. He was the Belle Zeller Chair for Public Policy and Administration at Brooklyn College. Kincheloe is the author and editor of over thirty books and hundreds of articles. His areas of research involved urban education, research bricolage, critical pedagogy, cultural studies, school standards, and their relation to social justice. His recent books include *19 Urban Questions: Teaching in the City* (with Shirley Steinberg), *Multiple Intelligences*

Reconsidered: An Expanded Vision, and *Rigour and Complexity in Educational Research: Conceptualizing the Bricolage.*

CAROL KORN-BURSZTYN, is a psychologist and associate professor of early childhood education at Brooklyn College, City University of New York, where she provides leadership to the School of Education's lab school. She has worked as a child psychologist in New York City public and private schools and in clinical settings. Her research interests include the arts in education, the experience of cultural transitions, and the development of narrative in childhood.

CAROLINA MANCUSO teaches in the Graduate Literacy Program at Brooklyn College. In addition to scholarly work, she publishes personal essays and fiction and gives readings of her work. She has a background in theater and dance and focuses on the arts in teaching. Carolina became literate as a young child when she realized her four siblings were too old to play with her.

SHUAIB MEACHAM is an assistant professor at the University of Illinois, Champaign/Urbana with a research interest in literacy education. His research aims to apply insights from African American culture in general and literacy traditions in particular to address educational challenges broadly conceived. He is also a spoken word poet who has worked with community poets to introduce teachers to the writing processes implicit within spoken word poetry.

NICHOLAS M. MICHELLI is University Dean for Teacher Education for the City University of New York and professor in the University's Ph.D. program in urban education. He is responsible for the improvement of teacher education across the system. He serves on New York State's Professional Standards and Practices Board. Michelli's interests include urban teacher education, teaching for democratic practice, critical thinking, and educational policy.

WAYNE A. REED is an assistant professor at Brooklyn College, City University of New York. A passionate urban educator, his research centers on issues of social justice and poverty. Professor Reed is currently studying the influence of teacher residency on schools in low-income contexts. By understanding the practice of teachers who are residents of their school's neighborhood, he hopes to develop programs that recruit and prepare urban educators to serve in their local community.

ALMA RUBAL-LOPEZ is an associate professor at Brooklyn College where she is the Bilingual Program Head and the Undergraduate Deputy in the School of Education. She earned her Ph.D. in bilingual developmental psychology with an additonal concentration in linguistics, sociolinguistics, psycholinguistics and applied linguistics at Yeshiva University. She is the co-author of two very distinct books, one that addresses the global spread of English, *Post-imperial English: Status of English after Colonialism*, and the other that depicts her childhood in the South Bronx, titled *On Becoming Nuyoricans*.

FLORENCE RUBINSON has been teaching in the School Psychologist Graduate Program since 1991 and is currently program head. She is interested in promoting the importance of psychology in schools and especially supports the need for psychologists to play a major role in school reform.

SHIRLEY R. STEINBERG is an associate professor of education and the program chair of Graduate Literacy at Brooklyn College. Raised in Los Angeles, going to school in Canada, and finally settling in New Jersey and New York, she claims she can only live and work in urban chaos. Her areas of research include youth literature, popular culture, queer theory, improvisational social theater, cultural studies, and critical pedagogy. She is the author and editor of many books and articles, including *Kinderculture: The Corporate Construction of Childhood* (with Joe Kincheloe), *Multi/Intercultural Conversations: A Reader*. Steinberg is the founding and senior editor of *Taboo: The Journal of Culture and Education*.

Index

187 96

Academic tradition 3
Action research 236
Adorno, T. 33
Affirmative action 104
Agency 205
Alverman, D. 120
Alienation 115
American Apartheid 96
American Sign Language 150
Americans with Disabilities Act 149
Anticolonial activity 38
Antiwar movement 38
Apple, M. 242
Apprenticeship 231
Arendt, H. 254
Aristotle 56
Arts and sciences xi, 17, 18, 20, 45
Assessment 184, 188
Assistive technologies 150
At-risk children 153
Au, K. and Jordan, C. 120
Authentic dialogue 44
Autism 152

Banks, J. and Banks, C. 120, 152, 153
Banking education 104, 105
Baugh, J. 115
Bay Area Project 197
Behavior-shaping 142
*The Bell Curve: Intelligence and Class
   Structure in American Life* 95, 256, 257
Bernstein, R. 145
Bilingual classes 201
Bilingualism 182
Biliteracy classes 201
Binet, A. 143

Black codes 95
The Black Underclass 96
black youth 96
Bourdieu, P, 259
Braille 150
Brown, A. and Campione, J. 237
Brown v. Board of Education 94
Buber, M. 53, 57

Cahill, M. 68
Callister, T. 55, 56
Cartesian modes of research 98
Cartesian-Newtonian physical science 15
Changing demographics 182
Chavis, D. and Wandersman, A. 126
Chernin, K. 217
Child study movement 184
Children of color 181
Children with special needs 151
Chomsky, N. 218, 219
Christian dominance 38
Christian Right vii
Citicorp 8
Civil Rights Acts 97
Civil Rights movement 7, 38
CKC (community knowledge-centered)
   model 124, 125, 126, 127, 129, 130,
   131, 132
Class privilege 38
Classroom management 252
Classroom practice 232
Cobern, W. 238, 239
Coca-Cola 8
Code-switching 201, 215
Cognitive apartheid 238
Cognitive understandings 21
Coleman, J. and Hoffer, T. 76
Collaboration 188

Colonization 1
Columbine High School 179
Communities of color 131
Community development 74, 77, 125
Community empowerment 131
Community engagement 131
Community faculty 131
Community knowledge-centered model of
    teacher education 130, 131
Conservative reeducators 8
Constructivism 184,185
Contextualizing dimensions of teacher
    education 10
Cooperative learning 152
Corporate advertisers 8
Corporate schooling 210
Corporatized information environment 25
CPDS (Community Professional
    Development Schools) 128, 129, 132
Craft culture 21, 22
Critical complex analysts 15
Critical complex empiricism 30, 31, 32
Critical complex practitioners 41, 44
Critical complex questions 15
Critical complex teacher education 2,3, 6,
    13, 14, 16, 20, 22, 25, 32, 33, 35, 36, 37,
    39, 41, 46, 225
Critical democratic teaching 24
Critical domains 27
Critical knowledges 35, 39
Critical literacy 202
Critical literacy texts 202
Critical pedagogy 33, 151, 259
Critical reflection 85
Critical theorists 32, 57, 214
Critical theory 33, 224
Critical thinking 99, 114
Cultural context 7, 21
Cultural diversity 182
Cultural empwerement 152
Cultural wars 38
Culturally diverse children 122
Culturally diverse learners 120
Culturally diverse school contexts 123
Culturally diverse teacher preparation 119
Culture 259
Culture of positivism 35
Culture wars
Cummins, J. 120
Curricular change 195
Curriculuar modifications 120, 121
Curriculum and pedagogy 150

Curriculum development 21
Curriculum reform model 121

Dangerous Minds 96
Darling-Hammond, L. 234
Degradation of teaching 7, 11
Delpit, L. 107, 201, 219
Democracy 5, 34
Democratic education 29, 43
Democratic society 26
Democratic, transformative pedagogy 25
Demographic differences 115
Demystification process 107
Desocialization 39
Develomentalist tradition 4
Dewey, J. 54, 59, 60, 106, 145, 196, 199,
    202, 233, 244, 255, 258
Disabilities 141,146, 148, 150, 151, 257
Disciplinary power 36
Discursive power 36
Disempowered technicians 29
Diverse cultural groups 152
Diverse urban populations 117
Dominant culture 71
Dominant language 215
Dominant power 25
The Dreamkeepers: Successful Teachers of
    African American children 82, 83
Du Bois, W. 257
Duckworth, E. 236

Early childhood education theory and
    practice 159
Early childhood pedagogy 159
Early childhood teacher praxis 157, 158
Early literacy 200
EBD (Emotional/Behavioral Disorders)
    140,147, 216, 219
Ebonics 216, 219
Economic assumptions 60
Economic context 7
Economic foundations of the new standards 53
Educational colonialism 38
Educational knowledge base 27
Educational purpose 21
Educational reform 71
Educational theory 232
Egalitarian spirit 22
ELL (English Language Learners) 148,
    153, 201
Ellison, R. 92
Eminent critique 33

Empirical domains 27
Empirical knowledge 30, 31, 34
Empirical methodology of higher education 22, 23
Empiricism 16, 28
Empowerment 25, 38
Empowerment of teachers 24
English First programs 216
English Only 216
Epistemological assumptions 60
Epistemological awareness 29
Epistemological inconsistencies 34
Epistemological mistake 24
Epistemological standards 53
Epistemological understandings 23
Epistemologies of practice 21
Epistemology 14, 15
Epistemology of practice 24
Equity pedagogy 152
Ethnic and linguistic minority students 185, 186
Ethnographic research 28
Ethnographic studies 210
Eugenic ideology 256
European intellectual canon 38
Evaluation 21
Existentialists 57
Experiential approach 122
Experiential domains 27
Experiential knowledge about education 39, 40, 41, 42
Exxon 8

Factory model of school organization 256
Faculty of urban public schools 68
Fagan, T. and Wise, P. 181
Fair Housing Acts 97
Fanon, F. 99
Feiman-Menser, S. and Floden, R. 116
Feminist Marxist theory 219
Feminist theorists 33
Fenstermacher, G. 12, 23
Financial aid 94
Fine, M. 115
Formal learning 20
Foster, M. 120
Foundations and curriculum theory 45
Freire, P. viii, 33, 57, 59, 99, 100, 202, 209. 213, 215, 218, 224, 259
Freud, S. 109

Gay rights 38

Gee, J. 201, 219
Giroux, H. 59, 151, 259
Glasgow, D. 96
Goodlad, J. 6
Gopnik, A. 160, 161
Grammar 214, 215, 221
Grammar and pedagogy 215
The Grammar Book: An ESL/EFL Teacher's Guide 209
Gramsci, A. 216
Grant, C. 120
Greene, M. 252, 253
Gresson, A. 7, 96
Growth through English model 197
Grumet, M.151
Guiliani, R. 24

Haberman, M. 114
Hall, G. 184
Head Start 170, 171, 172
Hegemonic curriculum on minority children 151
Hegemonic grammar 221
Hegemony 36, 210, 216
Heidegger, M. 52
Henning-Stout, M. 184
Herrnstein, R. 95, 256, 257
Heterosexual normality 38
High-quality teaching 24
High-stakes testing x, 114
Hip-hop music 202
Hirsch, E. 258
Historical processes 38
Historical research 28
Historically marginalized communities 125
The Holmes Group 118
hooks, b. 55, 95
Hopkins, D. 232
Horkheimer, M. 32
Hyland, N. 67

IDEA (Individuals with Disabilities Education Act) 180, 182
Ideological disembedding 39
Ideology 36, 213
Ideology and language 214
Ideology and the curriculum 59
Ideology of dominant groups 151
IEP (Individualized Education Plan) 138, 146, 147
Illich, I. xi
Indeterminate zones of practice 40

Inner-city neighborhoods 88
In-service teacher education 17
Interdisciplinary curricula 130
International Federation for the Teaching of English (IFTE) 197
Interpretive research 28
Intervention strategies 189
The Invisible Man 92
IQ Tests 15, 143, 256
Itard, J. 142

James, W. 145
Jefferson, T. 255
Jim Crow 95
Johnson, S. 243
Justice 8

Kane, J. 53
Kincheloe, J. 56, 60, 96, 107, 125, 152, 215, 224, 259, 260
Klein, J. 175
Kliebard, H. 242
Knowledge 15, 121
Knowledge base 39
Knowledge circles 128
Knowledge production 15, 21, 28
Kohlberg, L. 109
Kozol, J. 92, 93, 94, 95, 96, 97, 198

Lacanian linguistics 218
Ladson-Billings, G. 82, 120
Language 214
Latino youth 96
Lean on Me 96
Learning and Writing across the Curriculum 197
Learning communities 66, 78, 79, 80, 83, 84, 85, 86
Learning community model 82
Learning community school 88
Least restrictive environment 144
Lewis, M. 107
Liberal arts core requirements 116
Liberation movements 38
Litearacy block classes 201
Literacy 199
Literacy of grammar 213
Literacy of power 36
Literacy practices 202
Literacy theory 197, 203
Litmer, L. 184
Local culture of school 169

Lortie, D. 232
Low-income communities 74, 75, 131
Low-income neighborhoods 65, 67, 81, 85
Low-income students of color 115
Low-income, minority neighborhoods 87

Macedo, D. 94, 224
Magnet programs 150
Mann, H. 35
Marcuse, H. 33
Marginalization 136, 151
Marginalized communities 131
Mass media 202
Massey, D. and Denton, N. 96
McCarthy hearings 257
McCarthy, C. 121
McDonald's 8
McLaren, P. 59
Measured Lies: The Bell Curve Examined 96
Meiklejohn, A. 79
Mental health 189
Mental health interventions 186
Mental health programming 187
Meta-epistemological perspective 26, 27, 28, 29, 30, 40
Minority children 144, 151
Minority communities 141
Moll, L. 122
Moral assumptions 60
Moral standards 53
Moral, ethical, and political issues 16, 17
Morrison, T. 35
Multicultural education 258
Multicultural education requirements 116
Multicultural illiteracy 120
Multiglobal corporate capitalism 210
Munby, H. 27
Murray, C. 95, 256, 257
Museum/school partnerships 238
My Mother's House: A Daughter's Story 217
The Myth of Black Progress 96

NAEP (National Assessment of Educational Progress 198
NAEYC (National Association of the Education of Young Children 171
National Association of School Psychologists 179, 189
National Council of Teachers of English 199
National Writing Project 197
Nature of education 32

NCATE (National Council for Accreditation of Teacher Education vii
Neighborhood revitalization 74
New Criticism 198
New Literacy 199, 200, 202
New York State Regents Task Force on Teaching 3
Nieto, S. 120
No Child Left Behind vii, ix, 140, 203
Normative domains 27
Normative knowledge 32, 34, 35, 39

OCR (Office for Civil Rights) 139, 140
Ontological domains 27
Ontological knowledge 37, 38, 39
Ontological standards 53
Oppression 151, 210
Oppressive ideologies 27

Pailliotet, A. 55, 56
Paradigmatic awareness 27
Paranoiac 253
Parent support 166
Passivity 20
Patriarchy 38
PDS (Professional development schools) 118, 119, 128, 132, 234, 235
PDS model 118
Pedagogical knowledge 26, 116
Pedagogical purpose 30
Pedagogy 209
Pedagogy of poverty 114
Pedagogy of the Oppressed 99
People with disabilities 136
Performance-based assessments 186
Perry, T. 219
Person-centered planning 150
Phenomenological research 28
Philips, S. 120
Philosophical mindset 60
Philosophical research 28
Philosophical rigor 58, 59
Philosophies of education 52
Phonics 200
Piaget, J. 109, 233
Pinar, W. 151
Pinkney, A. 96
Pizza Hit 8
Plato 56
Political assumptions 60
Political context 7
Political linguistic theory 219

Politicization of education 34, 35
Politics 7, 38, 239
Politics and education 59
Poor communities 76
Poor public schools 153
Poor urban children 140
Popular media 202
Positivism 14, 15, 27, 28, 34, 39
Positivist process of knowledge production 29
Positivist teacher educators 16, 17
Positivistic epistemology 40
Positivistic teaching and learning 259
Positivistic technical rationality 40
Postcolonial discontent 38
Postcolonial translation theory 218
Poststructural grammatical perspective 219
Poststructural theorists 214
Poststructuralist vision of school reform 259
Poverty 75, 76, 97, 107, 117, 209, 210, 223, 259
Power 7, 13, 30, 38, 39, 69
Power relations 35
Practice 242
Practitioner as scholar 5
Prejudice 136
Preservice teachers 122
The Principal 96
Problem-solving paradigm 183, 184
Process writing 198
Professional development 129
Psychoeducational assessment 181
Psychological clinics 184
Psychological evaluation 143
Public Law 94-142 136, 144, 151, 182
Pugash, M. and Warger, C. 148

Qualitiatve interpretation 188

Race, class, gender, sexuality, religion, geographic place 7, 33
Race, class, and urban containment 114
Racial segregation 150
Racism 107, 210
Racism, class bias, sexism, and homophobia 9
Racist policies 98
Radical emancipatory pedagogy 259
Rational, positivist paradigm 28
Rationialism 14

Ravitch, D. 255, 258
Reader-response theory 197
Reconceptualization of teacher knowledge 28
Reductionism 16
Reductionist technician orientation 12
Reeducation 25
Reflective gaze of the teacher 158
Reflective practice 151
Reflective practitioners 100
Reflective teacher 234
Reflective-synthetic domains 27
Reflective-synthetic knowledge about education 42, 43
Reflexively aware teacher researchers 44
Reform movement 188
Reggio Emilia approach 258
Regulatory power 36
Relation of theory and practice 54
Research culture 21
Responsive practice 183, 185
Rich, A. 253, 254
Right-wing-sponsored proposals 94
RJR Nabisco 8
Rodriguez, E. 151
Rorty, R. 260
Rosa, J. 210
Russell, T. 27

Savage Inequalities 96
Schema theory 197
Schön, Donald 40, 42
School alienation 116
School psychologists 183, 186
School psychology 180, 182
School reform 11
School violence 179, 187
Schooling enterprise 9
Schools in a democratic society 32
Schoolteacher 232
Scientific managerial forces 14
Scientific method 31
Scripted curriculua 114
SEEK (Search for Education, Elevation and Knowledge) 104
Severe speech impediments 152
SFA (Success for All) 17
Simon, T. 143
Skinner, B. 142
Slave trade 1
Sleeter, C. 120
Smith, D. and Kaltenbaugh, L. 82

Social activists 10
Social and cultural theory 197
Social and emotional learning 186
Social assumptions 60
Social capital 66, 73, 74, 75, 76, 77, 88, 89
Social capitalists 74
Social change 252
Social context 7
Social Darwinism 95, 256
Social efficiency tradition 4
social justice 7, 13, 21, 34, 86, 132, 147
Social reconstructionist tradition 4, 5
Social vision 22
Socially just educational transformation 113
Socially just, democratic notion of schooling 24
Sociolinguistics 218
Sociolinguistictransactional model 200
Sociopsycholinguistic models 197
Special education 135, 136,140, 141, 142, 143, 144
Special education in urban schools 147
Special education pedagogy 142, 143
Special education movement 181
Standard English 214
Standard language 201
Standard writing216
Standardized tests 183, 184, 185, 239
Standardizing 9
Stanford-Binet Tests 256
State standards 239
Steinberg, L. 105
Steinberg, S. 56, 60, 96, 215, 259, 260
Student disengagement 105
Students of color 115
Stupidification 9, 10, 94
Subjugated community knowledge 127
Subversion 10
The Substitute 96
Syntax 214, 215, 216
Systemic functions 21, 23

Teacher as technician 5
Teacher education 174
Teacher empowerment 28
Teacher quality ix
Teacher research 158
Teacher-researchers 44, 237
Teachers as knowledge producers 21
Teachers for diversity 118
Techne 56

Technical rationality of positivism 31
Technically rational model 27
Technicism 12, 18, 19
Technicist and deskilling tendencies 27
Technicist tendency in teacher education 16
Television 238
Terman, L. 256
Testing Movement 256
Theory/practice link 233
Thinking philosophically 52
Thorndyke, E. 142
Tomlinson, S. 150
Traditional values 7
Transference of knowledge 100
Transformational reading 197
Transformative multicultural education 152
Triangulation 161, 162
TSWBAT 10
Tyack, D. and Cuban, L. 257

U.S. Department of Education xi, 139
Understanding 26
University of Chicago Lab School 255
Urban communities 122, 127, 136
Urban educational reforms 114
Urban educational systems 117

Urban school educational cultures 116
Urban schools 86, 119, 147
Urban teacher preparation 119
Urban Teaching: The Essentials 86, 98

Vouchers 94
Vygotsky, L. 94, 202, 233, 237

Walker, A. 35
Watson 142
Weaver, C. 200
Weiner, L. 86, 98, 231, 233
Western canon 36
Western thinking 222
Western view of history 53
Where We Stand: Class Matters 95
White males 8
White supremacy 38
Whole language 197, 200
Willinsky 196,199, 200
Winters, W. 69
Women's movement 7, 38
Wretched of the Earth 99
Writing Process Movements 197

Zone of proximal development 237

Questions about the
Purpose(s) of Colleges
and Universities

Norm Denzin,
Joe L. Kincheloe,
Shirley R. Steinberg
General Editors

What are the purposes of higher education? When undergraduates "declare their majors," they agree to enter into a world defined by the parameters of a particular academic discourse—a discipline. But who decides those parameters? How do they come about? What are the discussions and proposed outcomes of disciplined inquiry? What should an undergraduate know to be considered educated in a discipline? How does the disciplinary knowledge base inform its pedagogy? Why are there different disciplines? When has a discipline "run its course"? Where do new disciplines come from? Where do old ones go? How does a discipline produce its knowledge? What are the meanings and purposes of disciplinary research and teaching? What are the key questions of disciplined inquiry? What questions are taboo within a discipline? What can the disciplines learn from one another? What might they not want to learn and why?

Once we begin asking these kinds of questions, positionality becomes a key issue. One reason why there aren't many books on the meaning and purpose of higher education is that once such questions are opened for discussion, one's subjectivity becomes an issue with respect to the presumed objective stances of Western higher education. Academics don't have positions because positions are "biased," "subjective," "slanted," and therefore somehow invalid. So the first thing to do is to provide a sense—however broad and general—of what kinds of positionalities will inform the books and chapters on the above questions. Certainly the questions themselves, and any others we might ask, are already suggesting a particular "bent," but as the series takes shape, the authors we engage will no doubt have positions on these questions.

From the stance of interdisciplinary, multidisciplinary, or transdisciplinary practitioners, will the chapters and books we solicit solidify disciplinary discourses, or liquefy them? Depending on who is asked, interdisciplinary inquiry is either a polite collaboration among scholars firmly situated in their own particular discourses, or it is a blurring of the restrictive parameters that define the very notion of disciplinary discourse. So will the series have a stance on the meaning and purpose of interdisciplinary inquiry and teaching? This can possibly be finessed by attracting thinkers from disciplines that are already multidisciplinary, for example, the various kinds of "studies" programs (women's, Islamic, American, cultural, etc.), or the hybrid disciplines like ethnomusicology (musicology, folklore, anthropology). But by including people from these fields (areas? disciplines?) in our series, we are already taking a stand on disciplined inquiry. A question on the comprehensive exam for the Columbia University Ethnomusicology Program was to defend ethnomusicology as a "field" or a "discipline." One's answer determined one's future, at least to the extent that the gatekeepers had a say in such matters. So, in the end, what we are proposing will no doubt involve political struggles.

For additional information about this series or for the submission of manuscripts, please contact Joe L. Kincheloe, 1 Sand Piper Drive, South Amboy, NJ 08879. To order other books in this series, please contact our Customer Service Department at: (800) 770-LANG (within the U.S.), (212) 647-7706 (outside the U.S.), (212) 647-7707 FAX, or browse online by series at: www.peterlangusa.com.

DISCARD

EXPECTATIONS
GAME

ol

DATE DUE

AUG 0 1 2005			
			DEC 0 2 2004
GAYLORD			PRINTED IN U.S.A.

Published in the United States of America
by ScarecrowEducation
An imprint of The Rowman & Littlefield Publishing Group, Inc.
4501 Forbes Boulevard, Suite 200, Lanham, Maryland 20706
www.scarecroweducation.com

PO Box 317
Oxford
OX2 9RU, UK

British Library Cataloguing in Publication Information Available

Library of Congress Cataloging-in-Publication Data

Tucker, Barbara, 1942–
    Expectations game : a staff development tool / Barbara Tucker, Mary
Jackson.
        p. cm.
    Includes bibliographical references.
    ISBN 1-57886-114-4 (pbk. : alk. paper)
1. Teachers—In-service training. 2. Activity programs in education. 3. Group
work in education. 4. Teachers—Attitudes. I. Jackson, Mary, 1947– . II. Title.
LB1731.T75 2004
370'.71'5—dc22   2004000497

∞™ The paper used in this publication meets the minimum requirements of
American National Standard for Information Sciences—Permanence of Paper
for Printed Library Materials, ANSI/NISO Z39.48-1992.
Manufactured in the United States of America.